Sponsored by
SRI International

Funded by
Studies of Education Reform
Office of Educational Research and Improvement
U.S. Department of Education
under contract number RR 91-172010

Technology and Education Reform

Technology and Education Reform

The Reality Behind the Promise

Barbara Means

EDITOR

Jossey-Bass Publishers • San Francisco

Substantial discounts on bulk quantities of Jossey-Bass books are available to corporations, professional associations, and other organizations. For details and discount information, contact the special sales department at Jossey-Bass Inc., Publishers.
(415) 433–1740; Fax (415) 433–0499.

For sales outside the United States, contact Maxwell Macmillan International Publishing Group, 866 Third Avenue, New York, New York 10022.

Manufactured in the United States of America. Nearly all Jossey-Bass books, jackets, and periodicals are printed on recycled paper that contains at least 50 percent recycled waste, including 10 percent postconsumer waste. Many of our materials are also printed with vegetable-based ink; during the printing process these inks emit fewer volatile organic compounds (VOCs) than petroleum-based inks. VOCs contribute to the formation of smog.

Library of Congress Cataloging-in-Publication Data

Technology and education reform : the reality behind the promise / Barbara Means, editor.
    p.   cm. — (Jossey-Bass education series)
    The chapters in this book were prepared as part of an SRI International project, the National Study of Technology and Education Reform, sponsored by the Office of Educational Research and Improvement of the U.S. Dept. of Education.
    Includes bibliographical references and index.
    ISBN 1-55542-625-5
    1. Educational innovations—United States. 2. Educational technology—United States. 3. Educational change—United States. I. Means, Barbara, date. II. Series.
LB1027.T355   1994
371.3′078—dc20   93-45336
                                       CIP

FIRST EDITION
HB Printing 10 9 8 7 6 5 4 3 2 1   *Code 9423*

The Jossey-Bass Education Series

Contents

Preface

The school reform movement and the introduction of technology into classrooms are two of the most significant trends in education today. Public concern over education is at an all-time high, and there is an unprecedented willingness to consider radical changes in the ways schools are structured. At the same time, technology has saturated workplace, home, and commercial environments to a high degree and has become so powerful and inexpensive that its accelerated introduction into schools appears inevitable.

Unfortunately, these two innovative trends do not always (and some would argue do not usually) occur in concert. In many places, serious school reform is being undertaken without any real consideration of the facilitating role that technology might play. Even more common is the introduction of new instructional technologies without any serious consideration of how these technologies might further school reform goals.

Background of Technology in Schools

Electronic technology has been hailed as a powerful agent for transforming schools at least since the heyday of radio. Television in the 1960s, computer-assisted instruction in the 1970s, and the microcomputer, videodisc, and artificial intelligence in the 1980s all were supposed to create a new kind of classroom—yet they did not. Nevertheless, the authors of the chapters in *Technology and Education Reform* suggest that technology does have the potential to support education reform and that there have been changes both in the political climate and in people's understanding of instructional technology and its implementation that provide grounds for optimism. Specifically, the political will to rethink the entire educational system and the basic organization of schools is combined with a renewed emphasis on teaching advanced skills to all students. At the same time, schools are increasingly using technology as a tool to support student and teacher inquiry rather than as a substitute lecturer or workbook.

Rather than expecting, as many pioneers in technology did, that the introduction of powerful new technologies will be the driving force that transforms the U.S. school system, I have come to believe that the causal relationship flows at least equally strongly in the other direction—that is, that education reform makes a school ripe for technology. Teachers who rethink their curricula, replacing short pieces of didactic instruction on separate topics in discrete disciplines with multidisciplinary projects in which students tackle meaningful, complex tasks over extended periods of time, are establishing the prerequisites that will allow them to apply technology meaningfully to support student work. In classrooms where such meaningful education goes on, technology can amplify students' skills and make students' tasks more authentic—that is, more like real-life tasks. Students will approach their tasks with the same tools and access to information available to practitioners in the world beyond the schoolhouse. Students will engage in high-level planning and problem solving as they choose technological tools appropriate to their tasks and apply these tools in flexible ways. At the same time, as teachers become comfortable with technology, it can inspire them to think of new projects and activities and can raise their expectations for their students. Conversely, in schools and classrooms that rely upon conventional lecture and drill-and-practice approaches, teachers find little incentive to undertake all the hard work involved in introducing new technologies.

Audience

Technology and Education Reform reflects the editor's and authors' belief that instructional technology and school reform can, under the right conditions, become mutually reinforcing partners in support of student learning. As schools, districts, and states begin to build a body of experience in bringing these two forces together, educators and researchers are learning about the issues that arise and the additional forces that can undermine even carefully thought out efforts.

The book addresses individuals who seek to change their schools through education reform or through the introduction of technology. It is intended to help them think about ways in which education reform and new technologies can be interwoven and can support each other. The chapters were prepared by leading researchers as part of the National Study of Technology and Education Reform, an SRI International project sponsored by the Office of Educational Research and Improvement of the U.S. Department of Education.

Of particular interest for teachers and parents will be the discussion of ways in which technology can support the changed roles of students and teachers envisioned by the education reform movement. Teachers interested in incorporating new technological applications into their practice will find inspiration in chapters describing the use of technology to provide multimedia environments that support learning for disadvantaged students, to connect the classroom with the information resources of the world at large, and to formulate challenging multidisciplinary classroom projects.

Administrators and local policymakers interested in technology and education reform will find discussions of such important issues as the use of technology to conduct more authentic student assessments and the evaluation of technology-supported school reform projects. Educational policymakers will find discussions of such important policy issues as the kinds of training that can prepare teachers for classrooms in restructured schools and the kinds of support that technology-oriented education reform efforts need from the local, state, and federal levels of the educational system.

Overview of the Contents

Chapter One introduces a conceptual framework for thinking about technology and education reform. It classifies technologies as they are used in education and describes the kinds of learning experiences advocated by school reformers. From the characteristics of these desired learning experiences, I present implications for the kinds of technology that are most likely to have a lasting impact on classrooms.

Chapter Two, contributed by the Cognition and Technology Group at Vanderbilt University, describes what the group calls MOST environments (Multimedia environments that Organize and Support learning through Teaching). The members of the group describe their recent work in creating multimedia tools that help students who are at risk of school failure due to serious reading and literacy problems. In MOST environments, these students are able to select, understand, and learn from text-based resources, turning the resources into multimedia presentations that communicate information about AIDS, recycling, substance abuse, and other topics important to young people.

In Chapter Three, Denis Newman provides a thoughtful analysis of the effects associated with introducing telecommunications into schools. He argues that, thus far, network technology has in fact been a conservative force within schools. Most schools installing local area networks have used them in conjunction with integrated learning systems, which tend to reinforce teachers' practices of dividing instruction into short episodes on discrete subject areas and testing for students' mastery of specific competencies. Relatively few schools have access to wide area networks, and those that do generally lack connections to the local area networks that would make resources beyond schools' walls available to large numbers of students. Newman discusses recent network technology that is making such linkages easier and the growing interest in using Internet as the standard for a national school network.

In Chapter Four, Linda C. Barron and Elizabeth S. Goldman discuss the challenges that restructured classrooms pose for teachers and describe some ways in which pioneering schools of education are harnessing technology to provide more appropriate training for new teachers. Drawing on their own experiences in preservice training at Vanderbilt University and the experiences of others who use multimedia technology for teacher training, Barron and Goldman argue that teacher training programs should not teach prospective teachers *about* technology (as is done in the still-popular computer literacy courses), but instead, should *use* technology throughout the programs so that prospective teachers not only gain skills in working with equipment and software but also experience how technology can support the exploration, organization, and communication of knowledge.

Karen Sheingold and John Frederiksen argue in Chapter Five that a key to making education reform happen is rethinking instructional goals and the ways in which we assess progress toward those goals. As educators focus on teaching all students to think strategically and to apply higher-order skills concepts to solving problems, teachers need forms of assessment that top these skills. Sheingold and Frederiksen describe ways in which new technology can support more authentic assessments of performance than teachers have been able to give in the past. They also argue that technology can be particularly useful in helping teachers and students to share examples of complex work and discuss the merits and weaknesses of that work, even when the teachers and students are physically separated. Through such technologically enhanced conversations, a common language for describing work and a shared set of values and evaluation criteria can emerge.

The issue of how to evaluate the effects of technology within a school reform effort is the focus of Chapter Six, by Joan L. Herman. Reflecting on her experiences in evaluating technology-oriented school programs, Herman contends that policymakers' "simple" questions (such as, "What are the effects of technology on student learning?") are usually not answerable as they are stated. In reformed programs, different teachers use different technologies in different ways for different purposes. Moreover, the introduction of technology is almost always just one of a whole set of changes implemented simultaneously. Under these circumstances, it is seldom defensible to attribute changes in gross performance measures, such as standardized-test scores, to any one factor. Herman discusses evaluation methods in detail and offers guidelines for evaluation strategies that will effectively study the results of technology when it is only one among several school reform efforts.

Chapter Seven, by Jane L. David, considers the issue of technology and education reform from the policymaker's viewpoint. David argues that, despite technology's unfulfilled promises in the 1980s, the systemic reform movement in the 1990s increases the likelihood that technology will have a significant impact on the kinds of instruction large numbers of students experience. She discusses the local conditions needed for appropriate use of technology and provides "rules of thumb" for policymakers to use to make such conditions a reality. David argues for a flexible, iterative approach to technology planning; decentralization of technology decisions; and significant investments in the professional development of teaching staff.

Technology and Education Reform concludes with Chapter Eight, in which I and Kerry Olson describe some of the schools we have observed for the National Study of Technology and Education Reform. We present detailed descriptions of two classrooms in two different schools in which teachers are providing the kinds of learning experiences advocated by education reformers and are supporting these activities with technology. We also define the context for these two classrooms, describing the education reform and technology implementation efforts that exist elsewhere in the two schools. These implementation stories are contrasted with the history of a school designed from the bottom up as an innovative, technology-rich "school of tomorrow." The chapter also includes guidelines for planning school reforms supported by technology.

Acknowledgments

Preparation of the chapters for *Technology and Education Reform* was supported by the U.S. Department of Education.

This work is part of the Studies of Education Reform program of the Department of Education's Office of Educational Research and Improvement, under contract number RR 91-172010. The program supports studies and disseminates practical information about implementing and sustaining successful innovations in American education. The opinions in the document do not necessarily reflect the position or policy of the U.S. Department of Education, and no official endorsement should be inferred.

I am thankful for the counsel of Ram Singh, the monitor for this project, during the selection of topics and authors for the book. Preparation of the manuscript was ably supported by Augustina Biosic, Carolyn Estey, Katie Ann Kaattari, and Klaus Krause at SRI International and by the editorial and production staff at Jossey-Bass.

Menlo Park, California   BARBARA MEANS
January 1994

The Editor

BARBARA MEANS heads the Learning and Technology Program at SRI International, where she is also executive director of the Health and Social Policy Division. Her research interests focus on the application of cognitive psychology to education and instruction. This concentration has led her to explore the ways in which technology can support students' learning of advanced skills. Her interest in the design of school programs based on the needs of learners has led her to the study of educational innovations and systemic reform efforts as well. She is project director for the National Study of Technology and Education Reform, sponsored by the Office of Educational Research and Improvement of the U.S. Department of Education. She is also principal investigator for a National Science Foundation grant to study how technology can support the process of learning through collaboration with an expert mentor. Her published work includes the books *Comparative Studies of How People Think* (1981, with M. Cole) and *Teaching Advanced Skills to At-Risk Students* (1991, with C. Chelemer and M. Knapp). Means holds an A.B. degree from Stanford University in psychology and a Ph.D. degree from the University of California, Berkeley, in intellectual development and education.

The Contributors

Linda C. Barron is research assistant professor of mathematics education at Peabody College of Vanderbilt University, where she teaches mathematics methods courses for prospective elementary and early childhood teachers. Her research emphasizes the use of technology in instruction. Since 1987, she has worked with colleagues at Vanderbilt in developing integrated media materials for use in mathematics and science methods courses for prospective teachers. Barron is also a member of a multidisciplinary group of researchers at Vanderbilt's Learning Technology Center who are developing materials on videodisc to enhance middle school students' problem solving. She is author of *Mathematics Experiences for the Early Childhood Years* (1979), a mathematics methods textbook for prospective early childhood teachers, and has coauthored several articles pertaining to technology in education. She received her Ph.D. degree from Vanderbilt University in mathematics education.

Jane L. David is director of the Bay Area Research Group in Palo Alto, California. Her research and consulting activities focus on the connections between school change and education policy at all levels of education. David's current clients include Apple Computer, the National Governors' Association, SRI International, and several district and state agencies. She received her Ed.D. degree from Harvard University in education and social policy.

John Frederiksen directs the Bay Area Cognitive Science Research Group for the Educational Testing Service, where he is principal scientist. Frederiksen is also adjunct professor of education at the

University of California, Berkeley, in the Division of Education in Math, Science, and Technology. His recent work has focused on applying computer and video technologies to the development of collaborative-learning environments and integrated performance assessments that foster improvements in science teaching and learning. His National Science Foundation–sponsored research on performance assessment in middle school science focuses on the development of students' skills and knowledge for use in scientific inquiry. In his research for the National Board for Professional Teaching Standards, he addresses the use of video portfolios for both assessing and improving teaching. He received his Ph.D. degree from Princeton University in psychology and psychometrics.

Elizabeth S. Goldman is associate professor of mathematics education in the Department of Teaching and Learning at Peabody College of Vanderbilt University, where she teaches mathematics content and methods courses for prospective elementary teachers. She is also a scientist in Vanderbilt's Learning Technology Center, where she works with research and development projects that apply integrated media technology to mathematics education and mathematics and science teacher education. Goldman is currently serving as director or codirector of three technology-related teacher education projects funded by the National Science Foundation. She has taught high school mathematics and middle school mathematics and science. She holds a Ph.D. degree from Vanderbilt University in mathematics.

Joan L. Herman is associate director of the Center for the Study of Evaluation and the National Center for Research on Evaluation, Standards, and Student Testing of the University of California, Los Angeles. Her current research interests include the design and use of evaluation for school improvement, the effects of technology on school reform, and the development, implementation, and use of alternative assessments. Her recent books include *Making Schools Work for Underachieving Minority Students: Next Steps for Research, Policy and Practice* (1990, with J. Bain), *A Practical Guide to Alter-*

native Assessment (1992, with P. Aschbacher and L. Winters), and *Tracking Success: A Guide for School-Based Evaluation* (1992, with L. Winters). A past president of the California Educational Research Association and chair of the Stephen S. Wise Board of Education, Herman serves on advisory boards for the National Science Foundation, the National Council of La Raza, and California's education assessment and evaluation programs. She received her Ed.D. degree from the University of California, Los Angeles, in educational psychology.

Denis Newman is a division scientist at Bolt Beranek and Newman, Inc., where he directs research and development projects on communication networks for schools. Newman also works for the National School Network Testbed, a Bolt Beranek and Newman project that serves as an R&D resource for multiple projects that are investigating both the educational functionality and the implementation costs of a large-scale network of K–12 schools. He has written for a variety of journals, including *Cognitive Science*, *Discourse Processes*, and the *Journal of Educational Computing Research* and is author of *The Construction Zone: Working for Cognitive Change in School* (1989, with M. Cole and P. Griffin). He holds a Ph.D. degree from the City University of New York in developmental psychology.

Kerry Olson is a research social scientist in the Learning and Technology Program at SRI International. She is also deputy project director for the National Study of Technology and Education Reform. She has conducted extensive research in the use of technology within education, particularly in the area of early literacy and the use of the computer as a writing tool. Olson is a former teacher and early childhood program director. She is a Ph.D. candidate in the Combined Program in Education and Psychology at the University of Michigan.

Karen Sheingold is director of the Center for Performance Assessment at the Educational Testing Service (ETS). Her current research focuses on performance-based assessment as it is linked to the reform of schooling and the raising of educational standards. Before joining ETS, she was director of the National Center for Technology in Education and of the Center for Children and Technology at the Bank Street College of Education in New York City. She has coedited two books, *Mirrors of Minds: Patterns of Experience in Educational Computing* (1987, with R. Pea) and *This Year in School Science* (1992, with L. G. Roberts and S. M. Malcolm). Sheingold holds a Ph.D. degree from Harvard University in developmental psychology. She has taught at Wellesley College, Cornell University, and the State University of New York at Buffalo.

The Cognition and Technology Group at Vanderbilt is made up of interdisciplinary researchers who are examining relationships between human learning and technology. These researchers come primarily from the fields of cognitive science, education, computer science, engineering, and public policy. Members of the Cognition and Technology Group who contributed to this chapter are John D. Bransford, Laura I. Goin, Susan R. Goldman, Ted S. Hasselbring, Herbert J. Rieth, Diana M. Sharp, and Nancy J. Vye.

Chapter One

Introduction:
Using Technology to Advance
Educational Goals

Barbara Means

We are living in a time of great technological advance. Computing power is more available and affordable than ever before. Satellite transmission can beam instructional material to sites thousands of miles away. Computer graphics can create "virtual" environments in which the individual sees and interacts with an artificial yet three-dimensional world. Tools to support computer applications make it possible for school children to do everything from communicating with their counterparts on the other side of the world to building their own curriculum materials in hypermedia formats to collecting and analyzing data much as practicing scientists would. Although the most sophisticated technology remains in the hands of a few, it is becoming more and more affordable and available. At the same time, educators and researchers are finding educationally sophisticated uses of such now commonplace technologies as videotape and word processing.

One can easily make a case that use of technology in the schools has risen dramatically in the last dozen years. In 1981, only 18 percent of U.S. public schools had even a single computer for instructional uses; by 1991, estimates of this proportion reached 98

Note: This chapter is based on a paper presented at the Conference on Technology and Education Reform, held June 18–19, 1992, in Dallas, Texas, and conducted by SRI International under the sponsorship of the Office of Educational Research and Improvement of the U.S. Department of Education.

percent (Mageau, 1991; QED, 1992). More importantly, during roughly the same period, the average number of students per computer dropped from 125 in the school year 1983–84 to 18 in 1991–92 (QED, 1992). Although only 25 percent of school districts had modems in 1988–89, this percentage was expected to double by 1991–92 (Mageau, 1991). The number of schools using videocassette recorders has more than tripled, going from 31 percent to 99 percent since 1982 (QED 1992; Chen, 1991). Videodiscs and CD-ROM players were each found in about 9 percent of school districts in 1989; that number was expected to double in the 1991–92 school year (Yoder, 1991).

At the same time that the technology available to education has been rapidly increasing, the United States has been witnessing unparalleled general support for education reform. The stark warning in *A Nation at Risk* that the erosion of educational standards "threatens our very future as a nation and a people" (National Commission on Excellence in Education, 1983, p. 5) set off a series of state reforms aimed at raising educational standards through tougher course requirements and required scores on standardized tests. Disappointment with the results of these efforts provided the current impetus for a more fundamental reform focused on rethinking the structures and process of education itself, including what is taught and how. A new willingness to consider profound changes to the educational system is apparent in the current reform efforts of governors, state legislators, business coalitions, and teachers' associations. In 1991, in California alone, 1,500 schools submitted proposals to obtain planning grants for restructuring. On a national level, the Business Roundtable, an organization representing executives from 200 major corporations, has committed itself to a decade-long effort to help schools across the country restructure. The New American Schools Development Corporation's recent call for proposals to "break the mold" and rethink schools from the ground up garnered 686 proposals from forty-nine states. Educators, politicians, and citizens are now seriously debating structural reforms that would have seemed wildly idealistic just a decade ago.

There is no doubt that use of technology and education reform are major bandwagons in U.S. education today. The question I address in this chapter is the relationship—or the lack of it—between these two movements. A strong argument can be made that the movements are fundamentally disconnected. In and of itself, technology contains neither pedagogical philosophy nor content bias. Computers can present either dynamic simulations of complex phenomena or brief segments of text and tedious multiple-choice questions. Sophisticated fiber optics can deliver from a distance a German or geometry course that is totally traditional.

Although the state of the *art* in instructional technology has gone far beyond the provision of on-screen workbooks, the state of *practice* in many places has not kept pace. Many uses of technology either support the classroom status quo or occur at the margins of education (as enrichment, for example, or in special education or classes for the gifted) rather than in the mainstream academic program (Mehan, 1990; Oakes & Schneider, 1984).

At the same time, the majority of efforts to restructure schools appear to have little or nothing to do with technology. Ray (1991) studied restructuring schools in Maine and found that technology played a minor role at a few schools, but that most were redesigning themselves without any consideration of technology at all. Of the fourteen schools that won Next Century Schools grants from the RJR Nabisco Foundation in 1991, only three proposed any significant use of technology. Clearly, education reform efforts can go—and are going—forward without incorporating technology into the restructured schools.

In some ways, this state of affairs is not surprising. History suggests that whenever a new technology is introduced, be it a printing press or a horseless carriage, individuals' first inclination is to use it as they used the traditional technology it replaces. Certainly, this has been the case with educational technologies. Larry Cuban's *Teachers and Machines* (1986) contains a marvelous photograph that sums up this inclination. It shows a teacher and her class, circa 1927, availing themselves of the high technology of the time to support their study of geography. The class is up in an airplane cruising over the Los Angeles basin. But how are they using the technology of flight? As an off-site traditional classroom, complete with blackboard, student desks, teacher at the front, and all eyes facing forward instead of looking out the airplane windows at the geography below. If this example seems outlandish, consider the more recent cases of teachers who use computers only as typewriters or desktop publishing software only to turn out more beautiful overheads. Indeed, the majority of today's computer-based instructional programs do little more than put the ubiquitous student workbook on a computer monitor and automate the right/wrong scoring that a teacher would otherwise do by hand.

Are the use of technology and education reform destined to continue on separate paths? Probably not. There are enough cases in which technology and school reform have been successful partners to tell us that the marriage can be a productive one (Sheingold & Tucker, 1990; Stearns, David, Hanson, Ringstaff, & Schneider, 1991; Zorfass, 1991). The key to the partnership lies in educators' developing reformed sets of curricular and instructional goals and then using technology as a tool to support these goals. When this approach is taken, and the introduction of technology is viewed not as an end in itself but as a support for instructional goals related to increased student involvement with complex authentic tasks and new organizational structures within classrooms and schools, technology appears more attractive to those who must reach the new goals (Sheingold & Tucker, 1990).

Student Learning and School Reform

The primary motivation for teachers to use technology in their classrooms is the belief that the technology will support superior forms of learning. Learning theory and research are extremely important sources of ideas for teachers about instructional goals and strategies. Advances in cognitive psychology have sharpened educators' understanding of the nature of skilled intellectual performance and provided a basis on which teachers and researchers can design environments conducive to learning. There is now widespread agreement among educators and psychologists (Collins, Brown, & Newman, 1989; Resnick, 1987) that advanced skills of comprehension, reasoning, composition, and experimentation are acquired not through the transmission of facts but through the learner's interaction with content. This *constructivist* view of learning is the wellspring of ideas for many of the current curriculum and instruction reform efforts, calling upon schools to teach basic skills within authentic and, hence, more complex contexts in order to model expert thought processes and encourage the use of collaboration and external supports so that students thus supported can achieve intellectual accomplishments they could not attain on their own.

The experience of the 1980s tells us that serious reform efforts must look not just at the classroom but at the whole system within which education takes place. Nevertheless, the ultimate goal is to have a beneficial impact on students, and it is in making that impact that I believe technology can support the goals of education reform. Although variously described, the desired student outcomes of most reform efforts are increased learning, especially of advanced skills, and enhanced student motivation and self-concept. Naturally, there are various schools of thought as to how to achieve these ends, but the dominant thinking within the reform movement appears to stress teachers' moving from conventional instructional approaches to approaches based on the elements shown in the second column of the list on page 6.

In my view, the catalyst for the transformation of conventional instruction into reform instruction is the decision to center instruction on *authentic, challenging tasks*. These tasks will contain within them the characteristics of reform instruction. There is a strong sense among today's educational researchers that schools have decomposed tasks into discrete component skills (learning algorithms for finding square roots, for example) that have no obvious connection with anything students do outside of school. This traditional way of handling tasks demotivates students and makes it unlikely that they will transfer learned skills to real-world tasks (Resnick, 1987).

*Comparison of Conventional and
Reformed Approaches to Instruction*

Conventional Instruction	Reformed Instruction
Teacher directs.	Students explore.
Instruction is didactic.	Instruction is interactive.
Students receive short blocks of instruction on single subject.	Students perform extended blocks of authentic and multidisciplinary work.
Students work individually.	Students work collaboratively.
Teacher is knowledge dispenser.	Teacher is facilitator.
Students grouped by ability.	Students grouped heterogeneously.
Students who have demonstrated mastery of "the basics" work on advanced skills.	All students practice advanced skills.
Students assessed on fact knowledge and discrete skills.	Students assessed on performance.

Reformers argue that all students should have the opportunity to *practice advanced skills* within the context of tasks that are personally meaningful and challenging to students (for example, students might practice various skills through the task of describing their city to students in another part of the world). Meaningful tasks will almost always be more complex than tasks assigned for the practice of discrete skills. Meaningful tasks will also tend to be multidisciplinary (the description of the city might require students to assemble geographic and historic facts as well as work on composition skills), a feature that conflicts with the standard middle and secondary school division of the curriculum into distinct disciplines. Further, the fact that the tasks will be more complex suggests that longer blocks of time will be required to work on them, again conflicting with the notion of fixed, short periods of time for distinct subject areas.

Given complex tasks, students take a more active part in defining their own learning goals and regulating their own learning. They explore ideas and bodies of knowledge, not in order to repeat back verbal formulations on demand but to understand phenomena and find information they need for their project work. When students work on complex tasks, their work will often cross over the borders of academic disciplines, just as real-world problems often demand the application of several kinds of expertise. In this *multi-disciplinary context*, instruction becomes *interactive*. The nature of the information and the support provided for students will change as the problems they work on change and evolve over time.

Such complex, authentic tasks lend themselves to *collaborative work*. Some students track down all the economic data on their city while others look into information on weather patterns. Students form groups to work through mathematics problems, or they serve as each other's editors when writing documents. There are many advantages to collaborative learning (see, for example, Lesgold, 1992). In the process of collaborating, students gain experience in negotiating the purpose of their work, the meanings of the terms they use, and so on. They have experiences that mirror the activities of professionals working together. Collaborative work also has advantages in terms of motivation: students get involved in tasks because they like to work together; further, if difficulties encountered are temporarily daunting to one student, another student's enthusiasm can carry the work forward. Another frequently noted advantage of peer collaboration is that it calls on students to justify their conclusions and to act as external critics for each other. In so doing, they become more reflective about their own thinking. Over time, students come to internalize the role of critic so that they can effectively review their own work.

Collaborative projects help teachers adjust tasks to accommodate individual differences. Students of different ability levels can work together, taking roles commensurate with their skills. Thus, it becomes feasible to teach *heterogeneous groups* of students who vary in age, ability levels, or expertise. For example, a group working on a project to describe their city might value one student's contributions as a video expert, while another student takes the lead on composing written reports or assembling statistics. Within such groups, more students have the opportunity to excel at something, and students' experiences of teaching each other can be educationally valuable.

In the reform learning model, the *teacher becomes a facilitator and coach* rather than a knowledge dispenser or project director. Teachers are responsible for setting up the inquiry units and for creating the organizational structure within which the groups do their work. But once work begins, teachers no longer have the total control of the direction of instruction that they exercise in conventional classrooms. Teachers serve as resources and provide guidance and suggestions, but they do not tell students everything they need to know.

Instruction that is organized around authentic, challenging tasks also invites new kinds of assessment of students' learning. When students produce major products, teachers can test learning through *performance-based assessments* rather than through lists of multiple-choice items with little relevance to the real world.

School Reform, Advanced Skills, and Disadvantaged Students

Although the reformers' vision of a transformed classroom is important for all students, the change is especially dramatic for those who have been characterized as "disadvantaged" or "at risk." An increasing proportion of the children in U.S. schools come from homes with incomes below the poverty line. Many of these children have been raised in homes where English is not the dominant language or is not spoken at all. Some come from homes with only a single parent, or they have little stability in their primary caregivers. Some must cope with physical, mental, or emotional disabilities. Statistically, students with these characteristics are more likely to fall behind in academic achievement, to drop out of school, or to turn away from the whole process of education. Conventional instruction has had diminished expectations for these students. While it has hoped to teach them basic skills, it has not expected them to attain high levels of accomplishment in the advanced skills of problem solving, scientific inquiry, or composition. As a consequence, curricula for these students have stressed discrete skills and extensive drill and practice on vocabulary, number facts, and writing mechanics. In effect, schools have given these students less instruction in the advanced skills and less opportunity to develop the advanced capabilities that are, in fact, those most important for all students' future lives.

Under school reform, these students would experience a dramatically different kind of classroom. Instead of treating basic skills as a hurdle that must be surmounted before attempting more complex reasoning, problem-solving, and composition tasks, this classroom would teach disadvantaged students basic skills in the context of challenging, authentic tasks (Means, Chelemer, & Knapp, 1991). Rather than emphasizing the practice of discrete skills such as spelling and punctuation on endless worksheets, the curriculum for disadvantaged students would stress composition, comprehension, and applications of skills. Rather than working in isolation, often in ability groupings or in pull-out classes for compensatory instruction, disadvantaged students would work in mixed-ability groupings, often of mixed ages. They would be judged on their ability to perform a complex task and to reflect on and describe the thinking that went into it rather than on their facility with multiple-choice tests. One of the basic messages of school reform is that challenging problems and sustained intellectual effort are appropriate for all students, not just those who are academically advanced, affluent, or older.

Educational Technologies

In trying to bring some structure to technology's broad domain, I have found it useful to categorize educational technologies not in terms of their root technology (microprocessors or fiber optics, for example) but in terms of *the way they are used for instruction*. From this perspective, educational technologies can be classified into four broad uses: they can tutor, they can explore, they can be applied as tools, and they can communicate.

Technology is used *as a tutor* when it does the teaching directly, typically in a lecture-like or workbook-like manner. Tutorial uses include expository learning, in which the technological system provides information; demonstration, in which the system displays a phenomenon or procedure; and practice, in which the system requires the student to solve problems, answer questions, or execute a procedure. In contrast, technology is used *to explore* when it allows students to move through information or obtain demonstrations upon request. Through the discovery or guided discovery that accompanies an exploration, the student can learn facts, concepts, procedures, and strategies as he or she interacts with the system. A microworld simulation is an example of using technology to explore something.

Technologies *applied as tools* provide students with the same kinds of tools generally found in the workplace or the home. These technologies, unlike technologies that tutor and explore, are not designed explicitly for school use but can be put to educational purposes. Examples include word processing and spreadsheet software, video cameras, and video editing equipment. Finally, use of technology *to communicate* encompasses programs and devices that allow students and teachers to send and receive messages and other information through networks or other technologies. These four uses of technology in education are summarized in Table 1.1.

Using Technologies to Teach

The literature on educational technology suggests that the use of modern technologies in the classroom has undergone an evolution. The first uses were predominantly tutorial, reflecting the idea that a teaching machine might instruct better, or at least more efficiently, than the typical human teacher. Although tutorial applications are still probably the most common in terms of hours of instruction, many of the educational technology developers who followed the initial developers of tutoring programs have produced technologies that allow students to explore. The *Palenque* Digital Video Interactive (DVI) project at the Bank Street College of Education, for example, allows students to take a simulated journey through a Mayan site or a museum data base. The materials foster browsing

Table 1.1. Classification of Educational Technologies.

Category	Definition	Examples
Used as a tutor	A system designed to teach by providing information, demonstrations, or simulations in a sequence determined by the system. A tutorial system may provide for expository learning (the system displays a phenomenon or procedure) and for practice (the system requires the student to answer questions or solve problems).	Computer-assisted instruction (CAI) Intelligent CAI Instructional television Some videodisc/ multimedia systems
Used to explore	A system designed to facilitate student learning by providing information, demonstrations, or simulations when requested to do so by the student. Under student control, the system provides the context for student discovery (or guided student discovery) of facts, concepts, or procedures.	Microcomputer-based laboratories Microworlds/simulations Some videodisc/ multimedia systems
Applied as a tool	General-purpose technological tools for accomplishing such tasks as composition, data storage, or data analysis.	Word processing software Spreadsheet software Data base software Desktop publishing systems Video recording and editing equipment
Used to communicate	A system that allows groups of teachers and students to send information and data to each other through networks or other technologies.	Local area networks Wide area networks Interactive distance learning

and a personalized approach to the journey, giving students simulated cameras, photo albums, and so on.

As exciting as such explorations are, they can be very expensive to develop. For high-end technologies such as DVI, their cost and the cost of equipment to display the optical disks will limit the technologies' availability. Moreover, although less expensive microcomputer-based exploration programs, such as *SimCity* or *Where in the World Is Carmen Sandiego?*, are available, an exploration program is seldom a good match to a particular classroom's core curriculum and, hence, tends to be regarded as "enrichment." As a result, technologies that help students explore various areas tend to have a limited impact on students' core educational experiences.

Using Technologies to Support Learning

The current trend in technology use in schools is toward the third and fourth categories of use: technology applied as a tool and technology used to communicate (see, for example, Becker, 1990). Unlike the technologies in the first two categories, these technologies are designed for general purposes and used predominantly to support students' work rather than directly to teach. Ironically, these latter technologies are, I believe, more likely to have wide-reaching effects on what happens in schools than the technologies specifically designed for instruction. Because they support communication and work, they are highly compatible with the project-based, constructivist approach to student learning goals that drives the reform movement. Moreover, because technologies used as tools and communication devices do not contain instructional content per se, they can be adapted to any local curriculum, and they do not become obsolete for a student after he or she uses them once or twice. In classrooms across the country, researchers are starting to see these technologies used to support student work on authentic, challenging tasks and, consequently, to support the other instructional features associated with education reform, that is, multidisciplinary work over extended time periods, collaborative learning, performance-based assessment, and a shift from teacher-directed to student-directed learning. In the following sections, I discuss the ways in which technologies used as tools and communication devices can function to support each of these instructional features.

Authentic, Challenging Tasks

If teachers engage students in complex tasks of the sort they may encounter in the world outside of school, it makes eminent sense also to equip them with knowledge of the tools they may work with in that world (see Collins, 1990). These tools include technologies as mundane as the telephone—prominent by its absence in most classrooms—but also technologies as rapidly changing as word processing capabilities and desktop publishing software, video cameras, and applications software for storing, manipulating, and presenting data.

However, these tools and communication programs and devices do not provide adequate instructional value in and of themselves. Instructional value lies in the educational activity that uses the tools and communication devices, an activity that must be planned by the teacher. For this reason, it seems important that teachers and researchers identify and communicate models of instructionally worthwhile activities supported by technology.

A notable example of giving students an authentic task and the technologies to support their work on the task is the NORSTAR program in the Norfolk, Virginia, school district. NORSTAR was initiated when middle school students in an extended day program responded to a National Aeronautics and Space Administration (NASA) challenge to design a tool that would be useful on the space shuttle. After NASA officials judged the Norfolk students' entry as the most promising and gave the students the opportunity to fly their experiment as a small self-contained payload, the students proceeded to refine their design and to build their experimental materials at the NORSTAR lab. The students used software that supports advanced mathematical computations, mechanical drawing, and communications. They presented findings from this and other projects at professional meetings and in journals.

Although not every classroom can be part of the U.S. space program, many teachers are finding that they can make the process of writing and editing more meaningful to their students with support from word processing software and distance learning networks. Riel (1989) describes how students in classrooms in California, Hawaii, Mexico, and Alaska formed Computer Chronicles, a student news wire service. Each class produced a local newspaper, drawing not only on its own work but also on selected pieces electronically transmitted from other sites. In this context, student writing and editing are authentic tasks; the importance of language mechanics becomes evident when poor skills in this area become barriers to communication.

Multidisciplinary Work and Extended Blocks of Time

As more schools move toward organizing instruction around similarly complex tasks, the boundaries between traditional subject areas make less sense, and the pressure grows to provide opportunities for sustained task efforts. At the Magnet Middle School at Rippowam in Stamford, Connecticut, for example, instruction is organized around the themes of water and the environment. School bells to mark periods have been done away with; instead, schedules are arranged around student projects. Students' study of ancient civilizations includes not only topics that would be classified as social studies in traditional instruction but also fine arts (students reenact ancient life in an all-night camping trip, complete with ancient wedding and dance rituals) and mathematics (students use technology to chart the direction and distance of ancient rivers).

Collins, Hawkins, and Carver (1991) have described how the eighth grade of a Rochester, New York, urban middle school was made over with the introduction of a project-based curriculum supported with technology. Students at Charlotte Middle School set out to design a display describing their city for a Rochester museum exhibit. Some student groups worked on a description of the city's environment while others focused on history, cultural attractions, and so on. As they explored their specific topics, students also worked on developing their skills in posing questions, gathering data, interpreting and representing data, presenting findings, and evaluating their work. Students used computer tools such as Mac-Paint, MacWrite, CricketGraph, and HyperCard to support their work. To accomplish their tasks, students spent two daily two-hour periods on their projects. After a year's experience with this Discover Rochester project, middle school staff decided to use the project-based approach for the entire eighth-grade program.

Collaborative Work and Differentiation of Student Roles

When students work in groups on major undertakings such as the NORSTAR space shuttle experiment or the Discover Rochester museum display, the social structure of the classroom changes. Rather than listen as a group to the teacher or perform independently, students actually work with each other to develop a shared product. Through such undertakings, students have the opportunity to share their expertise with each other. Through serving as critics and assisting and having the assistance of their peers, students become aware of the qualities that distinguish a good piece of work.

Another thing that happens when students carry out extended technology-supported tasks in groups is that students begin to specialize. In the Discover Rochester project, for example, one student became the group's expert in computer animation. Such specialization not only reflects the distributed nature of work in the world outside the classroom but also makes it possible for many more students to shine. The poor reader may be a wizard with the video camera or with computer graphics. Ann Brown (1992) talks about the legitimization of differences between students in collaborative learning groups and the opportunities the accepted differences provide for everyone in the group to be a teacher as well as a learner.

Beyond projects like NORSTAR and Discover Rochester, which involve explicit assignment of students to groups tasked with creating a joint product, there are also uses of applications software that encourage students with individual assignments to work with their peers. For example, researchers at the Ontario Institute for

Studies in Education have developed a networked hypermedia system, Computer-Supported Intentional Learning Environments, that fosters collaboration (Scardamalia, Bereiter, McLean, Swallow, & Woodruff, 1989). A student using the system builds software "stacks" representing his or her content knowledge in areas of science and social studies. An overview of everyone's work allows the student to see titles for the work classmates have produced as well as for the student's own work. The student can review classmates' work and copy portions of the information they have compiled to his or her own files or append comments to what classmates have written. When the student writes a comment on another student's file, the author of the file is notified, thus laying the groundwork for extended interchanges concerning the content.

Performance-Based Assessment

In addition to facilitating students' intellectual activity and production of meaningful products, technology supports the assessment of student work not only by teachers but also by parents, peers, and the students themselves. When students produce such authentic products as the NORSTAR space shuttle experiment, the Rochester museum exhibit, or the Computer Chronicles news wire service, there is less temptation for teachers to resort to the multiple-choice exam to obtain a record of student learning. Through such means as desktop publishing or video editing equipment, technology can support the development of a polished finished product that can be judged on its own merits. In addition, technology can support evaluations of the *process* through which a product was created. Computers can maintain records of the intermediate states reached and the decisions made in the process of creating that product, and these records can be inspected to assess the students' level of skill.

Student-Directed Learning

Finally, and perhaps most fundamentally, the use of technology creates a shift in a classroom's control structure. In conventional classes, teacher-led activities consume the majority of the time. When students do work independently, they are likely to be completing brief exercises assigned by the teacher. The teacher has authority not only for assigning work but also for giving it value by assigning a grade to it. Computers, of course, can be used in exactly the same way, with the technology presenting preset exercises and giving scores and congratulations for the number of correct responses. But use of technologies to explore, to be learning tools, or to develop new patterns of communication leads to a different model of student-teacher interaction. In projects such as those described in this chapter, students are actively engaged not only in solving problems but also in formulating them. In research currently being conducted by Ann Brown and Joe Campione, middle school students are developing their own science curriculum materials in HyperCard (Brown and others, in press). As students take on a more active role, the teacher becomes an advisor and a resource rather than the source of all classroom structure and fount of all knowledge.

This change does not make the teacher's job easier, quite the contrary. Because the path of student inquiry is less predictable than in a scripted lesson, the teacher faces a much wider range of potential questions. In classrooms where students have considerable control over the direction their learning takes, teachers need a thorough command of the subject matter and the self-confidence and willingness to be questioned in whatever areas student exploration uncovers. Teachers also need the intellectual confidence to reveal both their lack of absolute knowledge and their thinking processes to their students. When confronted with a question they cannot answer, teachers have the obligation to find the answer and, as they do so, to model the problem-solving and information-gathering processes they want their students to use.

Lessons from Studies of Technology Implementation

Technology has the potential to support learning in all of the ways I have described, but that support does not fall into place automatically when the computer box or the video camera hits the classroom. Some technology implementations do nothing to support the goals of education reform. For example, Newman (1990) makes the case that integrated learning systems that combine drill-and-practice software with tools for managing instruction have found a niche within U.S. schools because these systems fit readily into the existing educational structure of compartmentalized learning and drilling of selected students on basic skills.

What education reform is asking teachers to do is much harder than conventional teaching, whether or not the teachers use technology as a part of that reform. Teachers need time to experiment and to become comfortable with the new instructional techniques and with the technology. They need support in this process and a sense that they can experiment without putting their jobs or their professional standing in jeopardy.

Research suggests that top-down implementations typically fail (Berman & McLaughlin, 1978). There is no reason to believe that top-down implementations of technology will fare any better. Teachers cannot use technology effectively until they have thoroughly assimilated it into a larger instructional plan. Mechanical implementations of technology by teachers who do not believe that the technology will further their instructional goals are almost always fruitless. The implication of this finding is that implementations of technology need to start with the kinds of learning that *teachers* want to foster and recognition of the fact that *teachers* need to be the dominant players in selecting the technologies and applications they will use to help them meet their goals. The further implication is that there is a tremendous need for teacher training that shows teachers the potential of various technologies and for technical assistance that helps teachers identify the particular technologies and applications that will serve their purposes and that then shows teachers how to use the chosen technologies for instruction.

Nevertheless, the shortcomings of purely top-down approaches to innovation do not justify taking an opposite, purely bottom-up approach. If the U.S. educational system comes to depend on individual teachers to be "points of light"—donating their time, buying software, and creating new curriculum materials because they believe in the need for such actions—this nation will have given up on the goal of technology's having an enduring impact on the educational system as a whole. Policymakers, administrators, and parents cannot expect the majority of teachers to be heroes. When there is no systemic support, student exposure to technology-enhanced student-centered programs will be sporadic at best. And what happens to the student who moves from the technology-rich constructivist classroom to a more conventional didactic classroom in the next year or the next class? If schools are to provide students with a coherent educational program, teachers must come together and develop a shared set of principles, at least at the school level. In the same vein, support from the broader educational system is important. The chances for a reform effort to survive will be enhanced if it is understood and supported, or at least not thwarted, by state curriculum frameworks and assessment systems.

Conclusion

Studies of school innovations suggest that each school must reinvent itself. We cannot accomplish the goals of reform by giving a school technology or an implementation package. Nevertheless, technology can stimulate education reform by providing what Jane David has called "an invitation to change" (David, 1990, p. 81). The decision to devote considerable resources to technology affords an opportunity for deep thinking about what we want to teach and how. A decision to introduce microcomputers into science labs can lead teachers and curriculum directors to rethink the basic purpose of those labs. Introduction to new software can lead teachers to a different understanding of the field they teach. Moreover, funds for inservice training related to the introduction of technology can provide one of the all-too-rare forums for teachers to discuss what they teach and why.

To argue that school reform can be stimulated by technology, is not to argue for school reform through serendipity—bring on the technology and good things may follow. Instead, I am suggesting that educators and researchers now have a useful base of experience in applying technology in schools and classrooms and that this experience indicates important ways in which technology can foster the changes that are the goals of education reform.

References

Becker, H. J. (1990, April). *Computer use in the United States schools: 1989. An initial report of U.S. participation in the I.E.A. Computers in Education Survey.* Paper presented at the annual meeting of the American Educational Research Association, Boston.

Berman, P., & McLaughlin, M. (1978). *Federal programs supporting educational change.* Vol. VIII of *Implementing and sustaining innovations.* Santa Monica, CA: Rand Corporation.

Brown, A. (1992, April). *The cognitive basis of school restructuring.* Invited address at the annual meeting of the American Educational Research Association, San Francisco.

Brown, A. L., and others (in press). Distributed expertise in the classroom. To appear in G. Salomon (Ed.), *Distributed cognitions.* New York: Cambridge University Press.

Chen, M. (1991). *Educational video: What works?* A position paper for the Hughes Public Education Project. San Francisco: KQED Television.

Collins, A. (1990). The role of computer technology in restructuring schools. In K. Sheingold & M. S. Tucker (Eds.), *Restructuring for learning with technology* (pp. 29–45). New York: Bank Street College of Education, Center for Technology in Education; & Rochester, NY: National Center on Education and the Economy.

Collins, A., Brown, J. S., & Newman, S. E. (1989). Cognitive apprenticeship: Teaching the craft of reading, writing, and mathematics. In L. B. Resnick (Ed.), *Knowing, learning, and instruction: Essays in honor of Robert Glaser* (pp. 453–494). Hillsdale, NJ: Erlbaum.

Collins, A., Hawkins, J., & Carver, S. M. (1991). A cognitive apprenticeship for disadvantaged students. In B. Means, C. Chelemer, & M. S. Knapp (Eds.), *Teaching advanced skills to at-risk students: Views from research and practice.* San Francisco: Jossey-Bass.

Cuban, L. (1986). *Teachers and machines: The classroom uses of technology since 1920.* New York: Teachers College Press.

David, J. L. (1990). Restructuring and technology: Partners in change. In K. Sheingold & M. S. Tucker (Eds.), *Restructuring for learning with technology* (pp. 75–88). New York: Bank Street College of Education, Center for Technology in Education; & Rochester, NY: National Center on Education and the Economy.

Lesgold, A. (Rapporteur). (1992, January). *Report of a workshop on educational potential of wideband national network* (George Mason University, Fairfax, VA, November 1–2, 1991).

Mageau, T. (1991). Computer using teachers. *Agenda, 1,* 51.

Means, B., Chelemer, C., & Knapp, M. S. (Eds.). (1991). *Teaching advanced skills to at-risk students: Views from research and practice.* San Francisco: Jossey-Bass.

Mehan, H. (1990). Oracular reasoning in a psychiatric exam: The resolution of conflict in language. In A. D. Grimshaw (Ed.), *Conflict talk: Sociolinguistic investigations of arguments in conversation* (pp. 160–177). Cambridge, England: Cambridge University Press.

National Commission on Excellence in Education. (1983). *A nation at risk: The imperative for educational reform.* Washington, DC: Decision Resources Corporation.

Newman, D. (1990, April). *Technology as support for school structure and restructuring.* Paper presented at the annual meeting of the American Educational Research Association, Boston.

Oakes, J., & Schneider, M. (1984, November). Computers and schools: Another case of ". . . the more they stay the same"? *Educational Leadership, 42*(3), 73–79.

QED. (1992). *Technology in public schools, 1991–92* (QED's Annual Installed Base Report on Technology in U.S. Schools and Districts). Denver, CO: Quality Education Data.

Ray, D. (1991, March). Technology and restructuring—Part I: New educational directions. *The Computing Teacher, 18*(6), 9–20.

Resnick, L. B. (1987). *Education and learning to think.* Washington, DC: National Academy Press.

Riel, M. (1989). The impact of computers in classrooms. *Journal of Research on Computing in Education, 22*(2), 180–189.

Scardamalia, M., Bereiter, C., McLean, R. S., Swallow, J., & Woodruff, E. (1989). Computer-supported intentional learning environments. *Journal of Educational Computing Research, 5*(1), 51–68.

Sheingold, K., & Tucker, M. S. (Eds.). (1990). *Restructuring for learning with technology.* New York: Bank Street College of Education, Center for Technology in Education; & Rochester, NY: National Center on Education and the Economy.

Stearns, M. S., David, J. L., Hanson, S. G., Ringstaff, C., & Schneider, S. A. (1991). *Cupertino-Fremont Model Technology Schools Project research findings: Executive summary (Teacher-centered model of technology integration: End of year 3).* Menlo Park, CA: SRI International.

Yoder, S. K. (1991, October 21). Readin', writin', and multimedia. *Wall Street Journal,* p. R12.

Zorfass, J. M. (1991, April). *Promoting successful technology integration through active teaching practices.* Paper presented at the annual meeting of the American Educational Research Association, Chicago.

Chapter Two

Multimedia Environments for Developing Literacy in At-Risk Students

The Cognition and Technology Group at Vanderbilt University

This chapter describes a new project designed by the Cognition and Technology Group at Vanderbilt to accelerate the development of literacy skills in middle school and high school students who are at risk of school failure. *Literacy* is defined here as the ability to read, write, speak, listen, compute, think critically, and learn on one's own. The approach we advocate is highly motivating and helps at-risk students find the confidence, skills, and knowledge necessary to be successful in school and after they graduate.

Our work involves the design of what we call MOST environments. MOST stands for Multimedia environments that Organize and Support learning through Teaching. An important feature of MOST environments is that they are designed to support individuals' differences in linguistic and conceptual development. We want to make it possible for students at risk of school failure to increase their motivation, confidence, and generative learning by using multimedia to teach others.

MOST environments are effective because they engage students in authentic tasks that place the students in a position to create interesting and important multimedia products that *teach* their peers, parents, and others about important life topics. MOST environments also enable students to use a variety of visual-artistic,

Note: Members of the Cognition and Technology Group who contributed to this chapter include John D. Bransford, Laura I. Goin, Susan R. Goldman, Ted S. Hasselbring, Herbert J. Rieth, Diana M. Sharp, and Nancy J. Vye.

musical, oral, and written skills. In addition, MOST environments are scaffolds that support the learning activities necessary to create authentic products. This support occurs through such activities as selecting, comprehending, learning from, and communicating the essence of relevant text-based resources and turning the resources into exciting multimedia products that are shared with peers, parents, and the community. Because MOST environments help students learn to learn, and help them use technology to achieve authentic goals, students develop important sets of cognitive and technological skills that will be useful once they graduate.

In the discussion that follows, we first document the need for schools to dramatically improve the kinds of services that are available to at-risk students with learning problems in reading and literacy. We then present an example of a prototype MOST environment. Finally, we discuss the theoretical and empirical principles underlying MOST environments.

Significance of the Literacy Problem

This nation's need to focus on literacy is clear from the research literature and is reflected in the national goals that have been adopted by the U.S. president and state governors. Literacy skills are foundational for lifelong learning. Difficulties in learning to read, along with difficulties in acquiring the cognitive and metacognitive skills for learning through reading, are major reasons for students' referral to special education services (Means & Knapp, 1991; Vellutino, 1979; Wong, 1985). Success is particularly important at the beginning stages of reading because strategies, behaviors, and beliefs established early are very difficult to change (Palincsar & Klenk, 1991).

Students for whom literacy development is particularly problematic are often disadvantaged in several ways: in their social and economic status, in the support for school-based literacy that they receive at home, and in their experiences with everyday events and with language (see, for example, Heath, 1983; Pallas, Natriello, & McDill, 1989). Kirsch and Jungblut (1986) report that these problems are especially serious for minority students. For example, studies by the National Commission on Excellence in Education (1983) show that whereas 13 percent of all seventeen-year-olds can be considered functionally illiterate, illiteracy among minority youth may run as high as 40 percent. Further, studies by the National Assessment of Educational Progress suggest that populations historically considered at risk continue to do poorly relative to the national population at each grade level and that the performance gap between better and poorer readers widens as they progress through school (National Assessment of Educational Progress, 1988). It is also reported that at-risk students who leave school without having acquired functional literacy skills have only a 50 percent chance of becoming employed (Wagner, 1990).

The need for schools to tackle problems of literacy development becomes especially striking when one looks at demographic data. These predict a rapid increase in the number of children from the inner cities and minority groups whose values tend to conflict with traditional school norms (Pallas, Natriello, & McDill, 1989). Such children often suffer from the problems that accompany poverty, which is increasing in this country. In addition, about 4.6 million children who are not native speakers of English currently attend U.S. schools, and this figure is expected to increase by 10 to 15 percent by the turn of the century (Scarcella, 1988).

Minorities and children from the inner cities, however, are not the only populations at high risk of school failure. Many children from rural communities leave school with a limited range of literacy skills to draw on and, therefore, find it difficult to compete in the workplace. The number of students educated in rural America is not trivial. Elder and Hobbs (1990) note that school districts in U.S. rural areas serve about 25 percent of the nation's students. Overall, demographic data suggest that without a dramatic change in the success rate for literacy development among students considered at risk of school failure, the United States faces serious problems in the years ahead.

Rieth (1990) notes that whereas a significant effort has been made to provide literacy instruction to elementary-age students with learning problems, it has not been until recently that adolescents and young adults considered at risk of failure have received their fair share of support services (Halpern & Benz, 1987; Schloss, Smith, & Schloss, 1990). Nevertheless, these students continue to experience extensive academic and social difficulties (Maheady, Sacca, & Harper, 1988) that include the following:

- Severe deficits in basic academic skills such as reading, spelling, and math
- Generalized failure and below-average performance in content area courses such as science, social studies, and health
- Deficient work-related skills such as listening well in class, note taking, studying, and test taking
- Passive academic involvement and a pervasive lack of motivation
- Inadequate interpersonal skills

All these difficulties contribute to at-risk students' general lack of academic progress during high school (Schumaker, Deshler, & Ellis, 1986).

Related findings show that adolescents with learning difficulties are also at greater risk than their "normal" peers of receiving a failing grade, with almost one in three at-risk students receiving at least one failing grade in his or her most recent school year (Wagner, 1990). Factors that contribute to failing grades among adolescents at risk of failure include frequent class cutting and tardiness (Zigmond, Kerr, Brown, & Harris, 1984). In addition, teachers report that these students often arrive without a pen or pencil, notepaper, or textbook at least 30 percent of the time. Further, these students are characterized by teachers as poorly organized, inept at taking notes, unable to identify main ideas in lectures and texts, and poor at following directions and completing and turning in assignments (Zigmond, Kerr, & Schaeffer, 1988).

The consequences of students' failing courses, particularly those needed for graduation, are serious (Wagner, 1989). Students who fail to accumulate sufficient numbers of required credits to pass ninth grade frequently drop out of high school before graduation (Zigmond & Thornton, 1985). Passing ninth grade does not guarantee successful completion of high school, but failing ninth grade is devastating to students with learning difficulties. By leaving school early, they also may miss educational experiences that could benefit them in their transition to the world of work.

Edgar (1987) and Zigmond and Thornton (1985) both suggest that the endemic deficient academic skills, failing grades, high dropout rates, and depressed employment prospects demonstrated by at-risk and difficult-to-teach students warrant a major change in secondary education programs. And it will be a major challenge for schools to provide effective instruction and support services for these students that motivate them to stay in school and develop the skills, knowledge, and attitudes that are the basis for students' success after graduation.

Traditional and New Approaches to Helping At-Risk Students

As Rieth (1990) notes, the persistent problems that plague students considered at risk of school failure have led to several discussions about potential remedies. One approach proposed is to teach academic survival skills while focusing primarily on vocational education to help students learn a specific skill or trade. A second proposal is to attempt broad-based remediation of academic skills.

A problem with many variants of the approach that advocates vocational education plus academic survival skills is that skills training is often very narrow. It will not prepare students for the likelihood that, given the increasing pace of change in this country, most people will have to learn new skills many times during their lifetimes and, thus, will need learning-to-learn skills (see, for example, Bransford, Goldman, & Vye, 1991; Collins, Hawkins, & Carver, 1991; Resnick, 1987). A problem with the academic remediation approach is that it often involves the same type of instruction that was unsuccessful in the first place, and therefore, it is likely to fail once again to have the positive effects that education reformers desire (see, for example, Means & Knapp, 1991; Resnick & Klopfer, 1989).

During the past decade, researchers from several different areas have begun to formulate a general approach to instruction that appears much more promising than either the vocational or remedial approaches just discussed. It combines some advantages of each of these approaches while placing them in a larger, more meaningful problem-solving context. For example, the new approach focuses on the notion of *cognitive apprenticeships* (see, for example, Brown, Collins, & Duguid, 1989; Collins, Hawkins, & Carver, 1991; Cognition and Technology Group at Vanderbilt, 1990), a learning activity that emphasizes reflecting on and discussing strategies and procedures for knowledge transfer much more than do the typical apprenticeships that emphasize skills training (see, for example, Lave, 1988).

In addition, the cognitive apprenticeship approach acknowledges the importance of traditional academic skills and well-organized knowledge, yet it situates student learning in the context of authentic, meaningful problems so that students better understand why they are learning new information and when that information will be useful (see, for example, Bransford, Franks, Vye, & Sherwood, 1989; Brown, Collins, & Duguid, 1989; Cognition and Technology Group at Vanderbilt, 1990). A major feature of the cognitive apprenticeship approach is that it encourages sustained thinking about issues over significant periods such as weeks and months (see, for example, Brown, Collins, & Duguid, 1989; Cognition and Technology Group at Vanderbilt, 1990, 1991a, 1992a, 1992b).

Differences Between Traditional Instruction and Apprenticeships

An article from the 1940s is an excellent illustration of the difference between typical educational environments and cognitive apprenticeships. Entitled "Poor Scholar's Soliloquy" (Corey, 1944), it is written as the personal account of a student named Bob who is not very good in school and has had to repeat the seventh grade. Many would write Bob off as having a low aptitude for learning, but when you look at the kinds of learning Bob achieves outside of school, you get a very different impression of his abilities. Bob describes how his teachers do not like him because he does not read the kind of books the teachers value. His favorite reading includes *Popular Science*, the *Mechanical Encyclopedia*, and the Sears and Wards catalogues. Bob uses his books to pursue meaningful goals, and says, "I don't just sit down and read them through like they make us do in school. I use my books when I want to find something out, like whenever Mom buys anything second hand I look it up in Sears or Wards first and tell her if she's getting stung or not" (p. 219).

Bob also explains the trouble he had memorizing the names of the U.S. presidents. He knew some of them, like Washington and Jefferson, but there were thirty altogether, and he never did get them all straight. He seems to have a poor memory. Then he talks about the three trucks his uncle owns and the fact that he knows the horsepower and number of forward and backward gears of twenty-six different American trucks, many of them diesels. He comments, "It's funny how that Diesel works. I started to tell my teacher about it last Wednesday in science class when the pump we were using to make a vacuum in a bell jar got hot, but she said she didn't see what a Diesel engine had to do with our experiment on air pressure so I just kept still. The kids seemed interested, though" (p. 219).

Bob's discussion of other areas of his schooling includes his inability to do the kinds of (arbitrary) word problems found in his textbooks. Yet he helps his uncle solve all kinds of complex trip-planning problems when they travel together. He also discusses the bills and letters he sends to the farmers whose livestock is hauled by his uncle and notes that, according to his aunt, he made only three mistakes in his last seventeen letters, all of them comma errors. Then he says, "I wish I could write school themes that way. The last one I had to write was on 'What a Daffodil Thinks of Spring,' and I just couldn't get going" (p. 220). Bob ends by noting that, according to his Dad, he can quit school at the age of fifteen, and he feels that he should. After all, he's not getting any younger, and there is a lot for him to learn.

Bob's soliloquy is as relevant to the 1990s as it was to the 1940s. It contrasts the difference between students' attempts to learn in typical school environments and their opportunities to learn in the context of real-world apprenticeships such as the one that Bob served with his uncle. Many high school students considered at risk of school failure have the same troubles learning in school that Bob had, but they do not have the advantages of his out-of-school apprenticeship. As a result, their potential remains untapped. As Knapp and Turnbull (1990) argue, a major reason for this untapped potential is that typical instruction for at-risk students tends to

- Underestimate what students with learning difficulties are capable of doing
- Postpone more challenging and interesting work for too long— sometimes forever
- Deprive students of meaningful or motivating contexts for learning or using the skills that are taught

Overview of MOST Environments

Our MOST environments are designed to overcome the limitations of much of today's traditional instruction. MOST environments are consistent with the new cognitive apprenticeship approach to instruction, and they aim to achieve the following objectives (discussed by Means & Knapp, 1991, p. 8):

Take a new attitude toward learners with disabilities.

Appreciate the intellectual accomplishments that all learners bring to school.

Emphasize building on strengths rather than focusing solely on the remediation of deficits.

Learn about children's cultures to avoid mistaking differences for deficits.

Reshape the curriculum.

Focus on authentic, meaningful problems.

Embed instruction on basic skills in the context of global tasks.

Make connections with students' out-of-school experience and culture.

Apply new instructional strategies.

Model powerful thinking strategies.

Encourage multiple approaches to tasks.

Provide scaffolding that supports students in accomplishing complex tasks.

Make dialogue a central medium for teaching and learning.

Our implementation of MOST environments also recognizes that education reform must focus explicitly on learning by teachers and students. Researchers are now documenting the critical role of professional development in improving teachers' ability to carry out new approaches to instruction (see, for example, Collins, 1992; Duffy, 1992; Pressley, El-Dinary, & Marks, 1992). In part because each teacher's decisions reflect his or her individual past habits and beliefs, teacher decision making is now recognized by many researchers as the "missing link" in education reform (e.g., DeFord, Lyons, & Pinnell, 1991; Goldman & Pellegrino, 1987). Kamil (1991) notes that methods of teacher education have not kept pace with the vast changes in student population. Teachers must be helped to learn to deliver instruction to all students, especially those who have difficulty in traditional instructional settings. Most importantly, education reform requires a radical shift in teachers' views about who can succeed and how teachers can make that success a fact. One way to bring about this shift in views is to provide school environments that reveal more of students' potential. Our model of these new environments is discussed in the following section.

Description of a MOST Environment

Our goal in this section is to describe a MOST environment so that readers can better understand its key instructional features and the manner in which they are supported by technological tools. Our MOST environments are Macintosh-based and have three interdependent components: the Peabody Literacy Program, the Multimedia Producer, and two-way videoconferencing.

Peabody Literacy Program

The Peabody Literacy Program used in MOST environments is an adaptation of the Peabody Multimedia Adult Literacy Program (Hasselbring, Goin, Kinzer, & Risko, 1991). Based on several years of research, the original version of the program mediates instruction in word recognition and decoding as well as students' comprehension of text passages that are centered on contemporary topics and presented via videodisc. An animated tutor guides the learner and gives him or her instructions and feedback in a digitized human voice (see Figure 2.1). A voice recognition system allows learners to interact with portions of the program by speaking to the tutor. The program also tracks an individual's progress and adjusts the instruction accordingly. Following is a description of the two major components of the Peabody Literacy Program: comprehension instruction and fluency instruction.

Comprehension Instruction. At-risk students are typically unable to understand what they are trying to read; thus, a major component of the Peabody Literacy Program is comprehension instruction. The program's combination of computer and videodisc technology allows for a new teaching approach in which comprehension training is anchored to video segments that instruct students on contemporary topics of importance to the students. These topics were identified by surveying students considered at risk of school failure. Not surprisingly, the students identified issues that are often regarded as among today's important issues for the larger society: driving safety, AIDS education, substance abuse, teen

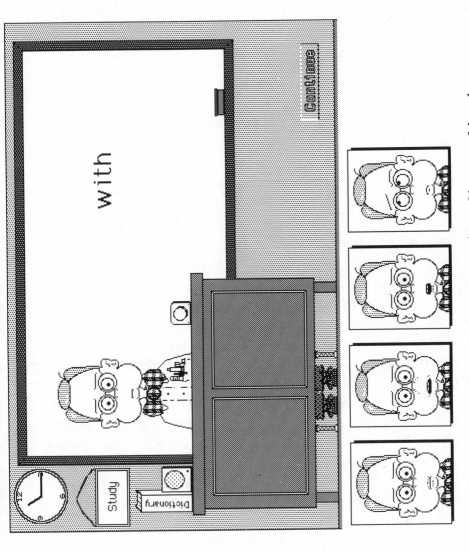

Figure 2.1. Animated Tutor Situated in a Classroom Metaphor.

sexuality, health education, consumer education, civil rights, and similar topics. Because so many poor readers lack the necessary experiential background to draw meaning from much of the text that they encounter, we use video as a way for these learners to gain the background knowledge necessary to understand a text passage.

During comprehension instruction, the animated tutor guides the student by having him or her view a short video segment (approximately one to two minutes) on a topic of the student's choice. Because the video material comes from a random access videodisc player attached to the computer, the program can virtually instantaneously access the video segments for the student to view. Further, the student can view the video several times if desired. After the viewing, the learner is presented with three text passages that we call *repeated reading discrepancy passages*. Although the three passages are similar, only one is an accurate description of what the learner has just viewed. It is up to the learner to read the passages for meaning and decide which one is accurate. This use of discrepancy passages was adapted from research on repeated reading (Rashotte & Torgensen, 1985). Reading the same passage several times is beneficial to poor readers in that both fluency and comprehension can be improved. Repeated reading is most beneficial when the level of the reading passage is equal to or slightly above the reading level of the reader and the reading is mediated by a teacher so that help can be given on words the reader does not know. The disadvantage of repeated reading is that most students dislike it, finding it tedious and boring to read the same passage repeatedly. Thus teachers are reluctant to use this technique.

The advantage of discrepancy passages, as we have designed them, is that the benefit of repeated reading is achieved without the associated tedium of reading the same passage multiple times. In addition, tying the passages to a video anchor gives students a schema for the passage, which helps them draw meaning from the text. We understand, however, that reading in the real world is much different from viewing a video and reading discrepancy passages, so we provide the student with additional comprehension tasks. Sometimes we have the learners read a passage first and then view several different video segments to choose the one that most closely represents what they have read. Here, they must draw meaning from the passage before they view the video. The program can also give students passages that are related to a video segment they have seen but are not just descriptions of that segment. Thus, students have to extend their thinking beyond what they have seen in the video and draw meaning from what they read.

The reading passages are written for three levels of difficulty, approximately fourth-, sixth-, and eighth-grade levels. The program is intelligent enough to match the difficulty of text passages to the approximate reading level of the learner, based on the number of words the student reads in the program's fluency component and the student's performance in selecting correct discrepancy passages. If necessary, the program can assess and target words from the passages for fluency training. The comprehension instruction is moderated by the tutor, and at any point the learner can ask the tutor for such help as the pronunciation or definition of a word.

Fluency Instruction. Most educators agree that the ability to decode words fluently is a requisite for being a competent reader. Previously, computer programs have been unable to teach reading fluency for one reason—an inability to monitor the reading process. Such monitoring requires that the computer present the student with a word, that the student say the word, and that the computer decide whether the word was read correctly and fluently. The Peabody Literacy Program takes advantage of a voice recognition device to overcome this monitoring problem. The device, a Voice Navigator connected to the Macintosh, is a speaker-dependent system (that is, a user has to train the system to recognize his or her voice). The device is somewhat limited in that it does not recognize continuous speech, but it does recognize single words and short phrases.

Initial fluency instruction in the program is focused on the 400 most frequently used words in the English language. After mastering the 100 most frequently used words out of the 400, the student can read between 30 and 40 percent of most text encountered and can begin comprehension instruction. After learning all 400 words, the student can read between 50 and 60 percent of most text encountered. In addition to the 400 most frequently used words, context-specific words from the comprehension passages can also be taught.

Four research-based instructional principles are incorporated into the fluency training:

1. Assessment prior to instruction
2. Systematic presentation of new information
3. Guided practice and corrective feedback
4. Independent practice

Fluency instruction follows this four-step format, as described in the following sections.

Assessment prior to instruction. The first time a learner works with this literacy program on computer and videodisc, he or she trains the Voice Navigator to recognize his or her voice, following instructions from the animated tutor. The tutor says to the student, "I am going to flash some words on the board; repeat these words after me. Say each word two times." The tutor then presents the first 25 words from the 400-word list, saying each one for the student to repeat. At the same time, each word appears on the blackboard next to the tutor (see Figure 2.1). As the student repeats each word, the program constructs a library of voice patterns, and from this point on, the Voice Navigator will use this library to recognize the learner's words as they are spoken. The library must contain a voice pattern for each word to be recognized; however, this library-building process is not visible to the student. It appears to students that they are previewing the words they will be studying.

When the first 25 words have been spoken by the student, the tutor says, "Now I will flash these words on the board again. This time I want you to read them to me." As each word is flashed on the board, the student attempts to read the word. If the reading is correct, the system records it as a correct response, along with the latency of the response. If the reading is incorrect, the tutor offers corrective feedback, saying the word for the student. This process of library building and assessment continues until the student has 15 words that are either incorrect or nonfluent (latency greater than one second). At this point, the assessment process stops and instruction begins. This is done to keep the program from frustrating a poor reader.

Systematic presentation of new information. To instruct the student, the program takes the student's first 5 nonfluent or incorrect words from the assessment list, and the animated tutor places these target words on the blackboard and repeats them for the student. Next, the tutor says, "Use the speaker and the dictionary to explore these words." The speaker and dictionary are located on the tutor's desk (see Figure 2.1). To access these tools, the student uses the mouse attached to the Macintosh to point and click on the word. Clicking on the word causes it to be highlighted, and once a word is highlighted, the student can cause the tutor to pronounce the highlighted word by pointing and clicking on the speaker. Thus, the student can have any problematic word pronounced by the tutor. By pointing and clicking on a word and then on the dictionary, the student can get a definition of the word; see the word used in context; get a phonetic analysis of the word; when appropriate, view a graphic depiction of the word; and also when appropriate, view a dynamic video that helps explain the meaning of the word (see Figure 2.2). Moreover, instead of using the speaker or the dictionary, the student can attempt to read the target words independently. If read correctly, the word will be highlighted.

The tutor systematically works with the student until the words can be read without error. At that point, the tutor provides the student with guided practice.

Guided practice. In the guided practice, the tutor simply presents the target words for the student to read. If the student makes an error, the tutor offers corrective feedback and asks the student to use the speaker and dictionary to explore the missed words. This practice continues until the student can read all the target words without error. Normally, reading the target words correctly is not a problem, given the small instruction set being studied by the

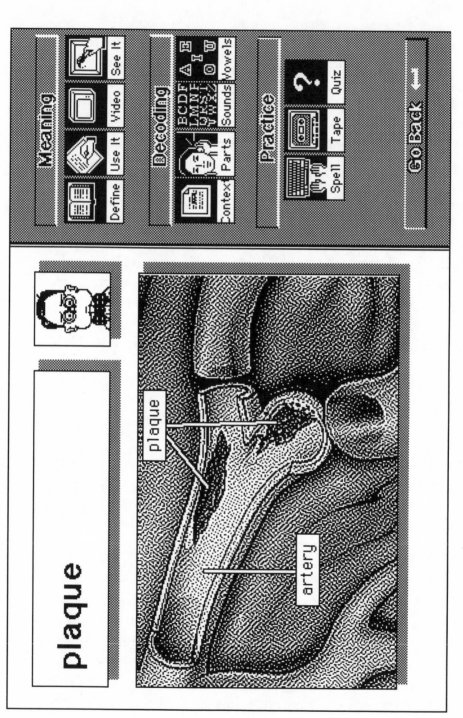

Figure 2.2. Graphic Depiction of a Word in the Dictionary Accessed from the Tutor's Desk.

student. During guided practice, the student's response latency is no longer monitored.

Independent practice. The final phase of fluency training is independent practice. Here, response latency is once again monitored as the student practices against a clock. The words are presented on the blackboard, and the student attempts to read each one within a one-second time limit. If the student can read a target word three times and be under the one-second limit each time, he or she is considered fluent in that word. After that, the word is reviewed intermittently during the student's independent practice sessions. Thus, even after a student is considered fluent in a word, the student still sees the word periodically.

Fluency training continues. When the student can read the 100 most frequently used words in the English language, the literacy program begins developing the student's comprehension, showing the words within the context of contemporary topics relevant to the student. Often students can already read the 100 most frequently used words fluently, so they begin working on comprehension immediately upon completing the assessment. However, fluency training remains part of the instruction. Even after reaching fluency on the 400 most frequently used words, the student receives fluency and decoding instruction on context-specific words drawn from the comprehension passages. Thus, fluency and decoding instruction is grounded in the context of comprehension instruction.

In sum, the ideas behind the Peabody Literacy Program are not radical but are based on effective teaching principles and empirically tested strategies. In addition, the program uses off-the-shelf video and computer technology in an innovative way to provide students with well-designed and engaging instruction.

The Multimedia Producer

Perhaps the most exciting component of the MOST environment is the Multimedia Producer, a Macintosh-based program that allows students to create their own multimedia productions. The software allows students to use digital video, still images, graphics, sound, and text to produce unique presentations on any topic. In addition, presentations can be transferred from the computer's digital memory to the analog medium of videotape to be shared by peers, parents, and the community at large.

Students using the Multimedia Producer have access to a wide range of excellent video materials that they can easily reshape to their own purposes by adding their own narration, music, artwork, and so forth. Sources of video from which students can borrow clips include public service announcements, government-sponsored videos that are in the public domain, and commercially available videodiscs. Besides these video sources, we have used videos made by corporations (for example, on recycling) that we have been given permission to use for educational purposes. Our pilot work with videos such as these has shown that students are extremely motivated to select relevant and appropriate video material to go with their narration. They also select or create appropriate music and art to support their presentation.

The Multimedia Producer is best thought of as a shell that allows the students to enter text, digital sound, digital video, or analog video by controlling a videodisc player. Developing the content for a presentation requires that the student research the topic, plan the presentation, gather the necessary materials, and then produce a product. This process requires a significant amount of planning and work, but the result is an authentic product that can be shared with teachers, peers, parents, and the community.

Student interviews have confirmed the importance of MOST students' generating a product of their own that is shared with others. We believe it is this public display that let the students feel that their products were authentic. When the products were to be publicly displayed, students reported, and demonstrated, that they took a great deal of pride in the product and were willing to work long hours to make it the best it could be. Students who typically spent little or no time on school projects reported spending entire weekends reading, researching, and finding appropriate media for their presentations. In addition, they reported that they actually had fun doing it!

Although MOST's goal is to improve literacy skills, MOST environments allow other content to be explored. For example, one group of special education students selected rain forests as the topic they wished to explore during their comprehension instruction. All of the video anchors and discrepancy passages involved information about rain forests, and the students learned a great deal about science, geography, and social issues relevant to the rain forest during their readings. In addition, each student had to select a rain forest topic he or she wished to explore in greater detail and about which he or she, as part of a group, would produce a multimedia presentation. Topics selected included medicines of the rain forest, endangered species, and biodiversity.

Clearly, the production process required that the students gain a deep understanding of their topic and forced them to think carefully about the messages they wanted to convey. The products were quite well done by any standard and were worthy of public display. In one case, after seeing the products that were produced, several students not in special education asked the teacher how they could get into the class.

Two-Way Videoconferencing System

The third component of our MOST environment involves a Macintosh-based two-way videoconferencing system called VISIT, developed by Northern Telecom. The VISIT system is so new that our tests of its capability are limited at present. The purpose of using this system is to bring MOST teachers and students into contact with content area specialists, designers, other schools, and the community at large. Traditionally, students and teachers are isolated within their classrooms and do not have access to these other groups unless both the teachers and the outside parties make a significant effort.

The VISIT system allows two-way videoconferencing to take place over the Integrated Services Digital Network (ISDN). The ISDN represents the final step of a major advancement in telecommunications, that is, the conversion of the worldwide telephone network from analog to digital signals. ISDN technology digitizes the worldwide telephone network's last remaining analog link: the signal that travels between the local telephone company's switching station and the individual user's computer and telephone. This final digitization makes it possible to send and receive data, visual images, and voice messages as easily as placing a telephone call. The emergence of an economical wide area ISDN network is providing researchers with tools for supporting education in new and exciting ways, and the VISIT system is one such tool.

The VISIT system requires an interface card in the Macintosh located in the implementation classroom, a small camera (about the size of a deck of cards) connected to the card and placed on the computer monitor, and an ISDN telephone line connected to the computer. In our tests, we have conducted teleconferences between a similar system in our Learning Technology Center and the implementation classroom. The system allows us to view the classroom in a window on the Macintosh screen, and anyone in the classroom can view us at the Learning Technology Center. In addition to interacting with students and teachers visually, we can also work collaboratively using a "whiteboard" feature that allows viewers on each end of the system to share a common workspace on the computer screen and work collaboratively on altering a shared document or visual. Also, using the high-speed data transfer rates of ISDN, we can share very large computer files in seconds; thus, students can send their multimedia presentations to us for comment, a feat that was very difficult before we had ISDN capability.

Unfortunately, ISDN deployment is in such an embryonic stage in most areas of the United States that this teleconferencing is not yet widely feasible and has been tested at only the most superficial level in education. Ours is the first such test in the state of Tennessee. Nevertheless, the advantages of ISDN are significant. To equip sites to conduct teleconferences using traditional equipment and transmission lines would cost from $30,000 to $50,000 per site, depending on the equipment used. A VISIT system currently costs about $3,000, and the cost promises to decrease annually.

We have used ISDN and the VISIT system in two important

ways. One is teacher support. If questions arise, the teacher is only a telephone call away from a face-to-face conversation with any of the project staff. Instruction on new topics can be carried out over the teleconferencing system, saving a staff member a trip to the classroom or the teacher a trip to our center. Also, students in the class can interact directly with the project staff to get help with their multimedia production or just to query individuals who have expertise in various areas. Over time, we believe that this two-way videoconferencing technology will transform our MOST environments from isolated classrooms into connected learning communities.

Design Principles of MOST Environments

The design principles that underlie MOST environments are consistent with constructivist approaches to instruction and are grounded in our own research with at-risk students conducted over the past several years. Specifically, our MOST environments are designed to address six critical student needs that must be met if students' literacy development is to be accelerated. These needs are described in the sections that follow.

Intrinsically Motivating Activities

The goal of motivating students to learn is a major challenge for nearly all teachers, but particularly for those who teach students who have difficulty learning, especially from text. When students perform learning activities solely to receive grades on tests, teachers often find it difficult to keep students engaged in these academic activities.

Our MOST environments are organized around the goal of students' creating authentic products that will be seen by other students, parents, and community members. The products are multimedia presentations about important and timely issues, such as drug and alcohol abuse, AIDS, and safe driving, and environmental concerns such as pollution and recycling. While using the Peabody Literacy Program for improving their literacy skills, student production teams do the research necessary to create first-rate products, and they also learn to evaluate and modify the products they create.

The multimedia products produced by students are developed at a multimedia workstation located in the classroom. As described earlier, visual images are made available from various video sources, and students combine the images with narration that they supply, as well as with music that they either select or create. Since the development of the student products involves a wide range of talents (in music, drawing, writing, and so on), the MOST curriculum allows students to use talents that often are not emphasized in school.

The fact that students in MOST environments are creating products to be shown to others is highly motivating. Researchers who have conducted similar types of authentic projects report that the motivation of at-risk students improves markedly in situations such as these (see, for example, Bransford, Goldman, & Vye, 1991; Collins, Hawkins, & Carver, 1991).

When completed, students' products are displayed on videotape in a kiosk in the school. In the future, we plan to place the presentations in other community locations, such as local shopping malls. In addition, as we expand the project to multiple schools, students at the different schools will receive opportunities to share products between themselves and with members of our group at Vanderbilt University.

Part of the task for the students is to get feedback on present products so that later ones can be improved. The model we are testing asks student production teams to present their products to a panel of experts. In a related pilot project, we have had student production teams first present their products to their peers, who serve as critical reviewers and help the production teams revise their products. After several iterations of the revision process, the students presented their products to a team of experts for judging. Thus far, experts from both Vanderbilt University and the community have served on the evaluation panel. Typically, each production team takes several minutes to present its work, and the panel may ask clarifying questions. Then, the panel rates the presentation on a set of predetermined criteria, which the team also used in developing the product. Each team is given feedback on its product, and if the product meets a threshold, the team is allowed to place it on public display in the school.

Emphasis on Higher-Order Learning

In MOST environments, students have to acquire the knowledge and skills necessary to conduct the background research for their products, and they also have to learn how to conduct research on product effectiveness. In addition, they learn how to work with technology. Through these various processes of acquiring and using knowledge, they also acquire important concepts and skills. Ideally, MOST environments allow students to develop integrated knowledge across content domains instead of simply acquiring a set of inert facts within a domain. Moreover, the topics that students can choose to explore are complex enough that they encourage students to integrate knowledge from a variety of curricular areas, such as science, mathematics, social studies, reading and writing, and health. Also, by working in one or two areas for significant amounts of time, students develop topic knowledge bases that facilitate their abilities to read and learn.

A number of studies have shown the advantages of sustained thinking about a topic. For example, Beck (1991) notes how a student's understanding of history is improved when he or she has the opportunity for in-depth exploration of important topics. Bransford, Kinzer, Risko, Rowe, and Vye (1989) discuss how a videodisc-based curriculum that involved exploration over a period of several months allowed students with learning problems to specialize in particular areas because the special topics remained relevant to the class topic. The class participation of these students rose dramatically, and their ability to read about their areas of specialization improved as they developed the knowledge and vocabulary necessary to understand the written materials.

Technology-Based Scaffolds for Learning

Students' abilities to acquire the knowledge necessary to create and evaluate their products are facilitated by several different uses of technology. Multimedia curriculum materials such as the videodisc-based curricula created by ABC News Interactive, the *Windows on Science* series created by Optical Data, and various special videodisc series produced by Nova, National Geographic, and others are particularly important uses of technology.

In our research to date, we have found that video-based contexts for exploration are particularly powerful when used with students who are poor readers, because the students can enter into discussions about issues highlighted in the video macrocontexts (see, for example, Bransford, Vye, Kinzer, & Risko, 1990; Cognition and Technology Group at Vanderbilt, 1992a). Also, just as initial language acquisition is facilitated when it takes place in a context rich in visual and auditory cues (see, for example, Chapman, 1978; Sherwood, Kinzer, Hasselbring, & Bransford, 1987; MacNamara, 1972), appropriate uses of video-based macrocontexts can greatly facilitate knowledge acquisition, vocabulary development, and the acquisition of strategies for comprehension and learning (see, for example, Cognition and Technology Group at Vanderbilt, 1991b; Sharp and others, 1992). We consistently find that events depicted in video-based macrocontexts motivate students to explore selected issues in more depth by consulting texts and other materials that help them pursue their learning goals (see, for example, Bransford, Vye, Kinzer, & Risko, 1990).

The Peabody Literacy Program used in our MOST environments also allows students to use a flatbed scanner and optical character recognition software to scan in relevant text and receive help (when needed) with pronunciation and vocabulary. This technology scaffold makes it much easier for students to learn from written documents that may be too difficult for the students to read without such help.

As students' knowledge about an area becomes greater, their reading is further enhanced by this increased knowledge base (see, for example, Juel, 1991). As mentioned earlier, the literacy program also provides instruction in decoding skills and allows students to supplement text with relevant video. Moreover, the program is designed in a way that makes it easy for teachers to assess the degree to which students are reading for meaning rather than simply engaging in "word calling." We noted earlier that an important advantage of the computer-based support scaffolding in MOST environments is that even students who are developmentally behind their peers can make important contributions to classroom discussions with the help of the technology (see, for example, Bransford, Vye, Kinzer, & Risko, 1990).

Cognitive Scaffolds for Learning

Besides technology-based scaffolds, students in MOST environments receive cognitive scaffolds for comprehension, learning, and transfer. In 1979, Durkin studied twenty-four classrooms and found a lack of instruction in reading comprehension strategies; more recent studies indicate that this is still a problem in U.S. classrooms, and one not easily overcome (Collins, 1992; Duffy, 1992; Pressley, El-Dinary, & Marks, 1992; Wong, 1985). One reason for the lack is that when students have questions about content, teachers have a natural tendency to explain the content rather than to help the students develop the skills necessary to clarify the content on their own (see, for example, Bransford, 1992; Langer & Applebee, 1987).

An important component of learning to learn is acquiring the skills of structuring, monitoring, evaluating, modifying, and checking performance. Lack of such metacognitive skills is often cited as a characteristic of individuals at risk of failure (see, for example, Wong, 1985). MOST environments have a well-organized and explicit user interface, which supports the development of students' metacognitive skills. When learning environments are well structured internally and externally, the development of students' metacognitive skills ought to be facilitated because more coherent mental models will result when the students use the environments. For example, in the comprehension instruction part of the Peabody

Literacy Program, learners acquire the skills necessary to detect inconsistencies, make decisions, and ultimately enter into mainstream conversations. It is to foster students' development of metacognitive skills that we employ the animated tutor—a dynamic, interactive external structure that is specific, provides assistance only when appropriate, and adapts to the learner's needs. In other words, the tutor's support fades as the learner improves, and increases when the learner's performance declines. Gradually the degree of structure needed for success decreases, as individuals gain extensive reading practice through working in the MOST environment.

Another metacognitive skill that is particularly important for interpersonal interaction and communication is the ability to monitor the impact of one's own communication efforts. Our MOST environments support students' efforts to build presentation products that other students evaluate for communication effectiveness. As described previously, the producer students then have opportunities to respond to the criticisms and to adapt their presentations to meet the evaluators' concerns.

Professional Development and Support for Teaching At-Risk Students

We noted earlier that professional development has been identified as the "missing link" in successful education reform (DeFord, Lyons, & Pinnell, 1991; Goldman & Pellegrino, 1987) and that many teachers are not prepared to work with diverse groups of students—especially students least ready for school. Without adequate preparation for and attention to effective professional development among the people who are expected to implement a project, the project will tend to remain a one-shot venture that is not replicated on a wide scale.

MOST environments use the same technology found in today's classrooms to provide the foundation for in-depth professional development and continuing support. For example, we begin teachers' professional development for our project by asking them to engage in the same production activities that their students will engage in. We supplement this activity with videotaped case examples that allow teachers to see firsthand a wide range of teaching approaches to learning activities for various children, and a range of the ways that teachers within the context of MOST environments interact with other teachers. In addition, videotaped cases can clearly show changes in literacy development over time in individual children. Several of our colleagues at Vanderbilt are also using videotaped cases for professional development (see, for example, Goldman, Barron, & Witherspoon, 1991; Michael, Klee, Bransford, & Warren, in press; Randolph & Evertson, 1992; Risko, 1992), and their data indicate that these programs can be highly effective. Data also suggest that videotaped evidence of students' changes over time is much more powerful in influencing teachers' beliefs about students' potential than is oral or written evidence of changes (see, for example, Vye, Burns, Delclos, & Bransford, 1987).

Continuing support for teachers who work in MOST environments is provided through the VISIT two-way videoconferencing system, which lets teachers actually show experts the problems they are experiencing with either the technology or the instruction and allows teachers to discuss possible solutions with other professionals. Sometimes these discussions take place with the project staff at Vanderbilt University; however, teachers can also hold discussions with peers at other schools with VISIT systems. To date, teachers using this system have told us that this form of immediate face-to-face communication is extremely helpful to them as a professional development tool.

Effective Connections to Homes and the Community

Recent research underscores that students' capabilities and motivation to learn are shaped by many influences, including their families, teachers, school climates, community organizations, and community values and expectations, each of which provides incentives and opportunities for further education and employment (see, for example, Comer, 1980; Heath, 1983; Nettles, 1991; Shields, 1991). Children's home environments are particularly important.

Although schools can compensate for some deficiencies in home environments, these influences still exert a significant impact on children's literacy development (Snow, Barnes, Chandler, Goodman, & Hemphill, 1991).

Our MOST environments use technology to help students make connections between their schools, homes, and communities. For example, the students' products provide a context in which parents and students can discuss ideas explored in the classroom, and students can make videotape copies of their multimedia products to share with their parents. Several studies have found that the existence of shared video-based contexts greatly increased the quality of the conversations between parents and children about important issues, especially when some instruction was provided to parents about how the macrocontexts could be used (see, for example, Cognition and Technology Group at Vanderbilt, 1992b; Pichert & Kinzer, 1992).

Conclusion

Our goal in this chapter was to illustrate how MOST environments can be useful for all students but especially for those at risk of school failure. It is our belief that MOST environments, used to develop literacy skills and to allow students to create authentic and meaningful multimedia products, can accelerate students' linguistic and conceptual development much more effectively than can typical school environments that are primarily language based. With technology as their scaffolding, MOST environments provide the following features:

- *Flexible technology.* Software can be tailored to provide support for students with a wide range of abilities and to elicit unique contributions from each student.
- *Authentic tasks.* Children can use literacy to teach, to learn, and to create products for effective communication.
- *Representational literacy.* Through videodiscs and computers, students can learn to communicate ideas flexibly, using multiple representations of spoken words, pictures, and print.

- *Mental model building.* With support from technology, students can practice deep comprehension and high-level verbal production.

- *Conceptualized development of phonemic awareness.* Students can learn to put sounds and letters together in meaningful contexts.

- *Content-based narrative and expository texts.* Students can practice literacy skills while building a base of useful, general world knowledge.

- *Professional development programs.* Teachers can acquire teaching skills through viewing video cases and can have ongoing support through videoconferencing.

- *Technology-based connections to schools and communities.* Schools and communities can be linked with students' learning through displaying student-produced multimedia presentations to parents and community members.

Our use of MOST environments is at an embryonic level. However, we have used some individual components of our MOST environments over several years, and we have conducted research showing that these components in and of themselves can be quite effective as teaching and learning tools.

But until recently, we had not put all the components of a MOST environment together in a comprehensive package. Thus, we are eagerly awaiting the outcome of our current research, which examines the impact of the complete MOST environment on the literacy skills of high school–age students at risk of failure. If our MOST environments are as successful as we believe they will be, the nature of these environments will make it easier to scale up our efforts to improve the literacy skills of many at-risk students. Over the next several years, we hope to demonstrate that one advantage of effective technology-based intervention programs is that the dissemination and scale-up problems common to more traditional teacher-based interventions can be more easily overcome than in the past.

References

Beck, I. L. (1991, March). *Reading and learning from social studies texts*. Paper presented at the Maryland Conference of Literacy in the 90's: Perspectives on Theory, Research, and Practice, Baltimore.

Bransford, J. D. (1992, April). *Improving cognitive strategy instruction: Pitfalls and promises*. Discussion at the annual meeting of the American Educational Research Association, San Francisco.

Bransford, J. D., Franks, J. J., Vye, N. J., & Sherwood, R. D. (1989). New approaches to instruction: Because wisdom can't be told. In S. Vosniadou and A. Ortony (Eds.), *Similarity and analogical reasoning* (pp. 470–497). New York: Cambridge University Press.

Bransford, J. D., Goldman, S. R., & Vye, N. J. (1991). Making a difference in people's abilities to think: Reflections on a decade of work and some hopes for the future. In L. Okagaki & R. J. Sternberg (Eds.), *Directors of development: Influences on children* (pp. 147–180). Hillsdale, NJ: Erlbaum.

Bransford, J., Kinzer C., Risko, V., Rowe, D., & Vye, N. (1989). Designing invitations to thinking: Some initial thoughts. Cognitive and social perspectives for literacy research and instruction. In S. McCormick, J. Zutrell, P. Scharer, & P. O'Keefe (Eds.), *Cognitive and social perspectives for literacy research and instruction* (pp. 35–54). Chicago: National Reading Conference.

Bransford, J. D., Vye, N., Kinzer, C., & Risko, V. (1990). Teaching thinking and content knowledge: Toward an integrated approach. In B. F. Jones & L. Idol (Eds.), *Dimensions of thinking and cognitive instruction: Implications for educational reform* (Vol. 1, pp. 381–413). Hillsdale, NJ: Erlbaum.

Brown, J. S., Collins, A., & Duguid, P. (1989). Situated cognition and the culture of learning. *Educational Researcher, 18*(1), 32–41.

Chapman, R. S. (1978). Comprehension strategies in children. In J. Kavanaugh & W. Strange (Eds.), *Speech and language in the laboratory, school, and clinic* (pp. 308–329). Cambridge, MA: MIT Press.

Cognition and Technology Group at Vanderbilt. (1990). Anchored instruction and its relationship to situated cognition. *Educational Researcher, 19*(5), 2–10.

Cognition and Technology Group at Vanderbilt. (1991a). Technology and the design of generative learning environments, *Educational Technology, 31*(5), 34–40.

Cognition and Technology Group at Vanderbilt. (1991b, May). Integrated media: Toward a theoretical framework for utilizing their potential. In *Proceedings of the Multimedia Technology Seminar* (pp. 3–27). Washington, DC: Center for Special Education Technology.

Cognition and Technology Group at Vanderbilt. (1992a). The Jasper series: A generative approach to improving mathematical thinking. In K. Sheingold, L. G. Roberts, & S. M. Malcom (Eds.) *This year in science series 1991: Technology for teaching and learning* (pp. 108–140). Washington, DC: American Association for the Advancement of Science.

Cognition and Technology Group at Vanderbilt. (1992b). The Jasper experiment: An exploration of issues in learning and instructional design. *Educational Technology Research and Development, 40,* 65–80.

Collins, A., Hawkins, J., & Carver, S. M. (1991). A cognitive apprenticeship for disadvantaged students. In B. Means, C. Chelemer, & M. S. Knapp (Eds.), *Teaching advanced skills to at-risk students: Views from research and practice* (pp. 216–243). San Francisco: Jossey-Bass.

Collins, C. (1992, April). *Facilitating teacher change: How teachers learn to teach in ways that they were not taught themselves.* Paper presented at the annual meeting of the American Educational Research Association, San Francisco.

Comer, J. P. (1980). *School power: Implication of an intervention project.* New York: Free Press.

Corey, S. M. (1944). Poor scholar's soliloquy. *Childhood Education, 33,* 219–220.

DeFord, D. E., Lyons, C. A., & Pinnell, G. S. (Eds.). (1991). *Bridges to literacy: Learning from reading recovery.* Portsmouth, NH: Heinemann.

Duffy, G. G. (1992, April). *Learning from the study of practice: Where we must go with strategy instruction.* Paper presented at the annual meeting of the American Educational Research Association, San Francisco.

Edgar, E. (1987). Secondary programs in special education: Are many of them justifiable? *Exceptional Children, 53*(6), 555–561.

Elder, W. L., & Hobbs, D. (1990). From reform to restructuring: New opportunities from rural schools. *Rural socialist,* 10(3), 10–13.

Goldman, E., Barron, L., & Witherspoon, M. L. (1991). Hypermedia cases in teacher education: A context for understanding research on the teaching and learning of mathematics. *Action in Teacher Education, 13*(1), 28–36.

Goldman, S. R., & Pellegrino, J. W. (1987). Information processing and educational microcomputer technology: Where do we go from here? *Journal of Learning Disabilities, 20*(3), 144–154.

Halpern, A. S., & Benz, M. R. (1987). A statewide examination of secondary special education for students with mild disabilities: Implications for the high school curriculum. *Exceptional Children, 54*(2), 122–129.

Hasselbring, T. S., Goin, L. I., Kinzer, C. K., & Risko, V. J. (1991). *Peabody Multimedia Adult Literacy Program* [computer program]. Nashville, TN: Vanderbilt University.

Heath, S. B. (1983). *Ways with words.* Cambridge, England: Cambridge University Press.

Juel, C. (1991, March). *Longitudinal research on learning to read and write with regular and at-risk students.* Paper presented at The Maryland Conference on Literacy for the 90's: Perspectives on Theory, Research, and Practice, Baltimore.

Kamil, M. (1991). A proposal for the National Reading Research Center. Submitted by College of Education, Ohio State University, Columbus, to the U.S. Department of Education.

Kirsch, I. S., & Jungblut, A. (1986). *Literacy: Profiles of America's young adults. Final report.* Princeton, NJ.: National Assessment of Educational Progress.

Knapp, M. S., & Turnbull, B. J. (1990). *Better schooling for the children of poverty: Alternatives to conventional wisdom: Vol. 1. Summary.* Washington, DC: U.S. Department of Education, Office of Planning, Budget and Evaluation.

Langer, J., & Applebee, A. (1987). *How writing shapes thinking: A study of teaching and learning* (Research Report No. 22). Urbana, IL: National Council of Teachers of English.

Lave, J. (1988). *Cognition in practice.* Boston: Cambridge.

MacNamara, J. (1972). Cognitive basis of language learning in infants. *Psychological Review, 79,* 1–13.

Maheady, L., Sacca, M. K., & Harper, G. F. (1988). Classwide peer tutoring with mildly handicapped high school students. *Exceptional Children, 55*(1), 52–59.

Means, B., & Knapp, M. S. (1991). Introduction: Rethinking teaching for disadvantaged students. In B. Means, C. Chelemer, & M. S. Knapp (Eds.), *Teaching advanced skills to at-risk students: Views from research and practice* (pp. 1–26). San Francisco: Jossey-Bass.

Michael, A. L., Klee, T., Bransford, J. D., & Warren, S. (in press). The transition from theory to therapy: Test of two instructional methods. *Applied Cognitive Psychology.*

National Assessment of Educational Progress (NAEP). (1988). *Who reads best?* Princeton, N.J.: Educational Testing Service.

National Commission on Excellence in Education (1983). *A nation at risk: The imperative for educational reform.* Washington, DC: Decision Resources Corporation.

Nettles, S. M. (1991). Community involvement and disadvantaged students: A review. *Review of Education Research, 61*(3), 379–406.

Palincsar, A. S., & Klenk, L. J. (1991). *Learning dialogs to promote text comprehension.* Ann Arbor: University of Michigan. (ERIC Document Reproduction Service No. ED 338 724)

Pallas, A. M., Natriello, G., & McDill, E. L. (1989). The changing nature of the disadvantaged population: Current dimensions and future trends. *Educational Researcher, 18*(5), 16–22.

Pichert, J. W., & Kinzer, C. K. (1992, April). *Embedded data in diabetes patient education.* Paper presented at the annual meeting of the American Educational Research Association, San Francisco.

Pressley, M., El-Dinary, P. B., & Marks, M. (1992, April). *Rites of passage: The perils of becoming a strategies instruction teacher.* Paper presented at the annual meeting of the American Educational Research Association, San Francisco.

Randolph, C. H., & Evertson, C. M. (1992, April). *Enhancing problem solving in preservice teachers' approaches to classroom management using video technology.* Paper presented at the annual meeting of the American Educational Research Association, San Francisco.

Rashotte, C. A., & Torgensen, J. K. (1985). Repeated reading and reading fluency in learning disabled children. *Reading Research Quarterly, 20*(2), 180–188.

Resnick, L. (1987). *Education and learning to think.* Washington, DC: National Academy Press.

Resnick, L. B., & Klopfer, L. E. (Eds.) (1989). *Toward the thinking curriculum: Current cognitive research.* Alexandria, VA: American Society for Curriculum and Development.

Rieth, H. J. (1990). *Curriculum issues in secondary school programs for students with mild disabilities.* Washington, DC: U.S. Department of Education, Office of Special Education Programs.

Risko, V. J. (1992, April). *Creating videodisc problem-solving environments to manage the complexity of literary instruction.* Paper presented at the annual meeting of the American Educational Research Association, San Francisco.

Scarcella, R. (1988). Conversational analysis in L2 acquisition and teaching. *Annual Review of Applied Linguistics, 9,* 72–91.

Schloss, P. J., Smith, M. A., & Schloss, C. N. (1990). *Instructional methods for adolescents with learning and behavior problems.* Boston: Allyn and Bacon.

Schumaker, J. B., Deshler, D. D., & Ellis, E. S. (1986). Intervention issues related to the education of LD adolescents. In J. K. Torgensen & B.Y.L. Wong (Eds.), *Psychological and educational perspectives on learning disabilities* (pp. 329–365). San Diego, CA: Academic Press.

Sharp, D.L.M., and others (1992). Literacy in an age of integrated-media. In M. J. Dreher & W. H. Slater (Eds.), *Elementary school literacy: Critical issues* (pp. 183–210). Norwood, MA: Christopher-Gorden.

Sherwood, R., Kinzer, C., Hasselbring, T., & Bransford, J. (1987). Macro-contexts for learning: Initial findings and issues. *Journal of Applied Cognition, 1,* 93–108.

Shields, P. M. (1991). School and community influences on effective academic instruction. In M. S. Knapp & P. M. Shields (Eds.), *Better schooling for the children of poverty: Alternatives to conventional wisdom* (pp. 313–328). Berkeley, CA: McCutchan.

Snow, C. E., Barnes, W. S., Chandler, J., Goodman, I. F., & Hemphill, L. (1991). *Unfulfilled expectations: Home and school influences on literacy.* Cambridge, MA: Harvard University Press.

Vellutino, F. R. (1979). The validity of perceptual deficit explanation of reading disability: A reply to Fletcher and Satz. *Journal of Learning Disabilities, 12*(3), 160–167.

Vye, N. J., Burns, M. S., Delclos, V. R., & Bransford, J. D. (1987). Dynamic assessment of intellectually handicapped children. In C. S. Lidz (Ed.), *Dynamic assessment: An interactional approach to evaluating learning potential* (pp. 327–359). New York: Guilford Press.

Wagner, M. (1989, March). *The transition experiences of youth with disabilities: A report from the National Longitudinal Transition Study.* Paper presented at the annual meeting of the Division of Research, Council for Exceptional Children, San Francisco.

Wagner, M. (1990, April). *The school programs and school performance of secondary students classified as learning disabled: Findings from the National Longitudinal Transition Study of Special Education Students.* Paper presented at the annual meeting of Division G, American Educational Research Association, Boston.

Wong, B.Y.L. (1985). Metacognition and learning disabilities. In D. L. Forrest-Pressley, G. E. MacKinnon, & T. G. Waller (Eds.), *Metacognition, cognition and human performance* (Vol. 2, pp. 137–180). San Diego, CA: Academic Press.

Zigmond, N., Kerr, M. M., Brown, G. M., & Harris, A. L. (1984, April). *School survival skills in secondary school age special education students.* Paper presented at the annual meeting of the American Educational Research Association, New Orleans, LA.

Zigmond, N., Kerr, M. M., & Schaeffer, A. L. (1988). Behavior patterns of learning disabled adolescents in high school academic classes. *Remedial and Special Education, 9*(2), 6–11.

Zigmond, N., & Thornton, H. (1985). Follow-up of postsecondary age learning disabled graduates and dropouts. *Learning Disabilities Research, 1*(1), 50–55.

Chapter Three

Computer Networks: Opportunities or Obstacles?

Denis Newman

Advocates of school technology are talking in glowing terms about the revolution that is about to take place in learning. Technology, it is said, will transform classrooms, provide patient tutors for each individual student, and enliven learning with graphics and interactive video. Seldom is it suggested that most school technology has either a fundamentally conservative impact or little impact at all. Although technology can be designed to support change in the curriculum or in the use of time and space for project-based or inquiry-based schoolwork, it is my view that most technology functions happily within the existing structures and supports the traditional compartmentalized curriculum.

The case in point that I discuss in this chapter is the use of computer networks, both within a single school, called *local area networking*, and between schools, called *wide area networking* or sometimes called *telecomputing*. Although networking technology has tremendous potential to support school restructuring, for the most part it has been counterproductive, or at best irrelevant, to any significant change. Of course, the acquisition of technology alone can never result in significant changes in a school. But technology can either support or inhibit the efforts of teachers and administrators as they attempt to foster change. Most worrisome are technologies that inhibit change. But as I also hope to illustrate, there are emerging models for the use of technology in ways that support change efforts. To illustrate these models, I have taken a different perspective than is usual on telecomputing, looking at it from within the school.

Shifting the Perspective on Telecomputing

The term *telecomputing* (a combination of *telecommunications* and *computing*) was adopted in the world of education to refer to using a single computer with a modem to access peers and resources outside the school. Telecomputing is most often described in terms of its ability to break down the walls of the school, opening it to distant resources as students communicate with students in other parts of the world or teachers communicate with teachers in other states.

Telecomputing has several benefits. Collaborative projects can be carried out between schools, as has been illustrated by the popular National Geographic Kids Network in which students experience hands-on science while contributing useful data for actual scientific investigations. Teachers working on similar problems can form geographically distributed communities to share information on effective implementations or to follow up with teachers they have met face-to-face in workshops. Students and teachers can obtain up-to-the-minute information from a large variety of resources relevant to their projects or professional work. In doing so, both students and teachers learn critical information-age skills while bringing authentic information into the classroom. In these ways, telecomputing can help build students' higher-order thinking skills while it also supports the community of teachers as they develop their own skills in using new resources for teaching.

If I were to leave the telecomputing story at this point, this technology would appear to be superbly situated to restructure schools toward the kind of project- and inquiry-based learning that fosters higher-order thinking skills. Unfortunately, the immediate prospects that telecomputing will have an impact on school restructuring are not as bright as we might hope. Although a large number of schools have the modems that are required for telecomputing, networking technology has had very little impact beyond isolated classrooms. The problem, for the most part, is that the local infrastructure, the networking technology *within* individual schools, either is not in a position to take advantage of outside resources or is designed in a way that makes using outside resources actually difficult.

Most schools that use a telecomputing system or wide area network (WAN) to link the computers inside a single building or campus with outside computers access the system through a single computer with a modem attached to a telephone line, located in a single classroom or at a teacher's home. It seems obvious that this single terminal cannot be adequate for the whole school. At best, it can serve a handful of classes, but most of the school's teachers and students will gain no firsthand experience with information sources available on the WAN outside the school. In these instances, telecomputing remains marginal as a force for restructuring the school.

In some rare cases, a local area network (LAN), connecting either all the computers in a computer lab or computers that are distributed among classrooms, is used to broaden access to outside resources, providing a WAN connection for every classroom computer. This is the equivalent of giving every computer its own modem and telephone line. These local area networks give many more students and teachers access to the wide area network than is possible with just a single point of connection, and do so far more efficiently than would be possible if every classroom had to be given its own telephone line and modem. This combination of LAN and WAN technologies can be very powerful, not only because it distributes students' and teachers' access to peers and resources outside the school but also because it increases the quality and value of the wide area connections. Collaborative projects within the school can contribute richer resources to other schools than is possible when telecomputing ability is limited to a single terminal. The idea behind combining LAN and WAN technologies is that internal and external communities can be mutually supportive. The excitement generated by external resources encourages experimentation within the school, and this spirit of experimentation, in turn, enriches the school's contribution to the external community.

LANs and WANs Are Unconnected
or Poorly Connected

Unfortunately, cases in which local area networks are used to broaden access to wide area networks are rare. Recently, in a project funded by the National Science Foundation, I and two of my colleagues conducted an informal search for such schools and found not more than a handful (Newman, Bernstein, & Reese, 1992). As part of this work, we followed up on a 1989 survey by the California Technology Project (CTP) (1990). The CTP survey assessed educational technology applications in a random sample of 1,000 California schools. The results of that survey gave us a glimpse of the current state of school networks. Four hundred and eighty-five schools had responded to the survey, which asked, among other questions, whether the school had a local area network and whether there was a modem or a wide area network connection available. With this information and an additional analysis of the data from CTP, we constructed a matrix (Figure 3.1) for the 407 schools for which appropriate data were available. Whereas 16.5 percent of the schools had LANs and 45 percent had access to WANs, only 10.6 percent had both. This 10.6 percent (43 schools) seemed like a good place to start our search since these schools had the potential to build on their LAN resources to make the best use of their WAN connections.

Wide Area Network
Connection

		Yes	No
Local Area Network	Yes	43 (10.6%)	24 (5.9%)
	No	140 (34.4%)	200 (49.1%)

Figure 3.1. LANs and WANs in 407 California Schools.

We were able to contact 30 of the 43 schools. The striking outcome of our follow-up research in these 30 schools, was that none of them made use of their instructional local area networks for distributing data coming from their wide area networks. (One school that approached such a use had a small single-purpose LAN that connected several terminals to a data base in the state capitol, but this setup was independent of the school's main LAN in a computer lab.) In more than half the cases, the modem used in instruction was not even on a LAN computer. When used for instruction in these schools, a computer with a modem was essentially a standalone device.

In business, higher education, government, and the military—that is, in all domains except K–12 schools—local and wide area networks are considered a single continuous technology applied to communication and sharing data. Telecomputing will be irrelevant to the restructuring of schools and education if schools do not learn how to use LANs and WANs together.

In the rest of this chapter, I will outline the two serious roadblocks to schools' using local area networks. First, I look at how the current uses of most LANs inhibit restructuring. This is the fundamental problem. Except in a small number of experiments, which I will also discuss, the current pedagogical purpose and the resulting management organization of existing LANs conflicts with an education reform goal of supporting acquisition of higher-order skills with LANs. Second, I look at how the current telecomputing technology inhibits wide access by the schools. Because of these two problems, there is a double mismatch that suppresses the school-restructuring potential of network technology. At the local area level, the technology is right, but the educational function is wrong. At the wide area level, the pedagogy is right, but the telecomputing technology presently used in schools does not allow for connections to the local area level. Although this state of affairs may sound discouraging, a rapid convergence of local and wide area networking is underway that promises both to break down the walls of the school and to help grow a new structure in their place.

Problem One: LANs That Restrict Restructuring

Except for a marginal use of telecomputing, network technology in schools typically takes the form of a local mechanism for instructional delivery. Painted in the broadest strokes, the distinction I am making here is between systems that *deliver* traditional instruction from a central repository and systems that enable teachers and students to *access and gather* information from distributed resources and communities of peers. Today's schools typically use computer networks for instructional delivery rather than accessing and gathering information. For example, a high school biology teacher who wants to learn to make the most of a new simulation of the cardiovascular system may be restricted because the school's network is designed simply to deliver courseware to students' workstations rather than to allow the teacher to use the network to learn from peers outside the school who are using the same simulation.

The delivery approach can be traced to the instructional paradigm that has dominated school computing from the first computer-assisted instruction (CAI) programs to the current advanced intelligent tutoring systems. The associated pedagogy puts the student in a passive role as the receiver of information. Often, the instructional goals emphasize basic skills, the usual items examined in standardized tests. Individualization of instruction is the major contribution of the technology, and students are isolated from peers (advertisements often show students wearing headsets) and from other resources such as remote data bases that would be necessary if students were to become involved in developing inquiry skills or performing open-ended real-world tasks whose results are not well assessed by standardized tests.

Conversely, the access-to-information approach is consistent with a pedagogy that gives learners active roles in exploring complex problems and that favors collaborative learning environments. In this approach, the computer often becomes a tool or stimulus for projects that let students delve deeply into subjects and sample problems. The previously mentioned simulation of the cardiovascular system, for example, makes improved information about a very complex organic system accessible to the biology classroom. In the access-to-information approach, a computing network could become a channel for the teacher's obtaining more information about that organic system, more peer collaborators, and additional materials that will make the most of the simulation when the student accesses it at the desktop.

How LANs Are Used for Instructional Delivery

Today, school LANs are dominated by the integrated learning systems (ILSs) that have evolved from the time-sharing CAI delivery systems of the 1970s. ILSs are usually sold as a lab consisting of enough computers that each student in the class can work individually. Courseware covers all major elements of the curriculum (thus the term *integrated*). Scheduling, tracking student progress, and managing instruction are the major functions of the LAN in this case. ILSs make it easy for schools to acquire and use computer technology without having to make major changes in goals or organization. A report by the EPIE Institute (Sherry, 1990), an independent consumer information organization, provides a detailed catalogue of this class of school technology and finds that it is growing in popularity.

In a sense, integrated learning systems can be considered a successful implementation of computers: one that serves a perceived need and fits well into the practices of the traditional school. The three aspects of ILS use that affect the way schools use their local area networks are the space in which the ILS is located, the curriculum to be taught, and the time frame of the ILS tasks. When work space, curriculum, and time frames are traditional, an ILS will conform to traditional pedagogical patterns. In this case, the uses of the LAN will actually support the traditional practices and make education reform all the more difficult.

Space. The EPIE report (Sherry, 1990) notes that it is an all but universal practice to put the integrated learning system in a lab. Although there is nothing inherent in the technology that requires this configuration, ILSs are sold as "labs," in units of about thirty, which is a sufficient number to simultaneously accommodate a whole class, assuming that students will work at the computers individually. In many ILSs, students also wear headsets, which further decreases peer interaction.

When an integrated learning system is centralized in a lab, the system can be more easily managed by a computer lab teacher or nonteaching paraprofessional than if the computers were spread through various locations. For a school starting with a low level of expertise, centralization also reduces the technical and subject matter training costs that would otherwise be necessary. Some educators also argue that having students occupied with computer tutorials offers teachers opportunities for dialogues with individual students who need more attention but are often ignored in traditional classroom teaching (Schofield, Evans-Rhodes, & Huber, 1990). Although these individual discussions are a fundamental change from the traditional lecture style, they do not change the traditional nature of the schoolwork, considered in terms of curriculum goals and class scheduling.

Curriculum and Assessment. Another way in which integrated learning systems are a good fit to traditional schoolwork is that the content organization of their courseware mirrors typical textbooks, offering separate categories of standard school subjects—math, reading, language arts, or science. For the most part, the content is also like the typical textbook in being presented as facts or procedures to be mastered in sequence.

This form of content and sequencing is necessary to the system's management and evaluation functions. Discrete tasks that result in a single correct answer can be evaluated by the system itself. More open-ended tasks, requiring, for example, formulation of a problem, research into sources outside the computer, or any kind of free-form response, cannot be handled by the system. Intelligent tutoring systems are a natural extension of the integrated learning system approach since they also operate best within confined subject domains and with a level of control over student responses similar to that of ILS courseware.

The division of topics into clearly defined subject areas also eliminates the need for teachers who handle different subjects to collaborate or for a teacher in a self-contained classroom to consider the integration of learning across the subjects. In this respect, too, ILSs strongly support existing work practices in most schools, where teachers are not expected to know much about what other teachers are doing.

Time. Integrated learning systems are designed on the assumption that each period will be self-contained. The tasks do not require preparation before the computer lab period, and call for a minimum of technical capability on the part of the student. Thus, the time frame assumed by ILSs is well suited to the structure of the traditional school day, broken into discrete periods. Teachers can easily schedule lab use into these preexisting time slots. A single task, such as an arithmetic problem, can usually be done in a matter of a few minutes. The short tasks of ILSs are also very similar to the kinds of tasks found on standardized tests. And the short, carefully constrained answer slots are ideal for automatic scoring in both instances.

How LANs Can Be Used for Access and Communication: The Earth Lab Project

However, there is an alternative to local area network use that restricts education reform. Integrated learning systems show that local area networks can support traditional schoolwork, which is highly compartmentalized into discrete subjects, grades, and classrooms. But LAN technology can also be used to break down barriers of time and space, providing a natural mechanism for extending teachers' and students' access to resources outside the school. In the school environment, barriers of time and space can also be reduced when teachers and students have flexible access to files (including data, text, reports, diagrams, and so on) across physical contexts (classrooms, computer labs, libraries, and homes) and time frames (periods, units, and grades). In essence, because files can be stored and retrieved from a file server on the LAN, it becomes possible to make data available wherever the student is working. This LAN capability makes project work more flexible and provides a sense of unity to the work, which is no longer limited by the time-and-place restrictions of the conventional school schedule.

These expanded uses and effects of LANs are illustrated by the work of the Earth Lab project, in which my colleagues and I have developed a local area network system for schools and conducted formative research on the system's functioning in several schools over the last four years (Newman, 1990; Newman, Goldman, Brienne, Jackson, & Magzamen, 1989; Newman, Reese, & Huggins, in press). The main school site is the Ralph Bunche School, a public elementary school (grades three to six) located in central Harlem in New York City. The school population of approximately 700 students is predominantly African American with a minority of Hispanic and other groups.

An AppleTalk network of approximately fifty Apple II and Macintosh computers includes a file server that allows central storage of data, text, and programs. The environment contains a variety of word processing, data base, desktop publishing, and other software, including electronic mail that connects students and teachers over both the local and wide area networks. Along with the technology, my colleagues and I introduced an earth science curriculum designed in collaboration with the teachers.

The primary means of supporting project work in Earth Lab are what we call *workplaces*. These are folders on the file server, in which the work of the project, in the form of text, data base, graphics, and code files, is stored. These workplaces, available to any computer on the school LAN, give groups a computer-based location for their work together. Figures 3.2 and 3.3 show the workplaces available to one sixth-grader, both within her class and at the schoolwide level. Schoolwide workplaces are set up to serve schoolwide clubs or other projects, such as Kid Witness News, a group

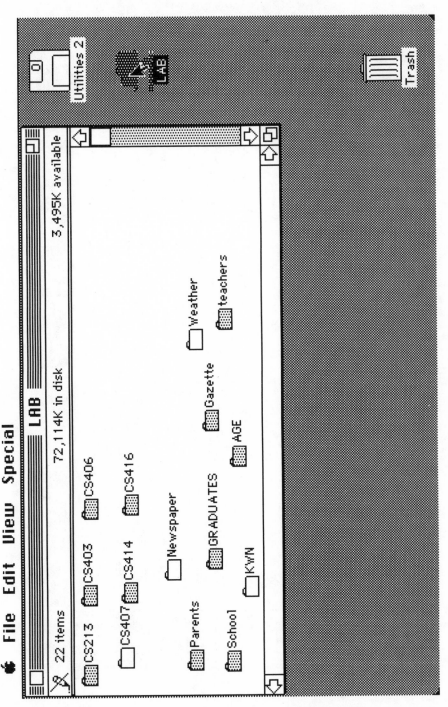

Figure 3.2. Sample LAN Workplaces at the Schoolwide Level.

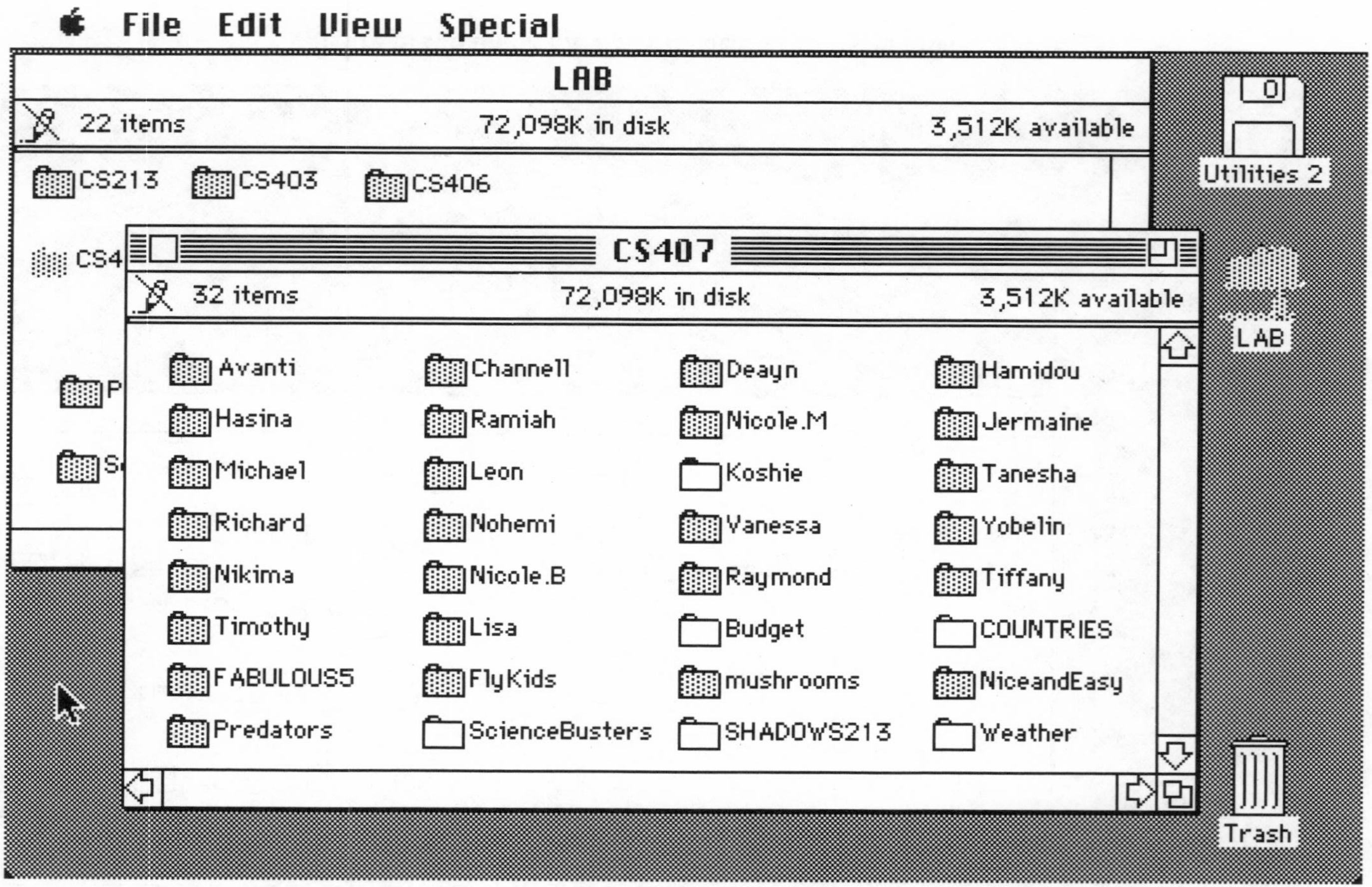

⚫ File Edit View Special

LAB

| 22 items | 72,098K in disk | 3,512K available |

CS213   CS403   CS406

CS4...

CS407

| 32 items | 72,098K in disk | 3,512K available |

Avanti	Channell	Deayn	Hamidou
Hasina	Ramiah	Nicole.M	Jermaine
Michael	Leon	Koshie	Tanesha
Richard	Nohemi	Vanessa	Yobelin
Nikima	Nicole.B	Raymond	Tiffany
Timothy	Lisa	Budget	COUNTRIES
FABULOUS5	FlyKids	mushrooms	NiceandEasy
Predators	ScienceBusters	SHADOWS213	Weather

P...

S...

Utilities 2

LAB

Trash

Figure 3.3. Sample LAN Workplaces at the Classroom Level.

involved in video production. Each individual also has a personal workplace within the classroom folder. The science work groups give themselves names that are used to identify group workplaces. Students share different data with different students or groups in the school—for instance, a science group, a noon-hour club, or their whole class.

We find that teachers who use this approach to a school LAN are better able to collaborate while students are better able to carry their work from one context to another. Moreover, the computer lab is increasingly used by a heterogeneous mix of students, with several projects or groups from different classes working simultaneously. The following examples, taken from our observations at the school, illustrate these changes.

Space. The Ralph Bunche School's computer network includes two separate labs, plus a satellite lab in a small room off one of the classrooms, and network connections in several other classrooms into which computers can be moved as needed. The way the computer-based project workplaces are set up for groups and individuals helps to develop a sense of continuity in work projects even though individuals may not work in the same room at the same time.

For example, several students from different classes and grades are editors for the school newspaper. The newspaper has a workplace on the network that students use for storing articles and other material for the newspaper. In addition, many students around the school contribute articles to the newspaper by sending them to the editors as electronic mail messages. The common workplace makes it easy for the editorial group to work on the newspaper at different times and places. In effect, the network makes the walls between classrooms permeable. The ease with which any student can contribute to the newspaper and the established identity of the group task that is supported by the workplace widen participation. Over time, students have become familiar with the network's function as a data organizer so that when other school projects, such as editing a video newscast, were started, students thought it quite sensible to create a computer-based workplace for their scripts, plans, and edit lists.

Curriculum and Assessment. The earth science curriculum developed for the initial field test and the curriculum materials that the teachers have continued to develop over subsequent years have been interdisciplinary. As students worked on weather and seasonal change projects, for example, they made connections to the disciplines of physics, math, writing, and social studies. The network system made classroom projects easier to manage and promoted collaboration among the teachers.

For example, at the beginning of the network's first year of operation, some teachers in this essentially traditional school had doubts about the students' capability to handle the autonomy involved in small-group project work. Having the small-group workplaces on the network helped communicate to the teachers that students were expected to work collaboratively. When interdisciplinary projects become a common feature of the curriculum, these electronic workplaces give students a clearer group identity or sense of project continuity, and thus, the workplaces help in classroom management. Instead of the centralized control of individualized instruction that is common in integrated learning systems, control in the reformed system can be distributed to the students.

The Earth Lab network made no attempt to provide a technological solution to the problem of assessing student progress or grading student projects, which is the central function served by the hierarchical nature of ILS courseware. We have, however, begun exploring the use of group and individual workplaces as portfolios of student work. The notion of a portfolio as an alternative vehicle for assessment is receiving growing attention among educators. The stages of work collected in a portfolio can provide insight to both teachers and students about the state of the students' projects and a retrospective look at the students' process of learning (Gardner, 1992). The workplaces at the Ralph Bunche School currently serve as archives of the groups' or individuals' project work and so can serve these functions of a portfolio. Assessment systems such as TextBrowser (Kurland, 1991), which serve a data base and analysis function for teachers' evaluations of students' work (their writing in the case of TextBrowser), provide a division of labor between teacher and technology that is appropriate for project-based schoolwork.

Time. The workplaces at the Ralph Bunche School provide continuity over time as well as location. Projects of collecting weather data and data on seasonal change extended over many months. In some cases, projects may extend over years, as new cohorts of students move through the school curriculum. Figure 3.4 shows a portion of the personal workplace of one sixth-grade student as it appeared during the first week of school. Notice that her writing and other data from fifth grade are still available to her, providing her with a powerful sense of her work's continuity and transcending the boundaries between grades.

The use of tool software requires a greater initial investment to bring students up to speed with the technology than is required for more traditional CAI programs, which present small tasks and simple interactions with the technology. However, the availability of the Earth Lab system to students at Ralph Bunche School over a period of years and consistency in the available tools has made it increasingly easy for teachers to introduce long-term projects as part of their curricula. In the first year of the system's operation, the sixth-grade class spent several months on fairly simple introductory projects designed to familiarize them with the word processing, data base, and communication tools. Several years later, teachers are able to start sixth-grade students immediately on substantial projects because they have learned the tools in the earlier grades.

The function of the Earth Lab local area network is to support project-based work. In contrast to integrated learning systems' functions, Earth Lab's functions are compatible with and supportive of telecomputing.

Problem Two: Current Telecomputing Technology

In addition to the functional incompatibility between reformed instruction and the resources that wide area networks offer on the one hand and the way local area networks are used in most schools on the other hand, there is also a difference in technology that makes many LANs used in schools incompatible with WANs. As long as this incompatibility persists, attempts to connect LANs and WANs, although not impossible, are very cumbersome. (The

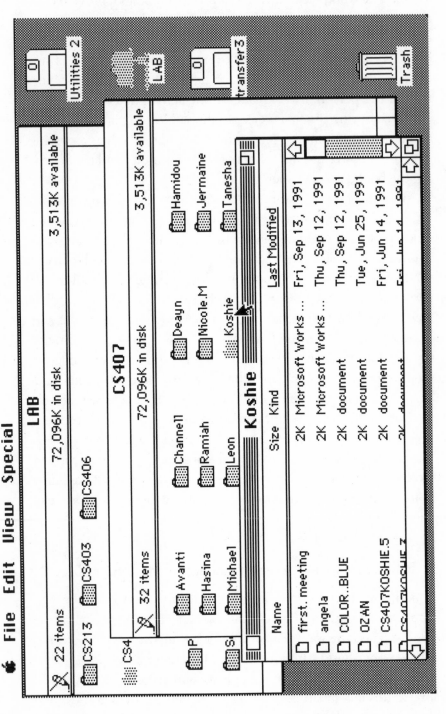

Figure 3.4. Sample LAN Workplaces at the Personal Level.

Appendix to this chapter presents a brief historical account that further explains the technical problems referred to in this section.)

The problem is that the current model for telecomputing is a network service that schools with WANs access via a terminal or terminal software on the classroom computer. Such network services have been available to schools, classrooms, and communities of teachers since the late 1970s (Kurshan, 1990a; Roberts, Blakeslee, Brown, & Lenk, 1990). The teacher or the school subscribes to the service, which may include conferencing with other teachers, weather reports, electronic mail, student pen pal communication, bibliographic data retrieval, and so on. Consumer services such as CompuServe, America Online, or Prodigy charge a connect-time fee. Electronic bulletin boards may offer similar services on a smaller scale and operate free of charge except for the telephone call. All these services (or *host* computers) are typically accessed through a single terminal on a classroom computer (or a teacher's home computer). Currently, practically all telecomputing projects use this kind of terminal-host connection.

The terminal-host connection has served the needs of isolated teachers and students attempting to access resources outside the school, but in most cases it cannot be extended to the school LAN in any straightforward manner because the connection between the terminal in the school and the remote host supports only the one interaction; other machines on the LAN cannot share the connection. Thus, telecommunication becomes an isolated, marginal activity. An individual teacher may conduct some projects with one classroom, but such activities will have little impact on the school as a whole. As our further analysis of the CTP survey indicated, even when a school has a LAN, its telecomputing computer is a standalone device.

However, local and wide area networks are beginning to converge in a way that will ultimately reinforce school restructuring. At the same time that LAN use is moving from the function of delivering instruction to the function of sharing and communicating information, WAN connections to the schools are beginning to employ a technology that connects the local area network directly into the wide area network. Instead of a single computer connected to the WAN as a terminal, all the computers on the LAN can be connected, as peers, to all the computers on the WAN, and the local area network can become a local extension of the wide area network.

The convergence between LAN and WAN technology follows from educators' growing interest in using the Internet as the standard for a national school network. As explained in the Appendix to this chapter, the Internet connects thousands of computer networks around the world. Although most of the thousands of teachers who use the Internet still make a terminal connection to a local host (at a nearby university, for example), some schools are beginning to explore direct connections between their LANs and the Internet and are taking advantage of the Internet's packet-switched system, which makes possible connections between schools' personal computers and the network.

Two advantages arise from this convergence of local and wide area networks. First, with a LAN connected to the Internet, a student or teacher can sit down at any computer to call up a mail server or other remote resource—data on Supreme Court rulings, for example. Many interactions between the local and wide area networks can be carried on simultaneously. Students or teachers can access the wide area network's resources at any time without concern for scheduling their turn in the computer lab where the single modem resides. The initiatives of individuals and groups in exploring resources will no longer have to be mediated by a single teacher.

A second advantage of the convergence is the integration of the school community with other widely distributed communities. With a mail server on the local school network, local and distant communications are supported by the same system from the students' and teachers' points of view. In these cases, local communication supports local project groups who are accessing remote resources. Teachers use local communications to coordinate their own work. The LAN becomes a medium for supporting communication and sharing information among the local community, not just a means of access to the wide area resources.

In a recently funded National Science Foundation research project, the National School Network Testbed, my colleagues and I are experimenting with direct network connections between school LANs and the Internet. This project will allow us to modify current software to make it more suitable for use in schools where the number of people using the network is quite large and changeable and where technical support staff are generally not readily available. Across a wide range of applications including staff development, collaborative curriculum development, and curriculum-related classroom projects, we will determine the main components of cost for and the educational benefit of the technology that allows a direct local area network connection to a wide area network.

The Ralph Bunche School is one of the research sites in which we have installed a direct network connection. This school had already been experimenting with the functionality of a LAN-WAN connection. Even without the more advanced technology required for a direct Internet connection, teachers and students had begun using their LAN as a vehicle for internal and external communication and sharing. For example, Ralph Bunche School students had engaged in collecting, sharing, and analyzing international data on changing sun shadow lengths, creating a guidebook that was shared with students in England, and obtaining and analyzing weather data from an information utility. We are using the network functions at this school as the basis for the design of a new kind of network system for schools.

From the perspective of the students and teachers, their electronic mail is connected directly to the communities outside the school. When a project group (which may be an individual, a small group, or the whole class) is carrying on a dialogue, the unit of communication is the group. Because in Earth Lab the group project is "housed" in a workplace, we are designing our new mail system so that the workplace, rather than the individual, will be the unit of communication in the mail system, as it is in fact. An electronic mail/conferencing system for schools that follows this design principle will be fundamentally different from the systems used in business contexts. As local and wide area networks used in education converge, we will have to address many such design issues to support project- and inquiry-based instruction.

Conclusion

It is far from true that technology automatically supports restructuring. Often technology is ineffective or irrelevant, as is the case with traditional telecomputing in schools. In other cases, technology actually works against desired changes, as is true of integrated learning systems. It is not enough to retrain teachers or to restructure work environments so the teachers can make better use of the technology. We may have to redesign the technology itself so that it becomes part of the solution rather than part of the problem.

Appendix: A Brief History of Network Technology

When educators talk about a "computer network," they are most often referring to a network service. This usage is reflected in several current surveys of school and educational networks (Kurshan, 1990a & 1990b; Kurshan & Harrington, 1991; McAnge, Harrington, & Pierson, 1990). For example, many teachers subscribe to CompuServe, America Online, Prodigy, or AppleLink, information services offered via a dial-up connection. Similarly, classrooms subscribe to the National Geographic Kids Network or to the AT&T Learning Network, which are more structured products provided by similar services. Local or dial-up bulletin board systems are also sometimes called networks. At other times, computer network refers to a community of people who use their access to a particular service as a means of communication within the community. For example, the "superintendents' network" consists of a group of administrators who dial into a computer at the Merrimack Educa-

Note: This Appendix is adapted from Newman, Bernstein, & Reese (1992).

tion Center in Massachusetts to communicate by electronic mail and share data base resources. This common usage implicitly accepts an antiquated notion of computer communication because it assumes that there is a particular computer service or host computer that all the members of the community use and that their common connection to that host is what defines the community. However, to fully understand the history of networks, it is necessary to get below the level of the services and communities that make use of networks, and look at the networks as systems of hardware, software, and transmission media.

The first thing resembling a computer network was the terminal-to-host system used on timesharing computers. First developed in the 1960s, the timesharing computer (the host) allowed many people simultaneous access from terminals (desktop consoles) wired directly to the host. In the late 1960s and early 1970s, the availability of modems, which turn digital into analog signals and vice versa, allowed the terminals to be located at the far ends of ordinary voice telephone lines. The model of centralized computing and communications between dedicated terminals and a host can be represented as illustrated in Figure 3.5. When personal computers (PCs) became widespread a decade ago, "terminal emulation" programs were developed so that a PC could serve as a terminal.

Terminals

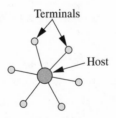

Host

Figure 3.5. Model of Terminal-to-Host Network.

Although the terminal-host connection let remote users use a single host, it did little for hosts that wanted to communicate with other hosts. If a data base were developed for one host, how could it be transferred to another host? How could a data base administrator sitting at a terminal on one host get files from or send files to another host? How could a scientist working on one host run a program that was on a host at a distant university? The answer was a distributed network on which hosts were not physically connected directly to each other but were connected to special-purpose computers called packet switches. Figure 3.6 represents these distributed computing and computer-to-computer communications as a complex mesh network. Packet switches serve to transmit the packets of data from one host to another. In this model, the hosts can be thought of as a network of peers, each of whom has a network address and can send and receive messages.

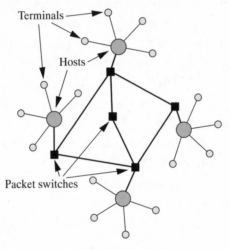

Figure 3.6. Model of Distributed Computing Network.

In the simple terminal-host connection, a stream of bits is transmitted between the terminal and the host. Since the line between terminal and host is dedicated to that connection (or, in the case of a dial-up, temporarily dedicated), there is no question where the bits are supposed to go. Anything from the terminal goes to the host and vice versa. In packet-switched networks, the bits from any one computer may want to go to any of the other computers, so there has to be a way to address the bits appropriately. Sending information in packets serves that purpose. Assembling a packet is like putting a group of bits in an envelope and addressing it to another computer. Each host has an address on the network. As the packets of data are sent out over the network, packet switches determine the most efficient route to the other computer.

The next major advance in computer networks occurred when local area networks connected PCs within a building to printers and other resources, including host computers. By the early 1980s, LANs were becoming commonplace on campuses and in corporations, as low-cost desktop PC systems and sophisticated desktop workstations became available. Like the wide area networks, LANs also use addressed packets to transmit information from one PC to another, as well as between each PC and the local host. Under these circumstances, the connection between the desktop PC and the host is just part of the local packet network, as illustrated in Figure 3.7.

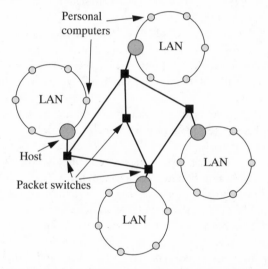

Figure 3.7. Model of Distributed Local Area Networks.

The development of different wide area network technologies and the need to interconnect multiple packet networks using different protocols led to the growth of internetworking. What is now called the Internet is an important development because it has extended the notion of internetworking internationally. The Internet consists of more than 5,000 networks that link together hundreds of thousands of computers and millions of users throughout the world.

References

California Technology Project. (1990). *An assessment of educational technology applications in California public schools.* Chico: California State University.

Gardner, H. (1992). Assessment in context: The alternative to standardized testing. In B. R. Gifford & M. C. O'Connor (Eds.), *Changing assessments: Alternative views of aptitude, achievement and instruction* (pp. 77–119). Boston: Kluwer.

Kurland, D. M. (1991, April). *TextBrowser: A computer-based tool for managing, analyzing, and assessing student writing portfolios.* Paper presented at the annual meeting of the American Educational Research Association, Chicago.

Kurshan, B. (1990a). *Home market for educational online services* (Research Report). Roanoke, VA: Educorp Consultants.

Kurshan, B. (1990b). *Statewide telecommunications networks: An overview of the current state and the growth potential* (Research Report). Roanoke, VA: Educorp Consultants.

Kurshan, B., & Harrington, M. (1991). *Statewide education networks: Survey results.* Roanoke, VA: Educorp Consultants.

McAnge, T., Harrington, M., & Pierson, M. E. (1990). *A survey of educational computer networks.* Blacksburg: Virginia Polytechnic Institute and State University.

Newman, D. (1990). Opportunities for research on the organizational impact of school computers. *Educational Researcher, 19*(3), 8–13.

Newman, D., Bernstein, S., & Reese, P.A. (1992). *Local infrastructures for school networking: Current models and prospects* (BBN Report No. 7726). Cambridge, MA: Bolt Beranek & Newman, Inc.

Newman, D., Goldman, S. V., Brienne, D., Jackson, I., & Magzamen, S. (1989). Peer collaboration in computer-mediated science investigations. *Journal of Educational Computing Research, 5*(2), 151–166.

Newman, D., Reese, P. A., & Huggins, A.W.F. (in press). The Ralph Bunche computer mini-school: a design for individual and community work. In J. Hawkins & A. Collins (Eds.), *Design experiments: Restructuring through technology.* Cambridge: Cambridge University Press.

Roberts, N., Blakeslee, G., Brown, M., & Lenk, C. (1990). *Integrating telecommunications into education.* Englewood Cliffs, NJ: Prentice Hall.

Schofield, J., Evans-Rhodes, D., & Huber, B. R. (1990). Artificial intelligence in the classroom: The impact of a computer-based tutor on teachers and students. *Social Science Computer Review, 8*(1), 24–41.

Sherry, M. (Ed.). (1990). *The integrated instructional systems report.* Water Mill, NY: EPIE Institute.

Chapter Four

Integrating Technology with Teacher Preparation

Linda C. Barron and
Elizabeth S. Goldman

New societal goals for education, recommendations from current educational research findings, and theories from cognitive and social psychology challenge a number of traditional beliefs about school learning: beliefs about *how* students learn, beliefs about *who* should learn (or is capable of learning), and beliefs about *what* is important to learn. Changing their instructional methods to conform to educational reform recommendations creates challenges for many teachers, but it places special demands on beginning teachers, whose framework for interpreting what goes on in a classroom is heavily influenced by their own school experience.

We take the position that teachers who are expected to redefine their ideas about teaching and learning must have opportunities to examine instructional methods in light of reform recommendations and current information about learning. But such examination, analysis, and reflection are often difficult or impossible in the complex, fast-moving environment of real classrooms. Therefore, our purpose in this chapter is to explore ways videodisc and integrated media technologies can be used in teacher educa-

Note: This work was supported in part by National Science Foundation grants TPE-8751472, TPE-8950310, and TPE-9053826. Any opinions, findings, and conclusions expressed are those of the authors and do not necessarily reflect the views of the National Science Foundation. We extend our appreciation to Barbara Means, Paul Cobb, and Joe Murphy for their review of and comments on early drafts of this chapter.

tion programs to help teachers rethink traditional instruction. We believe that certain types of technologically based materials can provide an environment that is more conducive to examination, reflection, and analysis than the real classroom, and we will mention several teacher education projects that are developing and using technology to provide such environments in which preservice teachers can learn about reformed teaching and learning.

Restructuring at the Classroom Level

Much of the attention that has been given to restructuring U.S. schools has been devoted to issues of school organization and governance (Elmore, 1992; Evertson & Murphy, 1992; Hallinger, Murphy, & Hausman, 1992). Restructuring discussions and guidelines have included such themes as school-based management, teacher empowerment, and parental choice (Hallinger, Murphy, & Hausman, 1992; Smith & O'Day, 1991). However, in recent publications, policymakers and researchers have suggested that initiatives in these areas alone are unlikely to produce the changes desired in educational processes and outcomes. They recommend increased attention to restructuring at the classroom level—specifically restructuring in student learning and in the teaching needed to bring about improvements in student learning (Elmore, 1992; Fishman & Duffy, 1992; Murphy, 1991).

Such recommendations for restructuring the teaching and learning processes are based on current educational research findings that support a view of learning that has come to be labeled *constructivist* or *student-centered*. In the constructivist model, learning is seen not as a transmission of information from teacher to student but as an active problem-solving process in which the learner builds on his or her prior understandings to construct new knowledge (Resnick, 1987; von Glasersfeld, 1987; Yackel, Cobb, Wood, & Merkel, 1990). Many modern researchers view learning as a process of enculturation (Brown, Collins, & Duguid, 1989) that is shared, developed, and refined through social interaction and conversation. Knowledge can be considered an individual property, but it can also be thought of as shared by a group, that is, as a *social construction* as well as an individual one (Cobb, Yackel, & Wood, 1992; Leinhardt, 1992).

Those who hold a constructivist view of learning believe that what a student learns depends to a great degree on the context in which he or she learns it (Cognition and Technology Group at Vanderbilt, 1990; National Council of Teachers of Mathematics, 1989); that is, knowledge is situated in, and inseparable from, the activity, context, and culture in which it is developed (Brown, Collins, & Duguid, 1989). When people learn in the context of meaningful activities, they are more likely to be able to use the information as a tool to solve problems (Bransford & Vye, 1989; Cognition and Technology Group at Vanderbilt, 1990). On the other hand, knowledge that is acquired through artificial activities (such as solving textbook mathematics problems) may be effective in certain school settings (passing tests on comparable problems), but not necessarily in the real world (Cognition and Technology Group at Vanderbilt, 1990, 1993; National Council of Teachers of Mathematics, 1989). A major goal of the restructured classroom is to provide settings in which all children have an opportunity to engage in meaningful and authentic activities, to explore complex problems, and to communicate about these activities with the teacher and peers in both the classroom and the larger community.

Technology can support students' acquisition of higher-order thinking and problem-solving skills in a number of ways. At one level, students' use of technology as a tool in school projects contributes to the authenticity of the projects, because technology pervades much of society today (American Association for the Advancement of Science, 1989; National Council of Teachers of Mathematics, 1989; Sheingold, 1991). For example, it is realistic to expect students to use desktop publishing software to produce a class newspaper, a spreadsheet to develop a budget for a class project, and telecommunications to share information with students from other geographic areas (see Newman, 1992).

At another level, technology can be used to introduce a problem for student investigation. For example, videodisc-based *anchors* or *macrocontexts*, such as those developed at Vanderbilt University

(Bransford, Sherwood, Hasselbring, Kinzer, & Williams, 1990; Cognition and Technology Group at Vanderbilt, 1990), are realistic stories with dilemmas or suggested projects included in them that allow students to experience a shared context in which they engage in sustained thinking about complex problems. In some instances, technology can simulate a real-world situation that is not feasible for youngsters to explore otherwise (for example, space travel) or one in which complex episodes must be revisited or examined for information in a way that real-time activity does not allow. Thus, technology affords opportunities for making teaching and learning more efficient, more applicable to real-world problems, and more accessible to students with different backgrounds than the materials and instructional approaches of the traditional classroom can afford (Fishman & Duffy, 1992; National Council of Teachers of Mathematics, 1991; Pea, 1987; Sheingold, 1991).

Challenges for Teachers

New educational goals that demand a higher level of literacy and subject-area understanding for all students, new theories about how individuals learn, and the potential that newly emerging technologies have for supporting learning all have important implications for teachers. For many teachers, the central fact in these implications is change. The student-centered classroom is quite different from the traditional classroom in which the teacher is the authority for information and students work independently on tasks that stress memorization of discrete facts and skills. As the teacher's role with students shifts from provider of information to facilitator of knowledge construction, classrooms must be reorganized to allow students to interact with the teacher and with each other. Redesigning classrooms so that *all* children (including those considered special or at risk) have opportunities to develop higher-order thinking and problem-solving skills requires teachers "both to give up long-held beliefs about teaching and learning and to devise instruction that embodies the new goals and approaches" (Sheingold, 1991, p. 19). For many teachers, this means replacing well-practiced teaching approaches, such as those associated with differentiated ability grouping, with less familiar ones, such as collaborative learning, inquiry-oriented instruction, and project-based curricula.

Their approaches and beliefs are not the only things teachers are being asked to change. Instruction designed around existing and familiar materials (for example, the spelling book or the word-problem worksheet) is often inconsistent with the goals of the redesigned classroom. Therefore, teachers must not only select or create new instructional materials but learn how to use them as well. Some of the new materials will almost certainly involve technology, and this technology places additional demands on teachers. Information and communication technologies heralded by many as exciting new conceptual tools for children and youth may be both unfamiliar and threatening to the teacher who has spent much of his or her academic and professional career in a technology-poor environment.

Teacher education, both inservice and preservice, and ongoing support for teachers throughout the restructuring process are critical to the success of any restructuring effort. Teachers tend to teach as they were taught (Ball, 1990; Lortie, 1975), and very few teachers have experienced as students the environment envisioned for the restructured classroom. Beginning teachers, in particular, have college courses as their most recent models of instruction in the subject areas they will be expected to teach, and these college courses have almost invariably been lecture based.

In addition to not knowing what student-centered instruction might look like, some teachers have a narrow, fact-based understanding of their subject areas (Ball, 1990; Borko and others, 1992; Shulman, 1986), and they are uncomfortable in a classroom environment that encourages students to ask questions that a teacher may be unprepared to address.

Educators and researchers familiar with emerging media and communications technologies believe that these can play important roles, both in conveying new images of schools and learning to teachers and in supporting teachers who are working, or preparing to work, in student-centered classrooms (Ball, Lampert, & Rosenberg, 1991; Everton & Harris, 1992; Fishman & Duffy, 1992;

Goldman & Barron, 1990, 1991; Lampert & Ball, 1990; Merseth & Lacey, 1992; Randolph, Smithey, & Evertson, 1991; Risko, 1992b; Risko, Yount, & Towell, 1991; Sheingold, 1991). Just as technology can anchor or simulate a real-world context for novices learning complex problem-solving skills in a particular specialty, technology can simulate a real classroom for novice teachers learning to teach. In the next sections of this chapter, we will describe in more detail what some such technologies look like and the status of their use in teacher education programs. Since a comprehensive survey of the use of technology in teacher education is beyond the scope of this chapter, we will restrict our discussion to applications that make use of integrated media systems.

Integrated Media Technology

The terms *hypermedia*, *multimedia*, and *integrated media* refer to a computer-controlled nonlinear integration of information from a variety of media such as text, audio, video, or computer graphics. (We prefer to use the term *integrated media* unless we are describing a project or citing a publication that uses one of the other terms.) In an integrated media format, a computer screen displaying text or graphics might look very much like a page of a book. However, unlike ordinary print material, which is linearly organized, these computer programs contain electronic links or "buttons" that allow a user immediate and random access to other information. For example, if the first section of this chapter were presented in an integrated media format, the reference citations might be linked to abstracts of the articles themselves. Moving an electronic pointer to any reference and selecting that reference (by clicking the mouse) could produce, on the screen, both the source and an abstract of the work. When a computer is connected to a videodisc player (or has access to other sources of video or audio), the electronic buttons on the computer screen can provide access to information in other formats. For example, a paragraph describing characteristics of the redesigned classroom might contain links to video segments illustrating instructional activities or to audio segments from interviews with teachers who are in the process of redesigning their approaches to instruction. The user can click on a word or icon (picture) and see the video segment on a video monitor—or in some systems, in a window on the computer screen itself.

Researchers and developers of prototype integrated media products cite several features of the materials that offer benefits for instruction. First, the integration of video with text and information from other media creates a rich context for student investigation and problem solving (Bransford, Sherwood, Hasselbring, Kinzer, & Williams, 1990; Cognition and Technology Group at Vanderbilt, 1990). Second, nonlinear linking of information makes it possible for a topic to be examined from multiple perspectives, and this examination helps students organize knowledge in ways that promote retention and transfer (Spiro & Jehng, 1990). Third, when appropriate tools are available in the system, learners can create their own integrated media products, thus becoming involved in interpreting or producing knowledge (Bransford, Franks, Vye, & Sherwood, 1989; Cognition and Technology Group at Vanderbilt, 1991; Hasselbring, Goin, & Bransford, 1991; Spiro & Jehng, 1990).

Integrated Media Technology in Preservice Teacher Education

This section looks in more detail at some specific challenges that the redesigned classroom poses for the beginning teacher, and examines reasons why integrated media technology holds particular promise for helping teacher educators address those challenges.

A Different View of Knowing

The way a teacher teaches is related to the beliefs that he or she holds about the nature of the subject and what it means to "know" the subject (Clark & Peterson, 1986; Lampert, 1987). If a teacher believes, for example, that mathematics is the process of applying rules, then that teacher is likely to teach mathematics by having children memorize rules (National Council of Teachers of Mathematics, 1991; Romberg & Carpenter, 1986). Teachers who spent their own elementary years memorizing terms in science class are not likely to view science as a social activity that "inevitably reflects social values and viewpoints" (American Association for the Advancement of Science, 1989, p. 29); nor are they likely to understand how to organize projects and activities in which children share responsibility for learning, come to common understandings, and communicate these understandings to others. Many preservice teachers bring from their own school experience strong beliefs about what it means to know a subject or about who is capable of knowing the subject (see, for example, Ball, 1990; Borasi, 1990). Their concepts of teaching, learning, and knowing in a subject area are often dysfunctional in a restructured classroom, where all pupils are expected to engage in exploration, communication, and problem solving in realistic contexts.

Technology can help these preservice teachers develop new models of teaching and learning in content areas. At Michigan State University, Magdalene Lampert and Deborah Ball have created integrated media materials to "help teacher education students learn to think in new ways about the nature of the work entailed in teaching elementary school mathematics" (Ball, Lampert, & Rosenberg, 1991, p. 1). These materials include videotapes and classroom artifacts (student products, teacher journals, and observer field notes) from the fifth- and third-grade mathematics classes Lampert and Ball teach. The Ball and Lampert tapes, by themselves, are useful examples of inquiry-oriented teaching in classes where students reason, solve problems, and engage in discussion about mathematical ideas. When annotated with teacher comments and supplemented with student products, the videotapes provide rich case studies that preservice teachers can use to explore the aspects of teaching "that are invisible: thinking, reasoning, deciding, and caring" (Ball, Lampert, & Rosenberg, 1991, p. 2). The developers of the materials state that integrated media environments make it possible to represent the complexity and the endemic dilemmas of the elementary school classroom and to integrate these representations with theoretical perspectives on teaching and learning (Ball, Lampert, & Rosenberg, 1991; Lampert & Ball, 1990). Lampert and Ball envision that the videotaped lessons they have taught will be used by teacher educators to present preservice teachers with "a replay of a real time lesson and then conduct an analysis of that lesson in a seminar discussion format" (1990, p. 6).

Videodisc materials developed at Vanderbilt University for use in mathematics and science methods courses for prospective elementary teachers use pairs of contrasting lessons to show the effects of different types of instruction on children's participation in the learning process (Goldman, Barron, & Witherspoon, 1991; Hofwolt, 1992). One of the science videodiscs contains edited versions of two second-grade science lessons taught by the same teacher. In the first lesson, the teacher and students "discuss" a chapter from the science text on change of state of matter; the second lesson is a hands-on investigation in which the children collect data on the insulating properties of cups made of different materials in order to decide which type of cup to use for a class party. The teacher is enthusiastic and encouraging in each lesson, and the class is well behaved in both. In the traditional lesson, most of the children are able to recite back to the teacher the terms or definitions that they have "learned." However, closer analysis of the two lessons (an analysis facilitated by the viewers' ability to contrast video segments by using the HyperCard stack associated with the disc) reveals substantial differences in the level of student involvement, the degree to which the children raised questions or offered opinions about the scientific phenomena they were studying, the level of interaction between children, the level of scientific thinking, and the general interest in the content of the lesson. The children's thinking processes and potential misconceptions are much more visible in the hands-on lesson. At specified places in the video, the lesson can be stopped and the viewer asked to interpret what a particular child was asking or suggesting. A methods course instructor might use these videodiscs, in a presentation format, as a context for class discussion on such topics as what it means to "know" science, the organization and management demands in a hands-on teaching environment, the role of the teacher in science investigations, children's misconceptions in science, how to make children's thinking visible, and the teacher's decision-making in a student-centered environment.

Recently one of the authors of this chapter used a videodisc containing contrasting mathematics lessons (see Goldman, Barron, & Witherspoon, 1991, for a description of these materials) in another format in her methods course. Instead of the instructor's developing the HyperCard stack and presenting the contrasts, students in the mathematics methods course were assigned readings on certain topics (such as the role of mathematical representations in children's understanding of mathematics), and the methods course students, working in groups of four at video stations in a computer laboratory, developed their own integrated media presentations on their topics using video segments that they selected from the videodisc to illustrate points in their presentations. They then presented their projects to their classmates using a presentation console in the lab. Text from HyperCard screens, displayed from the computer through an LCD (liquid crystal display) panel on the overhead projector, served as an outline of the points the methods course students wished to make, and video buttons in the program accessed the video segments, which were played through wall-mounted monitors in the classroom.

We believe that this exercise not only encouraged the methods course students to consider course information in the context of actual practice, but it took the methods course instructor out of the role of providing the initial interpretation and let the students explore differences in instructional methods for themselves. After the student exploration, the instructor capitalized on the student interpretations by leading class discussions on the topics the interpretations raised. We believe that preservice instructional activities such as this mirror the activities we propose that the methods course students use when they work with elementary school pupils. Thus, the students experience the method of teaching that we would like them to try for themselves. A byproduct of this type of activity, we are finding, is that the preservice teachers become more comfortable with computers (Goldman, Barron, & Witherspoon, 1992).

In Vanderbilt remedial reading methods courses, Victoria Risko (1992a) is using video-based case studies that allow preservice teachers to explore multiple sources of information about the teaching of children with reading difficulties. A videodisc with associated HyperCard stack focuses on one child and offers such information as video of the child reading, video interviews with parents and teacher, student products and assessment information, and related references and abstracts from the literature. Risko's case materials were designed to help change prospective teachers' views of the disabled reader: "Their understanding of remedial readers tends to be narrow, usually related to 'have not' characteristics (for example, limited mental ability, deprived family life, deficient skill development), which further restricts their understanding of low achieving students' capabilities and the multiple factors that might interact to produce disabled readers" (1992a, pp. 6–7).

Course instructors use these cases in whole-class and small-group sessions, both as a context for discussion of the factors that produce disabled readers and as a model for a case-based approach to diagnosing and addressing reading problems.

In each of the uses of integrated media technology described here, the technology provides a richer base of information and a more effective vehicle for analysis and investigation than do linear videotapes, which are usually passively viewed. To change teachers' views about what it means to understand a subject or what it means to teach for understanding, we believe that teachers must be able to see why traditional instruction is problematic, especially for certain children. For example, for some of our preservice teachers, the traditional text-based science lesson mentioned earlier is their *only* model of science instruction, and when they watch that lesson without seeing the contrast, they are impressed with the way the teacher is presenting the content. Allowing methods course students to focus on a single incident or child, to revisit parts of a lesson, and to access additional information is particularly useful in encouraging them to analyze how different children react to instruction.

Analyzing Pupil Understandings

Teachers, especially beginning teachers, have difficulty knowing
what their students understand and think; yet this knowledge is
essential if teachers are to base their interactions with individual
students on each student's prior knowledge. Leslie Steffe (1990,
p. 391), in describing teachers' mathematical knowledge, suggests
that "the mathematical knowledge of students as perceived by
teachers is an invention of the teachers." Beginning teachers have
limited experience in assessing pupil knowledge and understanding, and even experienced teachers are often unaware of intuitive
understandings and misconceptions that children bring to classroom instruction (see, for example, Carpenter, Fennema, Peterson,
& Carey, 1988).

Integrated media research environments, such as those being
developed by the Research Group on Mathematics Education and
the Computer Centre at the University of Utrecht (van Galen,
Dolk, & Feijs, 1990), should be especially useful in helping beginning teachers construct models of how children understand subjects, models that may be quite different from the teacher's "adult"
understanding of the material. These researchers have developed
interactive-videodisc teacher education materials that support the
"realistic mathematics" approach to teaching mathematics (see
Streefland, 1990, or Gravemeijer, 1990, for a discussion of realistic
methods). One of the University of Utrecht videodiscs contains
interviews with young children who are asked to perform various
counting tasks; another contains classroom footage of children
explaining how they solved a problem that involved finding the
number of tables needed to seat a certain number of people.
Through the computer program that controls the videodisc,
prospective teachers are asked to interpret children's thinking in
the counting tasks or to examine the differences between children's
written work and their verbal explanations of their strategies
for solving the problem of the tables. The software allows teachers
to isolate and replay student responses and explanations and to
type in comments. The developers believe that this use of tech-

nology offers an advantage over real-time observations of classrooms and activities since it allows prospective teachers to have focused practice in analyzing children's thinking "without the task of managing the class at the same time" (van Galen, Dolk, & Feijs, 1990, p. 3).

Improvisation and Instructional Choices

Orchestrating discourse, interpreting student contributions, helping students construct mature understandings, organizing cooperative learning and problem solving, and managing instruction in complex environments all require some degree of improvisation, yet improvisation is especially problematic for beginning teachers (Berliner and others, 1988; Borko & Livingston, 1989). Teaching is full of inherent dilemmas (see, for example, Lampert, 1987), and teachers must often make difficult choices. For example, on the one hand, teachers who teach from a constructivist perspective must be willing to "honor students' 'inventions,' or they will not share them. On the other hand, the teacher needs to guide students toward a more mature understanding, which frequently means challenging student constructions" (Prawat, 1992, p. 11). Furthermore, the acknowledgment that learning is a socially constructed act means that this guiding and challenging will take place publicly, and thus will require a high level of teacher sensitivity and judgment.

Randolph, Smithey, and Evertson (1991) have developed and used videodisc examples and HyperCard programs in a secondary education methods course at Vanderbilt University in order to engage preservice teachers in a problem-solving approach to classroom management. The videodisc examples emphasize planning for smooth classroom operations and highlight teacher decision making during the course of instruction. Results from studies concerning these materials indicate that the video examples contributed to the "preservice teachers' abilities to dimensionalize classroom events" and to sort through the "multiple layers of complexity that make up real life in classrooms" (Randolph & Evertson, 1992, p. 12).

Some Vanderbilt University materials use simulations of teacher decision points to help preservice teachers confront the types of choices they will be required to make during the course of instruction (Goldman, Barron, & Witherspoon, 1992). In these materials, the program stops the video at critical incidents and poses such questions as "Can you interpret what the student is asking?" or "If you were the teacher, how would you respond to this student's suggestion?" These incidents become minicases as groups of preservice teachers discuss options and the options' possible consequences. Some incidents are particularly rich in the different perspectives that can be taken on the decision presented. For example, one such incident occurs in the hands-on science lesson mentioned earlier. In the recorded lesson, each group of children had one metal, one glass, and one Styrofoam cup, with covers for each of the cups and an ice cube in each cup. At two-minute intervals, the children removed the covers from the cups and ranked the cups according to the size of the melting ice cube, with the cup having the largest piece of ice ranking number one. At one point, while waiting to record an observation, the teacher asked the children to feel the outside of each cup and say what they had discovered. "Kevin" responded: "Well, this cup [metal] is cold—and—and this one [Styrofoam] is hot—sort of warm—*but it got first place in ours.*"

Kevin had noticed that the Styrofoam cup had the largest piece of ice ("got first place"), but that the sides of the cup were warm. When one watches his response, it is clear that his observation is counter to his intuition and that there is a question implied: Why isn't the coldest cup keeping the ice frozen best? In this situation, a number of factors influence the teacher's next move. First, she may or may not recognize that Kevin is confronting a counterintuitive event. Such recognition requires that the teacher pay attention to Kevin's thinking as well as have some knowledge of children's misconceptions in science. Second, she must call on her own understanding of energy transfer in order to assess Kevin's understanding. The teacher must then decide whether this is a "teachable moment" that should be followed up, either with Kevin individually or with the whole class. The decision about follow-up may be influenced by theoretical issues such as the developmental level of the children (the teacher might consider whether a discussion of molecules is appropriate for second-graders) or practical considerations (the teacher might think that if she stops to deal with Kevin the class will miss the next timed observation).

At Vanderbilt, we use incidents such as this in methods courses with the instructor showing the video and the teacher education students working in groups to suggest and justify an action for the teacher. These suggestions and justifications are then debated among the groups. In a slightly different use of video lesson decision points, methods course students work in groups at video stations to review an edited version of a complete lesson, and the computer program stops the video at various points to simulate the decision-making process a teacher goes through in the course of a lesson. When the video stops, the computer poses the question, "If you were teaching this lesson, what would you do now?" The simulation software allows the methods course students to enter their comments about each lesson incident, and the comments can be retrieved and printed out for the students' own reference or for the instructor's review.

Materials and Methods

In traditional materials and methods courses in the past, prospective teachers devoted much of their time to learning about available curricular materials and developing lesson plans or resource files for using the materials. When classroom films and, later, videotapes became available for teacher education, they were used primarily for "showing" how to teach. Today, teacher education programs that view the teacher as a problem solver or decision maker in a complex and ill-structured domain are more likely to take an analytical approach to teacher education and to use integrated materials, like those we have been describing, in ways that encourage teacher reflection and the development of analytical skills (see, for example, Lampert & Ball, 1990, or Risko, 1992a). However, it is still important for prospective teachers to have access to information about available curricular materials and to be able to see examples of the materials' use.

Data bases being produced through three integrated media development projects offer resources for integrated media teaching materials and approaches for prospective and practicing teachers. Gary Bitter and his colleagues at Arizona State University have developed videodisc materials that focus on the methodology of using manipulatives in teaching elementary school mathematics, and these materials have been used in the ASU teacher education program (Bitter, 1992). The main goal of the project was to "provide instructors with a generic visual data base of vignettes that they could use during their instruction" (Frederick & Hatfield, 1991, p. 3). The materials show real classroom scenes from grades one, three, and five of teachers and children using geoboards and numeration blocks. The methods course lessons about the use of these manipulative materials emphasized both content knowledge and instructional strategies for preservice teachers. The videodisc materials are used by methods course instructors in presentation format and by teacher education students working individually or in small groups at computer stations. Data collected from interviews with the preservice teachers who participated in these lessons indicated that the teachers responded positively to them (Frederick & Hatfield, 1991).

Ronald Abate and his colleagues at Cleveland State University have developed a multimedia data base containing videodisc/ HyperCard modules showing five approaches to teaching reading. Preservice teachers using these materials can watch video examples of the different approaches, examine a teacher's written lesson plans (with electronic buttons to access relevant portions of the lessons), and read the teacher's comments about decisions the teacher made in the course of planning and teaching the lesson (Abate, 1990, 1992; Dowhower, 1992). These materials are in use in introductory teacher education courses at Cleveland State University (Hannah, 1992) and have been field tested with teacher education students at Miami University, Ohio (Dowhower, 1992).

Thomas Duffy at Indiana University and Beau Fly Jones and Randy Knuth at the North Central Regional Educational Laboratory (NCREL) are developing a prototype multimedia data base designed to assist teachers "in adopting new approaches to teaching" (Fishman & Duffy, 1992, p. 5). The system puts the video viewer in the position of an apprentice, observing an expert teacher using effective instructional and management strategies; the video lessons used in the prototype materials are from videotapes produced by NCREL. Associated with each lesson are such ancillary materials as the teacher's lesson plan, related research articles, and expert commentary on the lesson. The developers explain that the various real-life teaching experiences offered through the video classrooms with accompanying supplementary materials are designed to help teachers "develop a mental model of the instructional approach being demonstrated and to develop the capability for implementing the strategy in their classrooms" (Fishman & Duffy, 1992, p. 5). To develop the data base, the researchers conducted a needs analysis with practicing teachers who were attempting to restructure their classrooms, asking them what aspects of their teaching they thought they needed to improve.

Production and Communication Tools

Integrated media systems can link tools as well as information, and most of the materials we have mentioned incorporate tools of some type. For example, several of the systems (Ball, Lampert, & Rosenberg, 1991; Fishman & Duffy, 1992; Goldman & Barron, 1991; Goldman, Barron, & Witherspoon, 1992) have, or are developing, annotating software that allows the user to enter comments about the video. Another user (or course instructor) can then watch the video and access these comments, thus building a data base of multiple perspectives on teaching and learning. The Vanderbilt students who created the integrated media presentations mentioned earlier used authoring software that allows a user to first annotate video material and then convert the annotated video into a Hyper-Card stack to be used for presentation (Goldman, Barron, & Witherspoon, 1992).

Systems that incorporate data bases have data sorting capability. Most, possibly all, of the systems now have printer connections that allow supplementary lesson plans, teacher comments, student products, and other such materials to be printed. The NCREL/ Indiana University materials have links to communications software that will allow the user (when the system is fully functional) to watch video of a classroom and use electronic mail to communicate with the teacher who taught the video lesson. This two-way communication and ability to be an apprentice to another teacher may be especially important to beginning teachers or teachers who are trying new approaches to teaching (Fishman & Duffy, 1992). Systems with these capabilities provide not only realistic contexts for the study of teaching and learning, but tools for communicating about that study as well.

Integrated Media Environments and Preservice Field Experiences

The integrated media materials and activities described in this chapter are not designed to replace preservice field experiences; however, there are reasons why a simulated environment might accomplish certain goals of teacher education more effectively, particularly the goal of preparing preservice teachers to work in the restructured classroom. Here we discuss several of these reasons.

University-based teacher education programs often attempt to provide contexts for introductory professional courses by sending preservice teachers out into the schools to observe teaching and learning or to work with small groups of students. However, the literature on beginning teachers shows that novice teachers misinterpret or fail to notice many of the features and cues that experienced teachers use to make sense of the classroom environment (Berliner and others, 1988; Randolph & Evertson, 1992). Beginning teachers need help in learning how to observe teaching and learning, particularly if they are to understand how teachers in student-centered classrooms make interactive teaching decisions based on student thinking and understanding. Research conducted at Vanderbilt (Randolph & Evertson, 1992; Risko, 1992a) indicates that when videodiscs were used in methods courses to help preservice teachers focus on classroom factors that influence teaching and learning, these preservice teachers were able to write richer, more elaborative descriptions of video classroom incidents shown as a component of a posttest than preservice teachers whose courses did not incorporate the integrated media materials. Videodisc technology allows a complex classroom incident to be revisited over and over as novice teachers work with teacher educators (or mentor teachers) to isolate and examine different influences on teaching and learning.

We believe that it is important for preservice teachers to analyze and discuss teaching and learning with each other around a series of shared contexts or cases. It is useful for teacher education students to bring in descriptions of incidents from direct observations or field placements, but the others in the class (including the course instructor) often cannot know enough about the original incidents to offer different perspectives on the significance of an event. Integrated media cases offer all parties access to the same experience, and can also provide a richer context than text-based descriptions.

When preservice teachers observe in real classes, the teacher education program often has no control over the type of teaching they see. Educators and researchers hope to change the traditional view of teaching and learning that many preservice teachers bring to teacher education, but they are unlikely to accomplish this change if education students are sent to observe in traditional classrooms. Until teacher education programs have ready access to the type of instruction they want modeled for prospective teachers, video models serve as a useful alternative. In addition, today's teachers should have opportunities to explore the uses of various technologies in instruction, but many of the field sites have limited technological resources. Integrated media systems can both model a technology-rich instructional environment and give prospective teachers experience in using it.

Authentic practice (see Brown, Collins, & Duguid, 1989) in teacher education undoubtedly involves teaching classes with real students in them; however, classroom management is a primary concern for beginning teachers (Veenman, 1984). When novice teachers have responsibility for groups of children or an entire class, they are often so overwhelmed with managing the complex inter-actions that they are not able to focus on the way an individual student is thinking. It might be more effective to have beginning teachers practice certain critical teaching skills, such as interpret-ing student constructions of meaning, in a video-based simulated environment that is not as immediate as the real classroom. Integrated media systems are able to represent the complexity of the classroom while making it manageable (Ball, Lampert, & Rosenberg, 1991).

Obstacles to Implementation

Educators, technologists, and cognitive psychologists agree that integrated media technologies have the potential to create envi-ronments in which learners can explore, communicate, solve authentic problems, and organize knowledge in new ways (Ambrose, 1991; Cognition and Technology Group at Vanderbilt, 1990; Kozma, 1991; Nix & Spiro, 1990). But if researchers and school systems expect teachers to use these technologies in their own classrooms to support students' active learning and problem solving, the teachers will need time, training, and opportunity to work with the equipment and software.

Those who work with preservice teacher education programs have special opportunities and responsibilities to prepare teachers who understand both what technology can do and how to use tech-nology. A once-popular strategy for preparing teachers to use tech-nology is to provide workshops or "computer literacy" courses for prospective teachers. However, teacher education programs that attempt to inform teachers about instructional technology through special technology courses are open to the same criticism of inau-thenticity as the traditional classrooms where children learn facts and rules out of context. A more natural and theoretically sound approach is to infuse teacher education programs (including the lib-eral arts courses that provide teachers' content background) with the types of technological applications education reformers hope to see in the schools. The use of technology in teacher education should produce new teachers who are comfortable with the technology, appreciate its potential, and are able to create their own applications. More importantly, if courses in pedagogy are to prepare teachers to be effective problem solvers and decision makers in the complex domain of the classroom, then novice teachers should be provided the same kinds of rich learning environments that are advocated for children and youth in the restructured schools.

In the mid 1980s, the American Association of Colleges for Teacher Education (AACTE) appointed a task force to study and make recommendations about the use of technology in teacher education. That task force warned that "the credibility of programs which fail to practice the approaches they espouse will be suspect. Contact with electronic information communications technology as a natural part of the life of the [school, college, or department of education] is the most potent way to show how and why technology is used in educational environments" (American Association of Colleges for Teacher Education Task Force on Technology, 1987, p. 28).

Despite encouragement from professional organizations such as AACTE, Brooks and Kopp (1989) found that teacher education institutions were "behind schedule" in the broad application of existing technologies such as productivity software or electronic networks (p. 4). More recently, in a discussion of hypermedia in teacher education, Merseth and Lacey (1992) reported few examples of teacher education applications using these emerging technologies. Although annual meeting catalogues of professional organizations such as AACTE and the American Educational Research Association contain sessions in which teacher educators and researchers report on technology-based projects for teacher education (American Association of Colleges for Teacher Education, 1992; American Educational Research Association, 1992), few claim that technology is "a natural part of the life" of their institution's teacher education program (if, indeed, the presenter is even associated with a teacher education program).

Teacher educators have been slow to infuse technology into their courses and programs for a number of reasons. Lack of funding is perhaps the greatest obstacle (Brooks & Kopp, 1989). Funding buys more than hardware and software for classroom use; with adequate funds, a program can provide technical support, equipment for a faculty member's out-of-class use (for example, a computer and printer in the office or at home), adequate and convenient teaching facilities (so equipment need not be transported from place to place), and perhaps most importantly, release time for faculty who want to incorporate technology into courses.

We surveyed seventy teacher education faculty and administrators attending two Vanderbilt conferences on technology and found that lack of time to learn about the equipment and to prepare to use new materials in class is a critical obstacle, particularly for faculty from nonresearch institutions, where teaching loads tend to be heavy. Because descriptions and research-based information on the effectiveness of such materials are just beginning to appear in the literature, teacher educators and administrators still question whether the pedagogical benefits of integrated media or other technologies justify an institution's investment in equipment, facilities, and staff development.

Inadequate staff development opportunities and lack of technical support are other factors cited frequently as barriers to the use of technology by teacher education faculty. Institutions that are more successful than others in integrating technology throughout a teacher education program tend to have a critical mass of faculty who use the technology and can share ideas and expertise with novice users. Such institutions often have an administrative unit or degree program in instructional technology that is charged with providing support to teacher education faculty. Smaller or less well funded institutions may need to seek technical support and ideas through interinstitutional networks such as the National Science Foundation–supported consortium based at the University of South Alabama that provides support to mathematics education faculty using integrated media instructional materials in eleven Alabama state institutions (Tucker and others, 1992).

Lack of appropriate materials has been a particular problem for those who wish to use integrated media technology. Video of acceptable technical quality is hard to produce outside a studio; however, classroom video produced in a studio usually looks (and is) staged. With the exception of the NCREL tapes, the integrated media examples mentioned in this chapter were all produced by teacher education institutions, usually with support from external funding. But producing materials in-house is costly and time consuming, and there is often no overlap between individuals who have the requisite technical and design expertise to understand what the technology can do and the teacher education faculty who are in the best position to select pedagogical activities that are consistent with the goals of the teacher education program or an individual course.

Brooks and Kopp (1989) suggest that the absence of clear programmatic goals may be a more fundamental reason why teacher education programs are slow to incorporate technology: "Most preservice and inservice teacher education programs have not come to grips with what it is that they should be trying to accomplish. Very often, the justification for technology is based on idiosyncratic faculty demand, not designed program demand" (p. 5). In general, higher education faces the same types of barriers to the use of technology that the schools face.

Conclusion

Transforming schools to improve the education of students is engaging the productive energies of educators, researchers, and policymakers throughout the United States. Informing these efforts is new research on how children learn, research that suggests challenging new approaches to teaching. In our discussion of the theoretical framework that supports the use of technology in preparing teachers for the restructured classroom, we have taken the position that beginning teachers have instructional needs that are different from those of experienced teachers and that integrated media materials offer special pedagogical promise for meeting those needs. However, several conditions must be met if this promise is to be realized:

1. Usable materials that take full advantage of the power of the technology must be developed. Many of the features of the materials described in this chapter are still in the development stage.

2. Those who have access to the prototypes of classroom technology need to determine ways to evaluate their effect on pre-service teachers' understanding of the process of teaching and learning. Does use of these prototypes, for example, change the way prospective teachers view the teaching of mathematics or the nature of the disabled reader?

3. Materials must be distributed more widely than are the few prototypes now being implemented at various development sites. This wider distribution will probably happen when commercial publishers or software developers believe that it will be profitable to produce these integrated media materials for teacher education.

4. Despite recommendations from professional organizations such as AACTE, a number of teacher education programs do not have the resources or technical expertise to make use of *existing* technologies (such as camcorders, videocassette recorders [VCRs], computers, or electronic mail), much less emerging integrated media technologies. Education reformers must develop strategies for changing this situation.

5. Some technical limitations still must be overcome before the educators of teachers can make widespread use of integrated media materials. At present, it is not economically feasible to store large quantities of high-quality video for rapid random access by a computer (one side of a videodisc is limited to thirty minutes of running video).

Although it is not practical for each teacher education program to produce its own materials, we believe that it is important to have different examples of integrated media and a critical mass of developers and researchers to share ideas and evaluate each other's materials. From our own experience in using integrated media with preservice teachers and from similar research and development efforts at other institutions, we are encouraged about the use and potential of such materials in preparing teachers for the challenges of the classroom.

References

Abate, R. J. (1990). A multimedia environment for preservice teacher education. *The Journal of Interactive Instruction Development, 2*(3), 14–19.

Abate, R. J. (1992, March). *The development of multimedia instructional materials in teacher education.* Paper presented at the third annual conference of the Society for Technology and Teacher Education, Houston, TX.

Ambrose, D. W. (1991). The effects of hypermedia on learning: A literature review. *Educational Technology, 31*(12), 51–55.

American Association for the Advancement of Science. (1989). *Science for all Americans: A Project 2061 report on literacy goals in science, mathematics, and technology.* Washington, DC: Author.

American Association of Colleges for Teacher Education (Ed.). (1992). *1992 annual meeting program.* Washington, DC: Author.

American Association of Colleges for Teacher Education Task Force on Technology. (1987). The challenge of electronic technologies for colleges of education. *Journal of Teacher Education, 38*(6), 25–29.

American Educational Research Association (Ed.). (1992). *1992 annual meeting program.* Washington, DC: Author.

Ball, D. L. (1990). The mathematical understandings that prospective teachers bring to teacher education. *The Elementary School Journal, 90*(4), 449–466.

Ball, D. L., Lampert, M., & Rosenberg, M. L. (1991, April). *Using hypermedia to investigate and construct knowledge about mathematics teaching and learning.* Paper presented at the annual meeting of the American Educational Research Association, Chicago.

Berliner, D. C., and others (1988). Implications of research on pedagogical expertise and experience for mathematics teaching. In D. A. Grouws, T. J. Cooney, & D. Jones (Eds.), *Effective mathematics teaching* (pp. 67–95). Reston, VA: Erlbaum and National Council of Teachers of Mathematics.

Bitter, G. G. (1992). *Teaching mathematics methods using interactive videodisc* (Monograph No. 4: *Monograph Series of Technology Based Learning and Research*). Tempe: Arizona State University.

Borasi, R. (1990). The invisible hand operating in mathematics education: Students' conceptions and expectations. In T. J. Cooney & C. R. Hirsch (Eds.), *Teaching and learning mathematics in the 1990's* (pp. 174–182). 1990 Yearbook of the National Council of Teachers of Mathematics. Reston, VA: National Council of Teachers of Mathematics.

Borko, H., and others (1992). Learning to teach hard mathematics: Do novice teachers and their instructors give up too easily? *Journal for Research in Mathematics Education, 23*(3), 194–222.

Borko, H., & Livingston, C. (1989). Cognition and improvisation: Differences in mathematics instruction by expert and novice teachers. *American Educational Research Journal, 26*(4), 473–498.

Bransford, J. D., Franks, J. J., Vye, N. J., & Sherwood, R. D. (1989). New approaches to instruction: Because wisdom can't be told. In S. Vosniadou & A. Ortony (Eds.), *Similarity and analogical reasoning* (pp. 470–497). New York: Cambridge University Press.

Bransford, J. D., Sherwood, R. D., Hasselbring, T. S., Kinzer, C. K., & Williams, S. M. (1990). Anchored instruction: Why we need it and how technology can help. In D. Nix & R. Spiro (Eds.), *Cognition, education, and multimedia: Exploring ideas in high technology* (pp. 115–141). Hillsdale, NJ: Erlbaum.

Bransford, J. D., & Vye, N. J. (1989). A perspective on cognitive research and its implications for instruction. In L. B. Resnick & L. E. Klopfer (Eds.), *Toward the thinking curriculum: Current cognitive research* (pp.173–205). Washington, DC: Association for Supervision and Curriculum Development.

Brooks, D., & Kopp, T. (1989). Technology in teacher education. *Journal of Teacher Education, 40*(4), 2–8.

Brown, J. S., Collins, A., & Duguid, P. (1989). Situated cognition and the culture of learning. *Educational Researcher, 18*(1), 32–41.

Carpenter, T. P., Fennema, E., Peterson, P. L., & Carey, D. A. (1988). Teachers' pedagogical content knowledge of students' problem solving in elementary arithmetic. *Journal for Research in Mathematics Education, 19*(5), 385–401.

Clark, M. M., & Peterson, P. L. (1986). Teachers' thought processes. In M. C. Wittrock (Ed.), *Handbook of research on teaching* (3rd ed., pp. 255–296). New York: Macmillan.

Cobb, P., Yackel, E., & Wood, T. (1992). A constructivist alternative to the representational view of mind in mathematics education. *Journal for Research in Mathematics Education, 23*(1), 2–33.

Cognition and Technology Group at Vanderbilt. (1990). Anchored instruction and its relationship to situated cognition. *Educational Researcher, 19*(6), 2–10.

Cognition and Technology Group at Vanderbilt. (1991). Technology and the design of generative learning environments. *Educational Technology Journal, 31*(5), 34–40.

Cognition and Technology Group at Vanderbilt. (1993). The Jasper experiment: Using video to furnish real-world problem-solving contexts. *Arithmetic Teacher, 40*(8), 474–478.

Dowhower, S. L. (1992, April). *Using HyperCard and interactive videodisc technology for better teaching and advising in reading.* Paper presented at the annual meeting of the American Educational Research Association, San Francisco.

Elmore, R. F. (1992). Why restructuring alone won't improve teaching. *Educational Leadership, 49*(7), 44–48.

Evertson, C. M., & Harris, A. H. (1992). What we know about managing classrooms. *Educational Leadership, 49*(7), 74–78.

Evertson, C. M., & Murphy, J. (1992). Beginning with classrooms: Implications for restructuring schools. In H. H. Marshall (Ed.), *Redefining student learning: Roots of educational change* (pp. 293–320). Norwood, NJ: Ablex.

Fishman, B. J., & Duffy, T. M. (1992, April). *Strategic teaching frameworks: Hypermedia for strategic classroom change.* Paper presented at the annual meeting of the American Educational Research Association, San Francisco.

Frederick, H. R., & Hatfield, M. M. (1991, April). *Interactive videodiscs, vignettes, and manipulatives: A mix that enhances the mathematics methods class.* Paper presented at the annual meeting of the American Educational Research Association, Chicago.

Goldman, E., & Barron, L. (1990). Using hypermedia to improve the preparation of elementary teachers. *Journal of Teacher Education, 41*(3), 21–31.

Goldman, E., & Barron, L. (1991, April). *Using hypermedia to provide elementary classroom contexts for prospective mathematics teachers.* Paper presented at the annual meeting of the American Educational Research Association, Chicago.

Goldman, E., Barron, L., & Witherspoon, M. L. (1991). Hypermedia cases in teacher education: A context for understanding research on the teaching and learning of mathematics. *Action in Teacher Education, 23*(1), 28–36.

Goldman, E. S., Barron, L. C., & Witherspoon, M. L. (1992, April). *Integrated media activities for mathematics teacher education: Design and implementation issues.* Paper presented at the annual meeting of the American Educational Research Association, San Francisco.

Gravemeijer, K. (1990). Context problems and realistic mathematics instruction. In K. Gravemeijer, M. van den Heuvel, & L. Streefland (Eds.), *Contexts, free productions, tests, and geometry in realistic mathematics education* (pp. 10–32). Utrecht, Netherlands: Technipress.

Hallinger, P., Murphy, J., & Hausman, C. (1992, April). *Conceptualizing school restructuring: Principals' and teachers' perceptions.* Paper presented at the annual meeting of the American Educational Research Association, San Francisco.

Hannah, C. L. (1992, April). *Survey on faculty use of videodisc technology in teacher education.* Paper presented at the annual meeting of the American Educational Research Association, San Francisco.

Hasselbring, T. S., Goin, L. I., & Bransford, J. D. (1991, May). Integrated media: Toward a theoretical framework for utilizing their potential. In *Pro-*

ceedings of the Multimedia Technology Seminar (pp. 28–36). Reston, VA: Council for Exceptional Children.

Hofwolt, C. A. (1992, March). *Using hypermedia to develop effective elementary science teachers.* Paper presented at the annual meeting of the National Science Teachers Association, Boston.

Kozma, R. B. (1991). Learning with media. *Review of Educational Research, 61*(2), 179–211.

Lampert, M. (1987). How do teachers manage to teach? Perspectives on problems in practice. In M. Okazawa-Rey, J. Anderson, & R. Traver (Eds.), *Teachers, teaching, and teacher education* (pp. 106–123). Cambridge, MA: Harvard Educational Review.

Lampert, M., & Ball, D. L. (1990). *Using hypermedia technology to support a new pedagogy of teacher education* (Issue Paper 90–5). East Lansing: Michigan State University, National Center for Research on Teacher Education.

Leinhardt, G. (1992). What research on learning tells about teaching. *Educational Leadership, 49*(7), 20–25.

Lortie, D. C. (1975). *Schoolteacher: A sociological study.* Chicago: University of Chicago Press.

Merseth, K., & Lacey, C. (1992). *Weaving stronger fabric: The pedagogical promise of hypermedia and case methods in teacher education.* Unpublished manuscript.

Murphy, J. (1991). *Restructuring schools: Capturing and assessing the phenomena.* New York: Teachers College Press.

National Council of Teachers of Mathematics. (1989). *Curriculum and evaluation standards for school mathematics.* Reston, VA: Author.

National Council of Teachers of Mathematics. (1991). *Professional standards for teaching mathematics.* Reston, VA: Author.

Newman, D. (1992, March). *Turning telecomputing inside out.* Paper presented at A Conference on Technology and Education Reform, an SRI International project funded through OERI, Dallas, TX.

Nix, D., & Spiro, R. (1990). *Cognition, education, and multimedia: Exploring ideas in high technology.* Hillsdale, NJ: Erlbaum.

Pea, R. D. (1987). Cognitive technologies for mathematics education. In A. H. Schoenfeld (Ed.), *Cognitive science and mathematics* (pp. 89–122). Hillsdale, NJ: Erlbaum.

Prawat, R. S. (1992). From individual differences to learning communities—our changing focus. *Educational Leadership, 49*(7), 9–13.

Randolph, C. H., & Evertson, C. M. (1992, April). *Enhancing problem solving in preservice teachers' approaches to classroom management using video technology.* Paper presented at the annual meeting of the American Educational Research Association, San Francisco.

Randolph, C. H., Smithey, M. W., & Evertson, C. M. (1991). Observing in secondary classrooms: Piloting a videodisc and HyperCard stack for secondary methods students. In D. Carey, R. Carey, D. Willis, & J. Willis (Eds.), *Technology and teacher education annual* (pp. 84–87). New York: Haworth Press.

Resnick, L. B. (1987). *Education and learning to think.* Washington, DC: National Academy Press.

Risko, V. J. (1992a, April). *Creating video-based problem solving environments to manage the complexity of literacy instruction.* Paper presented at the annual meeting of the American Educational Research Association, San Francisco.

Risko, V. J. (1992b). Developing problem solving environments to prepare teachers for instruction of diverse learners. In B. Hayes & K. Camperell (Eds.), *Yearbook of the American Reading Forum* (Vol. 12, pp. 1–13). Logan: Utah State University.

Risko, V., Yount, D., & Towell, J. (1991, April). *The effect of video-based case methodology on preservice teachers' problem solving and critical thinking.* Paper presented at the annual meeting of the American Educational Research Association, Chicago.

Romberg, T. A., & Carpenter, T. P. (1986). Research on teaching and learning mathematics. In M. C. Wittrock (Ed.), *Handbook of research on teaching* (3rd ed., pp. 850–873). New York: Macmillan.

Sheingold, K. (1991). Restructuring for learning with technology: The potential for synergy. *Phi Delta Kappan, 73,* 17–27.

Shulman, L. (1986). Those who understand: Knowledge growth in teaching. *Educational Researcher, 15*(2), 4–14.

Smith, M. S., & O'Day, J. (1991). Systemic school reform. In S. H. Fuhrman & B. Malen (Eds.), *The politics of curriculum and testing* (pp. 233–267). New York: Falmer Press.

Spiro, R. J., & Jehng, J. (1990). Cognitive flexibility and hypertext: Theory and technology for the nonlinear and multidimensional traversal of complex subject matter. In D. Nix & R. Spiro (Eds.), *Cognition, education, and multimedia: Exploring ideas in high technology* (pp. 163–205). Hillsdale, NJ: Erlbaum.

Steffe, L. P. (1990). Mathematics curriculum design: A constructivist's perspective. In L. P. Steffe & T. Wood (Eds.), *Transforming children's mathematics education* (pp. 389–398). Hillsdale, NJ: Erlbaum.

Streefland, L. (1990). Realistic mathematics education (RME): What does it mean? In K.Gravemeijer, M. van den Heuvel, & L. Streefland (Eds.), *Contexts, free productions, tests, and geometry in realistic mathematics education* (pp. 1–9). Utrecht, Netherlands: Technipress.

Tucker, S., and others (1992, April). *Validating the use of hypermedia in elementary mathematics: A case study.* Paper presented at the annual meeting of the American Educational Research Association, San Francisco.

van Galen, F., Dolk, M., & Feijs, E. (1990, July). *Interactive video in teacher training*. Paper presented at the Fifth World Conference on Computers in Education, Sydney, Australia.

Veenman, S. (1984). Perceived problems of beginning teachers. *Review of Educational Research, 54*(2), 143–178.

von Glasersfeld, E. (1987). Learning as a constructive activity. In C. Janvier (Ed.), *Problems of representation in the teaching and learning of mathematics* (pp. 3–17). Hillsdale, NJ: Erlbaum.

Yackel, E., Cobb, P., Wood, T., & Merkel, G. (1990). Experience with problem solving and discourse as central aspects of constructivism. *Arithmetic Teacher, 38*(4), 34–35.

Chapter Five

Using Technology to Support Innovative Assessment

Karen Sheingold and
John Frederiksen

At *the core* of current efforts to reform education is a commitment to changing what students learn in school and how they learn it, in order to improve student achievement. It is now widely recognized by leaders, policymakers, and practitioners in education that schools must help students learn to think strategically, to understand concepts and ideas in curricular domains, to apply what they learn, and to pose questions and devise and solve problems. Such goals are viewed as mandatory for all of the nation's children (see, for example, National Governors' Association, 1990). At the same time, there is broad recognition that to change our expectations about what students should know and be able to do will involve also changing both the standards by which student achievements are judged and the methods by which students' accomplishments are assessed. For this reason, the redefinition of assessment is playing a pivotal role in the reform of education in the United States (National Council on Education Standards and Testing, 1992; Resnick & Resnick, 1992; U.S. Congress, Office of Technology Assessment, 1992). In the context of education reform, assessment matters more than it has in the past. It is more than simply one element that must change in order to transform teaching and learning. Instead, education reformers now find that assessment standards and methods have considerable power as the *agents* (or *inhibitors*) of such change.

We, moreover, believe it unlikely that any strong link can be forged between assessment and reform without considerable help from technologies such as computers, telecommunications, and multimedia data bases. In what follows, we argue that there are several ways in which assessment can foster reform: through the forms of the assessments, through the criteria and standards for judging student work, and most importantly, through the processes by which large numbers of people learn to apply criteria in judging, reflecting on, and valuing good work. Technologies are critically important to school reform because they increase the range of student work that can be used in instruction and assessment and because they provide the media through which students and teachers can have conversations that lead to shared understandings of the values and standards for student performance.

Forms of Performance Assessment

The power of assessment to assist in bringing about reform derives in part from the nature of new performance-based assessments that model challenging learning activities for students. Performance assessments (sometimes also referred to as *authentic* or *alternative* assessments) differ from traditional short-answer paper-and-pencil assessments in that they take as the object of assessment the actual work that students (or teachers) do. Moreover, standards and curricular guidelines now being developed increasingly emphasize such activities as carrying out research, constructing arguments, and debating conclusions, rather than recalling facts and applying algorithms in solving well-structured problems. Like tasks or activities that individuals carry out in the real world, the performance tasks to be assessed are expected to encompass extended activities that allow for multiple approaches and a range of acceptable products and results. In contrast, traditional forms of assessment examine single problems that call for particular, circumscribed elements of knowledge and problem-solving skill (Resnick & Resnick, 1992).

Performance tasks often require collaborative effort rather than only individual work. Performance assessment tasks may also require students to write investigative reports and debate conclusions (as history/social science assessments in the California Learning

Assessment System do) or to carry out inquiry projects in a chosen subject and create exhibitions that culminate in assessments in which students describe their projects to an audience and answer questions about them (Collins, Hawkins, & Frederiksen, 1990; Hawkins, Collins, & Frederiksen, 1990; McDonald, 1993). In other performance assessments, students solve open-ended problems in mathematics that include the application of knowledge and the building of mathematical models (Lesh & Lamon, 1992) or, as in the Arts Propel project in the Pittsburgh public schools, write critiques of their own ensemble musical performances (J. Waanders, personal communication, Nov. 1992). (For an excellent review of performance assessment activities being developed nationwide, see Mitchell, 1992.)

The new approaches to assessment also employ portfolios of student work, which include a collection of performances and products produced by a student over a school year or, in some cases, over several years. Portfolios contain work that students and/or teachers select according to a set of criteria. Because portfolios can include the full range of activities and projects the student has worked on, they provide useful evidence of the student's growth and development, as well as of the final levels of performance attained. Educators view portfolios as particularly valuable for the opportunities they give to students and teachers to reflect on a student's progress in a domain over a period of time. In assessment programs that rely on portfolios, students are often encouraged to consider what should go into their portfolios, why they have made their particular choices, and how their work has evolved over the period their portfolios cover (see, for example, Camp, 1992; Wolf, 1989).

A specific example of an extended, technology-enhanced performance assessment comes from a research project that Educational Testing Service (ETS) is carrying out in collaboration with the national Center for Technology in Education (Hawkins, Collins, & Frederiksen, 1990). At an alternative high school in New York City, students in a combined math/science course are given a phenomenon in physics to explain, such as the motion of a projectile. They are provided with a computer simulation environment in which they can manipulate variables so as to carry out experiments leading to an explanation of the phenomenon. Students keep records of their reasons for doing experiments, their library search for information pertinent to the problem, their hypotheses and experimental designs for testing the hypotheses, and their final results. They generate data using the computer simulation and graph their data in multiple ways using computer facilities. They also write a report that integrates their results using an explanatory model. And finally, from the materials they have developed in their project, they prepare and give an exhibition of the project to their teachers and fellow students (as they would at a science fair). The exhibition includes a question-and-answer session and is videotaped. Overall, the project may take from one to several weeks to complete. All the performance records (students' process documents, written reports, recorded data and graphs, and videotaped exhibitions) are sources of evidence for the assessment.

Performance Standards

The power of assessment as a reform agent derives as much from the standards for performance used in evaluating work as from the value of performance tasks themselves as learning activities. Performance assessments must provide evidence about students' learning and performance in relation to established standards. It is this evaluative perspective on student performance that makes assessments particularly powerful vehicles for learning as well as sources of information for students, teachers, and other audiences. In the context of the larger goals for education reform, it is through standards that the educational community defines what is valued.

Standards for Knowing and Doing

What, then, are the performance standards students are to meet? Educators are currently developing new standards in many disciplines. Importantly, these standards include both the content and the processes that students are expected to master. Within such domains as history, mathematics, and science, educators are attempting to define the "big ideas" and central themes that are worth knowing, along with the key methods for working, thinking, and applying knowledge within those disciplines (see, for example, American Association for the Advancement of Science, 1989; National Council of Teachers of Mathematics, 1989).

California is one state that is currently developing standards for its performance-based assessment system. State assessment guidelines for students' mathematical problem solving include such factors as producing clear and coherent diagrams and explanations, communicating effectively, understanding important mathematical ideas and processes, and presenting strong arguments that include effective examples and counterexamples (California State Department of Education, 1989). The standards that are being developed, therefore, extend well beyond considering a student's knowledge of the mathematics needed to solve a particular problem.

Defining and Applying Standards

The importance of standards, however, lies not only in what the standards are but also in the processes of defining and interpreting them. Across the nation, teachers, parents, curriculum specialists, policymakers, and businesspeople are all reconsidering what students should know and be able to do. This process of grappling with, arguing about, and coming to agreement on what matters is itself central to advancing the goals of reform. Indeed, it has been argued that this very process may be an essential component of what teachers do when they implement a performance assessment in their school (Darling-Hammond, 1992) or participate in assessment design.

To be more specific, in the math/science assessment project referred to earlier, the researchers are learning about how performance standards are interpreted by a group of high school teachers. When these science teachers met with project researchers to consider how to score students' physics projects, they first surrounded themselves with actual student performance records. As a group, they then began generating a list of valued features for science projects, including such desired characteristics as "makes connections," "makes use of knowledge," "gives detailed graphs and explanations," "tests preconceptions and assumptions," "takes a reflective stance," "uses hypothetical thinking," and so forth. The list grew quite long, reaching twenty-six separate features they were looking for in projects. In suggesting features, they used the students' projects to identify examples of the kind of performance taken as evidence of the presence of each feature.

At the end of the day-long meeting, the science teachers took this long list home with them and, several weeks later, produced a scoring rubric in which they had organized the twenty-six features under the following three broad categories:

1. "Organization of Work—the work as a whole. Does it hang together? Does it make its point? Is it easily understood?"

2. "Understanding of Math/Science Ideas—using 'habits of mind' to explore and develop Math/Science ideas and concepts."

3. "Process Skills—used to develop evidence, transferable to other academic investigations."

There was a strong feeling among the science teachers that this activity of considering how to value performance was at the heart of what their school was about. It is a testimony to the quality of the rubric they developed that state education departments have requested copies of this scoring guide.

Another example is the research and development the Educational Testing Service (ETS) is doing for the California Learning Assessment System. Teachers from throughout the state are being brought together to design performance assessments that are to be embedded in the ongoing curriculum and to become part of a statewide assessment system. Using the state's curricular frameworks as guides, the teachers are designing learning activities that will reveal what students know and can do, as called for within those frameworks. As part of the design process, teachers are asking themselves how these activities can generate valued performances, and by what criteria teachers will judge the evidence these activities provide. Having to work back and forth between the design of the activities and the criteria by which performances and products will be judged requires teachers to consider from the beginning what they are trying to help their students to accomplish. They consult state frameworks, model curriculum guides, and state scoring rubrics to ensure that what they design will contribute to the definition of statewide standards for student performance.

Transparency: What Good Work Looks Like

We have argued thus far that performance-based assessments provide a lever for reform because of their link to standards for student performance and because the evidence that is assessed is drawn from exemplary learning tasks and activities. More specifically, because they are designed to instantiate standards for student learning and performance, the new forms of assessment allow students to be evaluated with respect to valued goals and criteria. At the same time, assessments that invite students to demonstrate well-chosen "habits of mind" allow assessment itself to model and encourage valued activities and reflections on performance by students and teachers.

But achieving the goals of reform will require much more than creating new types of assessment activities and standards consistent with reform goals. Unless students and teachers genuinely come to understand what good work looks like and how they can foster it, the move to performance-based assessment will not succeed as a lever for change. The positive systemic effects of the performance assessments depend critically on the *openness* or *transparency* of the values and criteria used in those assessments.

What do we mean by transparency? To be transparent, an assessment must make students and teachers keenly aware of those characteristics of outstanding performance that exemplify shared values within the community and of the reasons these characteristics are valued. Criteria for outstanding performances do not become transparent simply by definition. Rather, they take on meaning the way most concepts do—by their use in describing instances and noninstances of the concept. Take, for example, one criterion for good writing: a sense of audience. Teachers and students learn what this "sense of audience" is by looking at writing and its effects (both intended and unintended) on its readers, and by discussing how particular examples meet or do not meet the criterion for "sense of audience."

Learning to describe performances is a social process in which meanings for concepts are negotiated between individuals and groups as they consider various performances in which the concepts may be found. Thus, the assessment system must provide examples of the ways values and criteria for good writing, painting, or scientific investigation are realized in actual performances at different levels of accomplishment. The system must also foster ongoing evaluation by teachers and students of their work in the light of these values, as well as continual refinement of the values themselves. An assessment system in which values and criteria are open and transparent is, by definition, a system in which these values and criteria are openly and widely disseminated and discussed.

Openness and transparency, then, are central requirements for an assessment system that can fuel education reform. What is evaluated in the assessment must reflect what is valued in student learning and, thus, what is emphasized in classrooms. Criteria and values become transparent to teachers and students, and to others who participate in the assessment system, both through materials (that is, examples, along with evaluations) and through multiple and varied opportunities to participate in the process of evaluation and reflection.

The goal of transparency is important precisely because it requires reflective practice. In order for the assessment to be transparent, students and teachers must participate in the process of understanding and valuing qualities of student performance. In addition, students and teachers must consider what kinds of tasks and projects allow students to develop and display the required qualities. For students, understanding and participating in the performance assessment process should encourage reflection on their own work—the personal style, strengths, and weaknesses it may reveal and the ways it can be improved. For teachers, understanding the performance assessment process should encourage reflection on their own and others' classroom practices and on ways to support students' development in a manner consistent with what is valued in the assessment system.

Conversations About Student Work

At the heart of assessment linked to reform are conversations about student work as evidence for learning and accomplishment. These conversations go on within and between school communities, and include all participants in the assessment system. They take place at the most informal level within classrooms, as teachers and students talk with each other about a piece of work in progress, and at completion, as students consult with each other about why and how to revise a joint project or as they reflect on their own progress over time in, say, history or physics. The conversations also take place when teachers share among themselves ideas for new assessment activities and their experiences with those activities already underway, and when teachers use student work as the basis for examining their own teaching and how it might change. The conversations occur when teachers work together in the construction and/or application of criteria to student work as they evaluate and score such work for assessments in their districts, regions, or states. The conversations occur as well when teams of people, including members of the larger community, make judgments about the quality of student work presented in public exhibitions of student accomplishment, or when teams of auditors review a school district's assessment process (Rothman, 1992). It is through inspecting, scoring, talking about, constructing, and internalizing standards for student work that communities come to agree on what constitutes good work.

It is only when educators, students, and the community develop a shared language about student work and a shared set of values and criteria that assessment can affect the larger educational system with the power and in the direction that reformers advocate. Thus, the design for a performance assessment system must involve many people. Teachers, in particular, must be enlisted as designers of tasks and rubrics, as scorers and judges of student work, and as central participants in the process of standards development. The task of designing and implementing an assessment system can become a catalyst for teachers, parents, and students to reconsider how valued habits of mind are acquired and how the achievement of standards can be demonstrated (Alverno College Faculty, 1979/1985).

Moreover, this activity of social construction should be an ongoing one, allowing for the constant renewal of the assessment system through the invention of new activities, the improvement of scoring frameworks, and the incorporation of new ideas about the goals of teaching and learning. Ideally, the resulting socially distributed assessment system will be a self-improving process for enriching the view of competence incorporated within the educational system.

To summarize, if assessment is to be linked with reform, all those involved in assessment's development must view it as a social process grounded in the following actions:

- Conversations about student work as evidence of learning and accomplishment

- Development of a common language for discussing learning, accomplishments, and standards

- Development of shared values and transparent criteria for evaluating student work

Given the foregoing analysis of the key characteristics of an assessment system that can be an instrument for educational change, how can technology be developed and used to promote the linking of assessment to reform? And if the development of a community of shared values is essential to this linkage, how can technology be enlisted to support its development?

Functions of Technology

As we see it, there are five central functions that technology can perform to help link assessment with education reform:

1. Support students' work in extended, authentic learning activities.

2. Create portable, accessible copies of performances and replay performances in multiple media.

3. Provide libraries of examples and interpretive tools.

4. Expand the community of assessment participants.

5. Publish selected student work and thus recognize accomplishments.

Supporting Extended, Authentic Learning Activities

Computer, communication, and video technologies support the kind of learning activities that link assessment and reform. The current dependence on text-based activities and products for student work limits both what students can do and the kind of evidence available for assessment. Technology can significantly broaden students' involvement in challenging, extended activities that require students' active participation and application of knowledge (Sheingold, 1991).

The technological possibilities include computer-based simulation tools; microcomputer-based laboratories; computer tools for representing knowledge and findings (such as graphing or drawing software); data analysis tools (such as video analysis software, spreadsheets, and statistics programs); writing and presentation tools; recording tools; tools that support collaborative inquiry and collaborative writing; data bases that contain data and phenomena not otherwise available in the classroom (videodisc data bases for example); and tools that facilitate remote collaboration (Sheingold, Roberts, & Malcom, 1992).

Creating Portable, Accessible Copies and Replayable Performances

In the past, and to a large extent in the present, performance assessment has been constrained in two ways. Either the work to be judged must be in written form, or the audiences/judges must be physically present to witness the performance or observe the products. Technology can help teachers and students overcome both of these hurdles.

Making Work Portable and Accessible. Technology allows the original versions of student work to take many different forms that include but go well beyond print media, including, for example, handwritten drawings and papers, group planning sessions, musical performances, demonstrations of mechanisms students have designed and/or built, question-and-answer sessions, student-developed computer programs or simulations, and students' reflective oral or written commentaries on their own or each other's work. Through photographs, videotape, film, audiotape, computer disks, and scanners, all these and many other forms of student work can be captured and preserved. Interactive multimedia formats can integrate many forms of information on one disk, and will become increasingly valuable for creating portfolios of student work in multiple media. Thus, technology permits assessments of products and processes that are not limited to text and writing.

Technology makes student work transportable to audiences and judges distant in time and place from the original performance or demonstration. And technology can ease problems of routing and transferring records of student work. The very physical problem of storing and moving around paper-based student portfolios from one year to the next is challenging to even the most inventive administrators. Technology can produce much less bulky versions of these portfolios, and ultimately, network technologies will largely eliminate the need for physically transporting student work to be assessed. However, the portability of recorded performances will be a boon to students and educators only if the performances are easily accessible to all parties. Of equal importance to schools' possessing appropriate recording technologies, therefore, will be their careful construction of data bases for holding and accessing recordings of performances. They will find it particularly important to create a user interface that will be accessible and understandable to the widest community of users.

Technological support will also be needed so that groups of system users can view recordings of performances together, for it is the social activity of interpreting performances in groups that leads to a common understanding of education's goals and standards. Group presentation technologies that will be needed include video image projection devices linked to a multimedia data base. Groups using such a system should be able to access and replay a recorded performance, as well as to classify and annotate that performance.

Making Performances Replayable. Analyzing and evaluating complex human performances such as students' presentations or teachers' lessons requires that the evaluators have multiple opportunities to observe the performances of interest, to develop and apply categories to these performances (we discuss this requirement more fully later in the chapter), and to reflect on the performances in relation to the categories. For these purposes, and also because analyses and judgments will often be made by several individuals in each case, it is very important for performances to be replayable. Conversations about student performance can be problematic if the performance is witnessed only once. Individual judges or audience members may have different recollections of what they saw or heard. And students or teachers who actually participated in the performance may have only a poor sense of how it affected others, because they were focused on moment-to-moment presentation issues. When performances are replayable, discussions about their merits can be significantly relieved of the burden of memory. If judges can see and/or hear again questionable parts of the performance, their discussions can focus appropriately on interpretation rather than on what actually occurred. For example, they may want to revisit a performance in order to view it with an alternative perspective. Videotape and audiotape technologies are most useful for these purposes.

Ownership and Access. In individual schools and school districts where performance-based assessment is taken seriously, one of its effects is to engage students in complex tasks and projects that become very important to them. Indeed, anecdotal reports from many districts around the United States reveal that, particularly where students are involved in creating, selecting, and reflecting on work in portfolios, the students value their work highly. They care about what they have accomplished, as do their teachers and parents, and because they prize it, they want to keep it.

This is just one aspect of the serious questions about ownership that can arise in regard to students' work. Who gets to have and keep the work students produce? For how long? If schools and districts need these records for accountability purposes, they cannot release them. Or can they? In most places, these debates are taking place on the assumption that there is only one right answer, since there is only one copy of the work. Here, again, is a place where technology (including such simple devices as copiers) can support a broader social ownership of and involvement in students' work. Without technological assistance, ownership issues must be imperfectly and often (from someone's perspective) unhappily resolved. If the performance records use computer and video technologies, it will be important to think about how they can be made accessible to all. Schools, public libraries, and community centers may all need to provide equipment and services for making student work more broadly accessible.

Providing Libraries of Examples and Interpretive Tools

The third important role for technology in making assessment a tool for reform is helping people to build and apply interpretive frameworks for viewing performance (Frederiksen, 1992). Consider for a moment the problem of interpreting a videotape of a student's exhibition of a science project. The videotape shows the student explaining the purpose of her project, the approach she took in undertaking it, how she dealt with problems that came up, and her findings and interpretations of them. The tape also shows how she made sure that her audience is following her ideas and how she answered questions from her teachers and peers. A judge evaluating the exhibition will view a continuous flow of events, activities, and remarks. Many things will be going on all at once, at many levels. There will be multiple aural and visual cues. A novice evaluator will be in essentially the same position as a novice student of botany or archaeology looking for the first time at a set of botanical specimens or a collection of fossils.

John Audubon is reported to have said that to train a naturalist, one first has "to teach him how to see." Seeing that differentiates among things seen requires an interpretive framework or conceptual model that serves as a lens to permit that differentiation between critical features of specimens or fossils or, in this case, aspects of a student's project exhibition. Moreover, the process of seeing and categorizing is knowledge based (Medin, 1989), and communication about what is seen, whether botanical specimens or performances, depends on a socially shared interpretive framework. The concepts and categories used derive their meaning from the collection of exemplars—ideal models—to which they refer (Brown, Collins, & Duguid, 1989). Thus, an interpretive framework is developed from looking at and discussing exemplars of the class of items to be interpreted, and the framework is then learned when groups of people apply it to interpret new instances of that class of items.

The challenge for technology, therefore, is to create tools to help teachers and students and other participants in the assessment system develop shared interpretive frameworks for perceiving and communicating about learning and teaching. Such tools should include multimedia data bases or libraries of performance exemplars that illustrate aspects of performance against an interpretive framework and that groups of teachers, students, or community members can study to learn how to interpret and evaluate student performances (Frederiksen & Collins, 1989).

To help people learn how to apply existing frameworks, the exemplar library should include a set of interpreted or scored performances, along with rationales for why they were scored as they were. These performances should be chosen to provide clear-cut and contrasting positive and negative examples for each of the assessment concepts to be employed. Groups of teachers or students can then learn to categorize these exemplars in the same way that they are classified within the library. The group approach allows the meaning of assessment concepts to emerge from conversations about performance and its interpretation.

These exemplars may be used for different purposes by teachers, expert assessors, parents, and other participants in the assessment system. Expert assessors will need to go beyond the study of the clear-cut exemplars in order to learn to score so they can achieve high levels of agreement with other experts. For purposes of classroom instruction and school-community discussions, however, teachers, students, and parents may use the library to develop an understanding of the assessment concepts and how they are manifested in performance.

The technology should also include software tools for annotating and interpreting student projects in accordance with the interpretive framework. These tools will be useful to teachers in grading students' projects and for communicating appraisals to students. Teachers may also use these tools for creating their own libraries of exemplars to document performance assessment tasks they and their students have developed and to show others their view of how important educational goals can be demonstrated. Tools for building libraries of examples should include tools for video editing and for creating multimedia data bases so that teams of teachers can create alternative interpretive frameworks that they can propose to others as ways of improving the assessment system.

Expanding the Community of Participants

If the link between assessment and reform is to have large-scale impact, the community of participants involved in creating and discussing the assessments and evaluating and interpreting students' work must be very large. Networking or interactive telecommunications technologies are key elements for the expansion of this community. First, these technologies enable teachers and students to develop and share assessment activities and experiences across time and space. Second, they establish scoring comparability within the wider community. Third, they foster the enrichment and evolution of the assessment system itself.

Developing and Sharing Assessment Activities. It will be very important for participants, particularly teachers, to be able to discuss, share, argue about, and swap assessment ideas informally with other teachers who have similar expertise and interests and who teach students at comparable grade levels. Because these teachers will often be either physically distant or hard to reach in real time, networking technologies can play a major role in supporting these teacher conversations. Other teacher-based networks have proven very helpful in promoting teachers' development and supporting their involvement in project-based classroom activities (Riel, 1990; Ruopp, Gal, Drayton, & Pfister, 1993), and the network approach should prove successful with assessment as well. A data base of libraries of performance examples and student work that teachers can access should be part of this telecommunications system.

Students as well as teachers will use the system to access and share assessment activities. The network will also serve as a browsing tool to help students choose, with the help of their teachers, appealing project ideas, courses, or research options. It can also support collaborative work among students in remote locations.

Establishing Comparability of Scoring. The success of a large-scale and widely distributed assessment system will depend in part on the ability of groups of teachers in separate locations to provide comparable scoring of student performance. To maintain such calibrated scoring, teachers must have opportunities to evaluate previously assessed performances from each other's districts and then to discuss any differences in their independent assessments in order to reach a consensus in their scoring methods. Applying such techniques of social moderation across districts requires technology that allows teachers to share performance recordings and appraisals. It also requires network technology to support the ensuing conversations and software to support collaborative video analysis, collaborative access to a data base, and video teleconferencing. The data base should support graphical and statistical comparisons among different groups' scoring of multiple performances. These comparisons will alert scorers to tasks that require discussion and moderation.

Fostering the Enrichment and Evolution of the Assessment System. Enrichment of an existing assessment system occurs through teachers' introducing new ideas for assessment activities and new ways to interpret students' performance within an existing interpretive framework. Evolution occurs through the introduction of new values and perspectives into the system by system users. Interpretive frameworks must be considered social documents that will undergo modification over time.

Publishing Good Work on the Network

When many teachers are working together to create engaging and challenging assessment tasks for students, and students are producing increasingly impressive work, there must be more ways than there are now to recognize and disseminate what teachers and students have accomplished. For teachers, we envision a technology-based system in which they submit assessment tasks that they have designed and tried in their own classrooms, along with scoring rubrics and evidence as to the value of the tasks. These materials are reviewed by committees of colleagues, and those deemed acceptable for publication are published on the network as valuable tasks for other teachers to use in their classrooms. Teachers whose tasks are published can cite this as an accomplishment on their résumés and include it in their portfolios. Of course, teachers could share tasks informally as well.

Similarly, students should have access to the same telecommunications system for publishing work that they have produced and that committees of students have reviewed and selected. Students could create journals for presenting their research, writings, or artwork. To the extent that these publications increasingly reflect larger and more diverse populations of students, they will provide both inspiration to other students about what to aim for and an interesting barometer of how much improvement there may be in students' best work. For students, too, having work published on the system will be a citable achievement that can be included in their portfolio of accomplishments. Journals can provide a means for celebrating good work, and publications can be used as credentials for the workplace and for higher education.

Conclusion

We have argued that, for assessment to be a significant tool of school reform, more is required than changing the form of the assessment and changing the standards by which students' work is assessed. Although these are critical changes, they are not likely by themselves to produce the kind of impact needed. An assessment system that can productively advance reform goals for student learning must be, in the first instance, a widely shared social system, in which large numbers of students, teachers, and community members participate. As we have described, it must be grounded in conversations about student work as evidence of learning and accomplishment; in the development of a common language for discussing learning, accomplishments, and standards; and in the development of shared values and transparent criteria for evaluating student work.

Technology can promote the linking of assessment with reform by supporting the development, functioning, and expansion of this social system. Specifically, technologies must be enlisted, designed, and developed that allow people in the system to engage in more authentic and complex learning activities, to have portable and replayable copies of student achievements, to use libraries of examples and tools for interpreting student work, to expand the assessment community by enlisting more participants, and to publish selected works.

Although many of the technologies that will be optimal to support an assessment system linked to reform are not yet available (or not widely so), simpler technologies are at hand that can fulfill some of the requirements we have described. Clearly, however, a serious development and research effort is required to create the kind of technological infrastructure we are urging.

Unfortunately, there is not yet a widespread understanding of the critical need teachers and students will have for technological support when they use an assessment system that is an agent of reform. Currently, many educators and test developers think of technology only as a tool for actually *doing* the assessment, for administering tests, scoring them, and reporting results. In the system we envision, technology will make it easier for the many participants in the system to communicate, to use and refine their judgment, to access a rich data base of student work, and to have lively and productive conversations about that work as evidence of student learning. Functioning in these areas, technology can indeed help to improve teaching and learning.

References

Alverno College Faculty. (1979/1985). *Assessment at Alverno College* (rev. ed.). Milwaukee, WI: Alverno College.

American Association for the Advancement of Science. (1989). *Science for all Americans: A Project 2061 report on literacy goals in science, mathematics, and technology.* Washington, DC: Author.

Brown, J., Collins, A., & Duguid, P. (1989). Situated cognition and the culture of learning. *Educational Researcher, 18*(1), 32–42.

California State Department of Education. (1989). *A question of thinking: A first look at students' performance on open-ended questions in mathematics.* Sacramento: Author.

Camp, R. (1992). Assessment in the context of schools and school change. In Hermine H. Marshall (Ed.), *Redefining student learning: Roots of educational change* (pp. 241–263). Norwood, NJ: Ablex.

Collins, A., Hawkins, J., & Frederiksen, J. (1990, April). *Technology-based performance assessments.* Paper presented at symposium on technology-sensitive performance assessment, annual meeting of the American Educational Research Association, Boston.

Darling-Hammond, L. (1992, April). *Reframing the school reform agenda*. Invited address given at the annual meeting of the American Educational Research Association, San Francisco.

Frederiksen, J. (1992, April). *Learning to "see": Scoring video portfolios*. Paper presented at the annual meeting of the American Educational Research Association, San Francisco.

Frederiksen, J., & Collins, A. (1989). A systems approach to educational testing. *Educational Researcher, 18*(9), 27–32.

Hawkins, J., Collins, A., & Frederiksen, J. (1990). Interactive technologies and the assessment of learning. In *Proceedings of the UCLA Conference on Technology Assessment: Estimating the future*. University of California, Los Angeles.

Lesh, R., & Lamon, S. (Eds.). (1992). *Assessment of authentic performance in school mathematics*. Washington, DC: American Association for the Advancement of Science.

McDonald, J. P. (1993). Three pictures of an exhibition: Warm, cool, and hard. *Phi Delta Kappan, 74*(6), 480–485.

Medin, D. (1989). Concepts and conceptual structure. *American Psychologist, 44*, 1469–1481.

Mitchell, R. (1992). *Testing for learning: How new approaches to evaluation can improve American schools*. New York: Free Press.

National Council of Teachers of Mathematics. (1989). *Curriculum and evaluation standards for school mathematics*. Reston, VA. Author.

National Council on Education Standards and Testing. (1992). *Raising standards for American education: A report to Congress, the Secretary of Education, the National Goals Panel, and the American people*. Washington, DC: Author.

National Governors' Association (1990). *Educating America: State strategies for achieving the National Education Goals*. Washington, DC: Author.

Resnick, L., & Resnick, D. (1992). Assessing the thinking skills curriculum: New tools for educational reform. In B. Gifford & M. O'Connor (Eds.), *Changing assessments: Alternative views of aptitude, achievement, and instruction* (pp. 37–75). Boston: Kluwer.

Riel, M. (1990). Cooperative learning across classrooms in electronic learning circles. *Instructional Science, 19*, 445–466.

Rothman, R. (1992). Auditors help Pittsburgh make sure its portfolio assessment measures up. *Education Week, 11*(40), 27–28.

Ruopp, R., Gal, S., Drayton, B., & Pfister, M. (Eds). (1993). *LabNet: Toward a community of practice*. Hillsdale, NJ: Erlbaum.

Sheingold, K. (1991). Restructuring for learning with technology: The potential for synergy. *Phi Delta Kappan, 73*(1), 17–27.

Sheingold, K., Roberts, L. G., & Malcom, S. M. (Eds.). (1992). *This year in school science 1991: Technology for teaching and learning*. Washington, DC: American Association for the Advancement of Science.

U.S. Congress, Office of Technology Assessment. (1992). *Testing in American schools: Asking the right questions* (Summary). Washington, DC: Office of Technology Assessment.

Wolf, D. (1989). Portfolio assessment: Sampling student work. *Educational Leadership, 46*(7), 35–39.

Chapter Six

Evaluating the Effects of Technology in School Reform

Joan L. Herman

Educational technology holds great promise in the quest to reform schools and their instructional programs, as other chapters in this book well attest. The enormous computing power now available in desktop form at relatively modest cost enables schools to provide exciting new instructional options for students: interactivity, multimodality, various new forms of communication, access to expertise, new varieties of resources, opportunities for simulation, enhanced productivity, and so on. These options seem to provide a means for achieving the dramatic transformations in curricula and in instructional processes that reformers and cognitive researchers advocate: active learning, apprenticeships composed of authentic tasks, sustained and challenging work, cooperative groupings, attention to complex problem solving, thematic and project-oriented approaches to subject matter, and student empowerment (Brown, Collins, & Duguid, 1989; Cognition and Technology Group at Vanderbilt, 1990; Collins, 1991; Scardamalia & Bereiter, 1991).

How does the reality of technology in school reform compare with this vision of technology's potential? Having been promised innovation and transformation, policymakers want answers to what they believe are simple questions. For example:

- What are the effects of technology on student learning?

- What are the effects of technology on students' workforce readiness?

- What are the effects of technology on teacher productivity?

- Is an investment in technology cost effective?

Yet, to date, research and evaluation of innovative and complex reform projects have failed to produce definitive answers to these questions. In fact, attempts to answer these questions empirically often end in conclusions that there is no significant difference or no measurable effects. Policymakers and others have been disappointed and have too often concluded that technology is a failure in education reform.

In this chapter, I shall argue that the fault for these results lies not with the technology-based innovations in education but with the methodologies and tools educators have used to assess their effects. I start with a reminder that some studies have produced evidence showing that technology in schools has positive effects on students' learning. Drawing a composite example from a number of intensive technology-based school projects I have studied, I then describe a variety of factors that render policymakers' "simple" questions essentially unanswerable in many innovative projects. Finally, I suggest alternative research and evaluation strategies that can better clarify the effects of technology in schools and better support sound policy and practice in this area.

Research and Evaluation Do Show Positive Examples

Studies of technology in schools have shown a number of positive examples, and these may well have implications for designing an effective assessment process. I will describe some of these success stories and contrast features of their design and evaluation with those of the broader reform efforts that have proven more difficult to assess. These examples, it should be noted, also suggest the variety of functions that computers and other technologies can serve in schools and classrooms; these different uses and functions, I shall later argue, need to be addressed by sound programs of research and evaluation.

Computer-Assisted Instruction

One area in which technology clearly shows significant positive effects, and in which research and evaluation have a long history, is computer-assisted instruction (CAI). Rooted initially in behaviorist theory and programmed instruction, CAI delivers drill-and-practice exercises on basic skills and immediate feedback on student performance, in tandem with either a teacher- or computer-delivered lesson on the topic—not the stuff to bring joy to constructivists' hearts. Typical studies of CAI, performed on students who have had almost daily exposure to highly structured CAI programs for a semester or more, show that it results in measurable effects on student learning, frequently as measured by standardized achievement tests. Well-controlled studies comparing students taught with CAI and those taught conventionally, in fact, have consistently favored CAI at the elementary, secondary, and postsecondary levels (Kulik & Kulik, 1991; Kulik, Kulik, & Bangert-Drowns, 1985).

In contrast to the broader reform efforts that I will discuss later, the standard drill-and-practice treatments on which these studies have focused are well defined and easily prescribed; the subject area (often mathematics) has an inherent structure; there is a good match between the desired outcome of the treatment and the outcome that is measured; and the intervention has been sustained over a long time, typically a semester to a year.

Higher-Order Thinking Skills Program

Stanley Pogrow has developed a thinking skills program called Higher-Order Thinking Skills (HOTS), based on information processing theories of learning (Pogrow, 1990). Five basic principles, used in "learning dramas," define the approach.

1. Concepts are not taught directly by the software but evolve from conversations about its use.

2. There is no direct instruction on technical issues surrounding use of the software. Discussions instead attempt to develop key thinking skills.

3. Dramatic techniques are used to pique students' interest and motivation.

4. Teachers receive training on the use of Socratic dialogue with students.

5. Thinking emerges from repeated interaction with ideas.

In the HOTS program, learning dramas are developed by instructors' selecting a piece of software that will interest students (for example, *Where in the World Is Carmen Sandiego?* or *Oregon Trail*) and formulating questions designed to provide students with practice in a number of specific metacognitive and thinking skills. The questions are tangential to the goal of the software and are centered around the words and phrases in the instructions for its use. In keeping with the dramatic character of this learning approach, teachers often dress in costumes and allow students to become emotionally involved with the subject in order to deepen their understanding.

Although not as well specified or as closely tied to standardized tests as the CAI programs described above, the HOTS program has been shown to have positive effects. Studies indicate that HOTS students gained nearly twice as much in reading and math as the national average for students in Chapter 1, the federally funded compensatory education program (Pogrow, 1990). It is also of interest that the software and technology appear to function as motivators and that, although learning to use them may be the platform for applying thinking and problem-solving skills, the software and technology themselves do not deliver the instructional strategy.

Jasper Series

A third example of an effective technology-based program, this one firmly grounded in cognitive theory, is the video-based *Jasper* series. Developed by the Cognition and Technology Group at Vanderbilt University, *The Adventures of Jasper Woodbury* focuses on math problem-solving skills for fifth-, sixth-, and seventh-grade students. The program's primary objectives are

- To raise students' interest in math and science and to teach them to generate and solve math problems
- To show students how separate content domains (for example, math and science) are integrated in application
- To motivate students to develop proficiency in the basic skills of math

The video portion of the program presents a narrative adventure and poses challenges or questions that the principal character or other characters need to solve, questions whose solutions require the use of mathematics. All the relevant information needed to solve the questions is included in the narrative. Programs are based on cognitive theory, which stresses the importance of active rather than inert knowledge; situated learning anchored in experiences shared between the teacher and the learner; and active construction of mental models.

Studies of the *Jasper* series, employing verbal protocols of individual student interviews, show that it improves students' complex problem solving skills (Cognition and Technology Group at Vanderbilt, 1990; Van Haneghan and others, 1992). Studies of group problem solving have also found positive results (Van Haneghan and others, 1992).

In contrast to other pioneering programs that have attempted to teach thinking skills through game-type formats, with disappointing results—for example, the early and popular *Rocky's Boots* (Burbules & Reese, 1984)—the *Jasper* program provides explicit instruction and/or guided inquiry techniques to support the development of thinking skills. Note, too, that *Jasper* program goals are circumscribed, the treatment is highly structured to support constructivist learning, and researchers and program developers have been heavily involved in introducing the program to classrooms, in order to assure appropriate, skilled, and theory-based implementation of the program.

Broader Education Reform Projects

In contrast to the controlled projects just discussed, where the target of instruction and methods of instruction are highly prescribed, the technology and school reform projects that have been launched with great expectations in a number of states and districts are much broader and much less sharply aimed. Consider Model Project X, a composite example drawn from several real cases, to highlight the challenge of detecting the effects of technology on education reform.

A Complex Project

Model Project X is set in an elementary school in a large urban school district. The student population can be characterized as inner city, Latino, and lower income. Over half the students who enter the schools in this community are classified as non- or limited-English proficient; as a result, the school operates a variety of classes to meet students' language needs: Spanish only, bilingual (the most common), and English only. Results of standardized achievement tests indicate that the great majority of students score well below the national average in reading and language arts, as well as in mathematics. Responding to identified student needs, Project X is intended to explore the ways in which new technologies contribute to the development of language arts skills and to the enhancement of students' attitudes about themselves, language learning, and the schooling experience. These skills and attitudes are believed to be the key elements that need to be improved if the educational disadvantage faced by the target student population is to be reversed.

The instructional philosophy underlying Project X is one of whole language. The philosophy rejects traditional intervention programs that focus on drill and practice, and curricula that seem insufficiently challenging. Instead, it stresses the importance of new, qualitatively different learning environments that are student centered and that enable students to use language and communicate in the context of real problems and authentic tasks. Some teachers understand this instructional philosophy and its methodology more deeply than others; similarly, the teachers exhibit a wide range of commitment to this new approach.

Although the intervention targets the student, the change strategy uses a collaborative, teacher-centered approach to project implementation. Central to the project is a belief in the importance of grass-roots, bottom-up exploration and development. Consistent with the change and reform literature (Berman & McLaughlin, 1977), the project believes that teacher empowerment and ownership are critical to the innovation process and that change works best when teachers are involved in making decisions and in transmitting new ideas to other teachers. Project X thus operates through the mechanism of a teacher development team, consisting of approximately twenty teacher volunteers, who represent about one-third of the total teacher population. The classes represented by these teachers range from kindergarten to fifth grade, and include Spanish-only, English-only, and a range of bilingual classrooms, and other classrooms designated as gifted. Assisted by a project manager and a site coordinator, members of the teacher development teams are charged with the responsibilities of planning, developing, trying out, and refining new technology-based strategies that can enhance their students' learning. Each teacher is free to use the available technology and incorporate it into the classroom curriculum as he or she sees fit.

Project X makes a variety of technologies available to teachers and students. The Technology (Tech) Center is the hub of technological activity at the school. It is equipped with enough computers (principally Macintoshes), scanners, printers, and other equipment to enable all children to be involved directly in computer-based activities; it also includes a variety of other technologies: videodisc players, CD-ROM players, camcorders, editing equipment, and modems, and access to several telecommunications options. By program design, each development team teacher is scheduled to bring students to the Tech Center twice a week for approximately an hour each time. Some teachers also have several computers permanently in their classrooms, and they can check out additional computer and video technology for their classroom or home use.

The original proposal for the project was developed with strong support from the school principal. Since the proposal was submitted, that principal has been transferred to another school, as has the principal author of the proposal. Meanwhile, the school's district is in the process of a dramatic reorganization; the horror of the district's deficit and the school board's attempts to make severe budget cuts are regular items in the newspaper; relations between the district and teachers are strained; and the threat of a teacher strike is omnipresent throughout the life of the project. The school district is also putting great pressure on the school to raise students' test scores. At the same time, state educational initiatives continue, and thus, a variety of other special projects are going on in the school: Chapter 1, Title VII innovative programs, bilingual education, a state science project, and so on.

Belief in Apparent Success

Despite the chaos sometimes surrounding Project X, however, the majority of project teachers are enthusiastic about its success. They have engaged students in a variety of stimulating and exciting technology projects and have innumerable anecdotes to tell that support their strong beliefs in the project's positive effects on students. Researchers' observations confirm the presence of qualitatively different modes of classroom interaction from the lecture- and worksheet-dominated classroom activities that have been documented by various researchers (Goodlad, 1984). The following interactions typify Project X classrooms:

- A fourth-grade class works in the Tech Center to produce collaborative reports about penguins. One group of students collects resource information on penguins by watching a videodisc and reading from textbooks. Other students, having already completed their research, compose their reports on the center's computers, while still others use a scanner to select and import visual images to complement their written work. Although most students are working independently, the teacher provides special instruction and direct information to a group that apparently requires more detailed guidance; she then walks around the room consulting with individual students and groups as needed. One girl, a recent immigrant from El Salvador, speaks not a word of English and is unable to read or understand the textual materials, but she has apparently easily mastered the HyperCard and scanning requirements of the report task and is able to contribute this expertise to her group.

•   Students work to narrate and dramatize poems from a book, producing what will become an award-winning video. Some poems are brought to life by the children's acting and dancing, others by the children's animated illustrations. The narration is in both Spanish and English.

•   Excited fourth graders busily and happily graph the data they have collected on acid rain. They electronically transmit their findings to student research partners across the country and thoughtfully discuss the geographic rationale for differences in findings, bringing in sophisticated concepts of climate, industrialization, and the like.

•   Students create their own HyperCard stacks in conjunction with a unit on weather. They scan an interactive videodisc containing examples of various cloud types and other assorted weather concepts. They write instructional units for second graders, integrating text with graphics, using both English and Spanish. Outside the classroom, students are observed pondering the sky, identifying cloud types with great interest and accuracy.

Teachers in such projects typically speak eloquently of the projects' effects. The following actual comments from teachers in several projects illustrate what Project X teachers would be likely to say:

> My teaching has changed. Even though we still have the [traditional] roles of teacher and student, my function in the classroom is as a facilitator, and often as a learner. Lots of times, the kids know how to do things I don't, or they show me things I haven't done before. Then, I can say, "Great, thanks for teaching me or for showing me how to do that."

My first-period class is classified as low-level seniors. They're the kids who have received D's and F's in English in the past. Anyway, these kids rush in here first period and go immediately to the computers. I can't even take roll because they're all sitting in cooperative groups around the computers. You should hear their conversations! In the past, these kids finished high school and got jobs at Ralph's [a local supermarket], if they were lucky. Now with computers, they talk about going to community college. They say things like, "Did you know that this class is being offered?" Working with computers has really motivated these kids to learn and strongly influenced, in a positive way, my perceptions about their abilities.

We are able to give the students so many different kinds of language experience using technology. We had no idea at the beginning of the project of the impact that the visuals would have on students, especially videotape. We thought the extent of the video use would be to take pictures of field trips, with a little animation, and that's it. But now we're teaching children language through video. They're learning language *themselves* through the use of the video. It's immeasurable what can be taught, in regard to technology.

[Parents] are realizing that their children have a future. They're realizing that [the students] will continue using technology in the workforce in a higher-level position or possibly continue their education at higher education facilities.

Students who tended to be shy, uncooperative, or uninvolved in traditional learning seem to feel less threatened by the technology. One girl who would not speak in front of others, or even directly to me, now will speak while I'm filming her on the camcorder.

I was actually amazed at what my students were capable of doing. Both my expectations, as well as their own expectations of themselves, rose dramatically in the course of the year.

A Complex, Multimethod Evaluation Strategy

Evaluation of projects that are similar to this composite Project X is complex. The evaluation discussed here as an example is also a composite, based on typical evaluations of similar projects.

The evaluation for Project X involved a multistage design, a range of data sources, and diverse quantitative and qualitative research methodologies. At issue were answers to basic questions about the project: How was the project implemented and managed? What were the effects of the project on instructional practices, on students, and on teachers? Table 6.1 summarizes the evaluation's data sources and research methods. The multistage design incorporated a three-level sample: all project teachers filled out questionnaires and were included in the pool for interviews; special student outcome measures and archival data, as well as parent data, were collected in a larger sample of upper elementary project and comparison classrooms; and a small case-study sample (four classes) was the subject of extensive observations and portfolio assessments. Note also the range of outcomes included in the evaluation: students' achievement in reading and language; achievement in writing, measured by special assessments; course grades; effort in classes as shown on students' report cards; absences; and attitudes, measured by a variety of scales.

Despite the credible design of the Project X study and the comprehensiveness of the data collection effort, those interested in the bottom line were disappointed in the results.

- Comparisons of standardized test scores over three years showed no project effects.

- Comparisons of students' grades over time showed no project effects in language-related areas or overall.

- Comparisons of students' effort, as shown on report cards, showed no project effects.

- Comparisons of direct writing assessments showed no project effects.

Table 6.1. Data Sources
for Evaluation of Project X Effectiveness.

Data Source	Method of Data Collection
Students	*Survey:* students in the selected project classes and comparison classes were administered an annual survey in their classrooms, in their choice of English or Spanish.
	Writing assessment: students in selected project classes and comparison classes were administered writing prompts each year in English or Spanish, as appropriate. These were administered along with the surveys by project research assistants. The writing assessments were scored by a group of trained teachers.
	Archival data: archival information on report card grades and standardized test scores was obtained from the cumulative files of students in participating project and comparison classes.
	Student portfolios: teachers in case study classes, as well as other interested teachers, maintained portfolios of students' writing and technology projects for students in their classes.
Parents	*Interview:* randomly selected parents were designated for telephone interviews each year, conducted in the parents' choice of English or Spanish.
Teachers	*Survey:* each teacher at the elementary, junior high, and high schools was asked to complete annual anonymous surveys.
Observers	*Observation:* structured observations were conducted throughout the case study classrooms and in the Tech Center.
Teachers, administrators, site coordinators	*Interview:* teachers, administrators, and site coordinators were interviewed periodically throughout the evaluation.
Teachers, site coordinators	*Focus group:* focus group sessions with teachers and site coordinators were conducted toward the end of the third and fourth years of the evaluation.

- Comparisons of student attitudes toward school and toward technology showed trends favoring project students, although statistically significant differences were only sporadic.

Why does the disappointed evaluator find no effects, even with his or her elaborate, multimethod design? Why does the policymaker sigh in dismay that school innovations never seem to work? Did the real-life equivalents of Project X truly have no effects on students? Observers and teachers in the program see differences in students. Why does the evaluation not document them?

Difficulties in Evaluating Technology's Impact on School Reform

The example I have described is quite typical of reform-oriented technology innovations. It is also filled with the research difficulties discussed in the following material. Individually, each research difficulty makes direct effects of projects on students hard to detect; in combination, these difficulties are formidable indeed.

Imperfect Research Environments

Real schools are messy and noisy environments for research, far from the pristine, controlled setting available in the research laboratory, the model on which most quantitative evaluation studies are based. The confounding variables are legion and include noncomparable comparison groups and the influences of the other interventions that are typically going on in any school.

Comparison groups are almost always noncomparable. Rather than randomly assign teachers to project classrooms, technology projects usually rely on volunteer teachers. If they do assign teachers randomly, in practice only the willing assignees participate in a meaningful way. In addition, students are not randomly assigned to project and nonproject classrooms. Thus teacher effects are fully confounded with the effects of technology.

Although the bilingual school setting in the example highlights the difficulties of identifying truly comparable students, the problem exists in all school settings. Small differences in the distribution of students by ability level or by language can make significant differences in the performances of different classes. Moreover, the relatively small number of classrooms involved in typical evaluations is rarely sufficient to allow such differences across programs and comparison classrooms to balance out. In one bilingual classroom, for example, the distribution may be weighted heavily toward those who have just transitioned from Spanish-only instruction, while the distribution in another class may be weighted toward those who are fully English proficient.

What might these differences in distribution mean when coupled with a small sample? Consider a dramatic example from a technology project in a nonbilingual school. Everyone connected with the school was surprised that the scores in the fifth-grade technology classroom took a nosedive from one year to the next when compared with a control classroom. Closer inspection found that the highest-scoring student in the technology classroom was present during the test administration for the first year but not the second. When his scores were excluded from the first year results, test trends were in the expected direction.

As if problems in comparing noncomparable groups were not enough, technology is rarely implemented in isolation from other school interventions, and disentangling the unique contributions of various mandates and other changes is nearly impossible. In Project X, the school was participating in various other innovative projects that involved some of the project's teachers as well as other teachers. At the same time, the school was under tremendous pressure from the school district to improve its test scores. Research suggests that when teachers feel such pressure, they are inclined to focus only on test content and to engage students primarily in worksheet exercises resembling the multiple-choice tests the students will be required to take (Herman & Golan, 1991; Shepard & Cutts-Dougherty, 1991). Because innovative learning activities are so far removed from the content of most standardized tests, one might even argue that the absence of a negative effect in project class-rooms when compared with nonproject classrooms actually suggests a positive impact. (I will discuss problems related to the mismatch between project goals and designated outcomes in greater detail later in the chapter.)

Implementation Strategies Differ from Evaluation Strategies

Standard experimental designs assume that the project interven-tion or treatment is a uniform independent variable that looks the same across classrooms. Yet projects like Project X are designed to *explore* the use of technology in schools; therefore teachers are encouraged to adapt the technology to their classroom needs in ways the teachers deem appropriate. In these projects, different technologies may be employed across classrooms and teachers, or the same technologies may be used in different ways.

From an innovation and change perspective, this is an effective strategy to build critical teacher ownership and to encourage the local adaptation that has been found to support change. Also, as all educators know (or should know), it is not the technology in and of itself but the way in which the technology is *used* that is likely to influence student outcomes. Furthermore, differences in how teachers use technology signal the teachers' different instructional targets and different goals for student performance. However, from a research perspective, this implementation strategy makes an oper-ational definition of program treatment impossible. There is no standard treatment to test, and without a standard treatment, any attempt to apply standard outcome measures is likely to be futile. Even under the best of circumstances, outcome measures are dif-ferentially sensitive and differentially match what actually goes on in different project classrooms.

From the perspective of time and duration, moreover, most school technology projects represent a relatively weak treatment. In Project X, for example, students were exposed to advanced and varied technological resources for only two hours a week. Although rich compared with typical school resources, such a time allocation still represents only a small proportion of available instructional time. How dramatic a change can one expect from such limited exposure, particularly when part of that time must be devoted to learning to use the technology and the relevant software programs? For example, in one project classroom, a single HyperCard project on health habits consumed essentially a full semester of allotted project time. Can one reasonably expect to see significant change in standard performance measures as a result of such a project?

Imperfect Longitudinal Study Environments

Looking at student effects over time could help alleviate the problem of testing results of limited exposure. Such longitudinal studies would also better simulate schools of the future, where technology will presumably be more cheaply and easily available and may be a routine part of regular school practice. But the practical constraints of current school environments are often at odds with such longitudinal plans.

Several technology-intensive projects in which I have been involved were planned initially to involve the same students over the life of the project; in some cases, this time would have covered the majority of their tenure in elementary school. But these were also projects that did not encompass the entire school, and thus the elegance of longitudinal study ran head on into issues of equity. Parents whose children were not part of the project were upset to learn that their children were excluded from what the parents viewed as an exciting and beneficial opportunity. In one school, in fact, when researchers alerted comparison parents to the existence of the special technology project, there was a deluge of calls to the school from parents demanding that their children be involved. In response, plans for longitudinal involvement and study fell by the wayside.

However, even if political problems had not compromised the longitudinal design, or if funds had permitted the whole school to be involved in the experimental group, the experimental rigor of the projected study would have been compromised by a number of other realities: student transiency, differences in implementation across classrooms, some teachers' resistance to any implementation, changes in the project over time, and breaks and uncertainties in the funding cycle. These and other problems render the conduct of a longitudinal study problematic.

Effective Implementations Require Time

The time dimension is important for another reason. In project after project, even under the best of circumstances, researchers find that teachers need a great deal of time to get comfortable with new technologies and to fully incorporate them into their classroom curricula. To the standard problems that accompany initiating change in schools, technological innovation adds problems associated with technical complexity and expertise, areas heretofore absent or treated only superficially in teacher preservice and inservice education (Scott, Cole, & Engel, 1992; Sheingold & Hadley, 1990). The problem of mastering the technology itself complicates the change process. Informal observations suggest that it takes most teachers several years to get comfortable with using and managing technology in their classes. Furthermore, it is not until teachers reach a comfort zone with the technology that genuine instructional innovation may begin to emerge (Dwyer, Ringstaff, & Sandholtz, 1990), a finding consistent with the literature on innovation and levels of use (Hord, Rutherford, Huling-Austin, & Hall, 1987). In short, searching for instant effects, as policymakers are prone to do, is likely to be futile.

Changing Primary Goals

Beyond advising patience in looking for effects, the findings just discussed highlight another elusive point in the search for measurable results. As teachers gain comfort with technology, they often explore new applications and try more radical changes in curricula and instruction methods. As new technology is marketed, an almost daily occurrence, even newer and more dramatic applications suggest themselves. Both teachers and technology developers, then, are constantly creating new possibilities for instruction and new goals for students (Baker, Herman, & Gearhart, 1989), making the goals of technology and technology's potential effects on students into moving targets; evaluators may carefully set their sights on evaluating the achievement of one goal, only to find that changes in teacher expectations about technology or in technical capabilities have led to substantial modifications in a desired outcome.

Insensitive Standard Measures

The insensitivity of standard measures in assessing the outcomes of innovative uses of educational technology is another challenging problem, and one that needs little explanation given current debates about the limitations of existing standardized tests (Herman & Golan, 1991; Linn, Baker, & Dunbar, 1991). When asked how technology is affecting students, teachers mention positive changes in such student abilities as sophisticated problem solving, writing, collaborative learning, global awareness, independence and efficacy, and engagement and motivation, as well as in students' specific technology skills (Baker, Herman, & Gearhart, 1989; Herman, 1988). Many educators believe, however, that current standardized tests do not measure complex thinking and problem-solving skills well (Baker, 1989; Resnick & Resnick, 1990), and of course, such tests are mute on other affective and social outcomes. Therefore, policymakers and educators should not expect standardized test scores to show the impact of many technology projects.

New alternative measures are in development but not yet available, and new learning theories suggest the challenge of assessing high-level skills. Cognitive research indicates that knowledge and skill development are context-sensitive (see, for example, Barron, 1989; Wittrock, 1986), a finding that raises fundamental questions about previously assumed transfers of skills across contexts. It is difficult, if not impossible, to measure problem solving without reference to particular content or specific topics, and a good problem solver in one area is not necessarily a good problem solver in another. This is a vexing problem for the whole philosophy of "standard" measures. If they are to detect effects, measures must be sensitive to particular interventions; they must match the domains of content, knowledge, skills, and dispositions that are the targets of instruction.

Even in the area of writing, where direct measures exist, results have been disappointing. Although teachers report improvements in students' writing as a result of experience with word processing, standard writing measures indicate little improvement (Gearhart, Herman, Baker, & Whittaker, 1992; Herman, Gearhart, Baker, & Whittaker, 1992; Sacramento City Unified School District, 1990). Why? According to one rationale, one-shot writing assessments in which students are given a topic and a single class period in which to compose an essay do not permit students who have learned word processing technology to show the capabilities they have developed. An important strength of word processing, say its advocates, is that it encourages students to engage in a thoughtful writing process and to revise their work. Standard writing assessments do not provide hospitable environments for reviewing and revising.

A final point well demonstrated by research in technological support for writing skills is that *one cannot separate the effects of technology from the quality of the instruction and curriculum in which it is embedded.* The fact that word processors may motivate teachers and students to engage in more writing does not ensure that students get appropriate instruction to improve and refine the quality of their writing (Gearhart, Herman, Baker, & Novak, 1992). To repeat, technology in and of itself can accomplish very little in education reform; the way technology is used, the functions it serves, and the extent to which it is grounded in and advances sound instructional practice are critical (Kulik, 1990; Scott, Cole, & Engel, 1992).

Toward More Effective Assessment Strategies

Research and evaluation in classrooms and schools will never have the pristine control of the laboratory; real schools are messy research environments, with some sources of "noise" more easily controlled than others. The multiplicity of problems cited above, in fact, suggest the shortcomings of using experimental paradigms and quantitative methods alone to study the effects of technology within broad school reform. Presumed controls are largely illusory, as is the scientific rigor often associated with quantitative studies.

Should policymakers and educators give up on research and evaluation? Absolutely not. But because of the flaws in evaluation designs, they cannot look to single studies of reform to provide definitive answers. Instead, schools might be better served by studies designed to deepen educators' understanding of how and why technology is working in particular cases and then building the knowledge base by aggregating data across similar cases. Everyone who is part of education reform also needs to get smarter about drawing on the insights and experience of those who have been involved in technology projects, about articulating the goals of specific technology applications, about matching those goals with innovative and appropriate measures of process and outcomes, and about demanding evidence of effectiveness before adopting new programs. In the sections that follow, I examine each of these suggestions in turn.

Merge Quantitative and Qualitative Methodologies

Good evaluation practice has long required the collection of implementation data as well as outcome data, so that evaluators can verify that programs actually have been implemented as designed before the evaluators reach conclusions about program effectiveness. Evaluators have also wished to better understand why outcomes are as they are, in order to make recommendations for future programs. And certainly, desires to aggregate findings across studies have long demanded good descriptions of program processes, so that similar programs can be identified.

Yet too often these standard dictums of evaluation practice are violated. Take a recent example I saw, an evaluation of technology in school reform that actually showed effects on standardized test scores. Enthralled, I quickly flipped to the implementation section to see how the technology was being used. Was it CAI that might be causing the effects, I wondered, or was this inner-city school site using technology in innovative ways? Much to my dismay, the report provided no information to fuel my hypotheses. It simply told me that the school had acquired computers, video equipment, modems, and the like, and that teachers had received some training in how to use the technology and how to integrate it into their classroom instruction. On the critical points of how the technology was being used and the nature of the curriculum and instruction in which it was embedded, the report was mute.

Build and Assess Theories of Action

Qualitative approaches to evaluation stress the importance of evaluators' understanding, from the inside out, the nature of the phenomena they study, paying attention to processes and effects as they evolve. Such understanding enables evaluators to build theories of action and to verify the appropriateness of those theories.

Theories of action are the rationales on which programs or projects are based. They identify the critical features, components, or variables of a program, how those features fit together and/or interact, and why those features are thought necessary to achieve success in a specific area, such as increased student learning, higher teacher satisfaction, greater efficacy, or change in routine practices. For example, some people believe that meaningful improvement in student learning requires substantial change in instructional and curricular practices, shifting the emphasis from discrete decontextualized skills to authentic real-world tasks, from students as mere recorders of factual information to students as creators of their own unique understandings of the world, from students' learning routine skills to students' using information in problem solving, and so on. Furthermore, people who have studied or successfully managed the change process in schools know that change requires strong leadership support, teacher ownership of the process, teacher training and follow-up on intended changes, time for reflection, adequate resources, appropriate materials, and the like. These elements (specific changes in instructional practice and specific supports for change) individually and in combination define a theory of action; consequently, these elements are useful targets for study.

In addition to defining the elements of program success, theories of action also define what "good" program implementation looks like. For example, if a project's theory reflected the kinds of meaningful instruction mentioned above, an observer walking into a project classroom would hope to see students involved in authentic tasks, students constructing their own meaning, and so on. An evaluation could then look for the presence (or absence) of such occurrences.

Consider this example from work performed by me and several of my colleagues. Combining our experience in a number of technology-intensive projects with constructivist views of how learning best occurs, one of our evaluation projects developed an implicit theory of how technology influences classroom instruction and ultimately affects student outcomes. Our theory suggested that technology implementation was likely to result in changes in teachers' roles, in more cooperative grouping and social learning among students, and in students' being engaged in complex projects that required them to integrate a variety of information sources and to construct their own meanings. These changes in instructional processes, we thought, were likely to influence students' learning and attitudes. So we built an observation instrument to begin to test our theory (Gearhart, Herman, Baker, & Novak, 1992). The observation was highly structured and required observers to document the nature of classroom activities every five minutes. The observers recorded a variety of elements describing the current instructional transaction: teacher role, social context (group, individual, cooperative, collaborative, and so on), nature of the work materials, complexity and length of required student responses, information resources available, amount of productive student interaction, and degree of student engagement. We also documented the subject area being addressed, instructional goals, and classroom context (grade level, time, ability level of group observed, if appropriate, and so on). The results enabled us to provide strong evidence on the effects of technology in instruction. They also highlighted differences in the use of technology across subject areas (for example, mathematics versus language arts), suggesting that these areas required separate analyses. Over time, such data could also be used to examine relationships between process and outcomes.

The Concerns Based Adoption Model (CBAM) (Hall & Loucks, 1981; Hord, Rutherford, Huling-Austin, & Hall, 1987) is another model evaluators use to look at program implementation and analyze the effects of specific interventions. Targeted innovation users (teachers or others) are categorized at one of six levels of innovation use, from nonuse to renewal. Subsequently, sensitive analyses of relationships between process and outcomes can be conducted that take account of these differences in degree of implementation.

Use a Variety of Indicators to Document Effects

If evaluators' theories of action are well founded, measures of process can also function as proxies for student outcomes. This is an important point, given the absence I mentioned earlier of good measures of students' complex thinking skills. Thus, although a number of evaluations my colleagues and I have conducted have not shown certain projects to have significant effects on student performance measures, the evaluations have nevertheless provided empirical evidence of instructional impact. Compared with regular (non–technology-using) classroom settings, technology-using classrooms exhibited dramatically higher incidences of complex learning tasks, teachers involved as facilitators rather than lecturers, students working in small groups, students interacting productively with one another, and students highly engaged in learning activities. From this evidence, we then were able to build a conceptual case, grounded in research and cognitive theory, about why such changes could be expected to affect student learning. The observations also provided evidence of technology-based activities that often are valued in their own right, such as cooperative problem solving, extended research projects, and facility with word processing.

The imperfections of existing measures and evaluation designs underscore the need for multiple indicators of effects. If standard measures show no effect, but observations, teacher and student surveys, and parent interviews point to similar impacts, then advocates of school reform can still begin to build the case for an innovation's effectiveness and can better understand the nature of these effects from the perspectives of students, teachers, and parents.

Articulate Goals Clearly

Theories of action require school teachers and administrators to be self-conscious as they use technology and to articulate the theoretical links between the uses and student outcomes. Why do they expect National Geographic Kids Network to improve students' knowledge and problem solving? On what aspects of students' performance do teachers and administrators anticipate an impact? How and why is word processing supposed to improve students' writing capabilities? What is the link between video projects and student outcomes? The *Jasper* series is a very good example of such theory building and a similarly good example of outcome measures that are carefully crafted to match intended objectives.

Sensitive measures of student outcomes require careful conceptualization and delineation of expected changes in student performance, yet this is often easier said than done. School personnel must ask themselves (beyond the "whiz bang"), how do we expect students to change as a result of technology projects? At the simplest level, what do we expect students to be able to do that they were not able to do before? What specific knowledge, skills, and predispositions do we expect them to acquire? Across what tasks or contexts do we expect their performance to generalize? If educators know what they are looking for, they can design appropriate measures or, at least, have a chance of doing so. However, without a specific target in mind, the probabilities of a hit go down exponentially.

Portfolio assessment (and other new alternatives) provides an intuitively appealing starting point for better measurement or, at least, for student assessment that better matches classroom instruction and curriculum. In several technology studies, I and my colleagues have encouraged teachers to keep student portfolios of both showcase and more routine technology projects. The portfolios have then become windows on curricula and instruction, and have stimulated teachers (and researchers) to think about the effects of these projects on student learning. Our next step was to structure the portfolios (or to build other alternative assessments) so that they could provide better measures of progress in identified areas. For example, if writing portfolios are to be used to assess student progress, then they need to include multiple samples of student work and the samples must be collected over time: monthly stories, bimonthly book reports, and so on. Alternatively, if portfolios are to be used to assess the quality of students' problem solving, then students must be assigned projects that require problem solving and that are consistent with some agreed-upon definition of what constitutes a problem-solving task.

Think-aloud protocols ask students to verbalize the thought processes they engage in as they go about solving a problem. In the context of technology-based projects, these protocols open another promising window on how students' knowledge structures and thinking skills may be changing as a function of particular applications, and/or how students' projects draw on certain processes or levels of cognitive skill. For example, what strategies do students engage to complete a LOGO project? What decision-making processes do they go through and what skills do they use in devising a multimedia project? How do they define the problem? Do they set parameters differently in these kinds of projects than in traditional projects? Are there differences in composing and decision-making processes when students are using word processing software compared with their composing by hand? In short, data from think-aloud protocols can help identify those skills and dispositions affected by specific technology-based projects. Those skills and dispositions can then form the basis of new assessments.

Demand Validated Applications

Articulating desired outcomes is one stepping stone toward documenting the effectiveness of technology-based reform projects. However, the compelling need to document effectiveness would dissipate substantially if validated applications were routinely available. Teachers involved in using technology in education reform are faced with an often bewildering array of software and hardware options. Which ones are effective for which purposes? Although there are some research-based exceptions, in most cases empirical evidence is scant. Rather than putting the onus on schools to provide evidence of effects, developers and publishers need to take responsibility for showing the effectiveness of their applications if used under specific conditions and for specific purposes. Then, at least, policymakers and practitioners could have confidence that specific applications, used under particular conditions, are likely to be effective, even if the precise impact of various combinations of applications is unknown.

Assess the Impact of Specific Applications and Projects

The notion of validating specific applications also has implications for teacher-developed units or for novel uses of existing applications. Rather than looking for omnibus effects of technology, educators can look instead for the effects of individual pieces or strands of applications. For example, rather than searching for overall school effects of various teachers' different uses of video, HyperCard projects, and telecommunications, project directors and administrators involve teachers and researchers and look to assess the effects of the teachers' individual projects. What is the effect of a second-grade teacher's use of word processing on students' writing attitudes and ability? How does a particular video project affect students' knowledge and understanding of the subject area of the project? How does it affect their observation skills? How does a particular pen pal network project influence students' motivation to write? How does it affect their communication skills or their progress in mechanics? Does a graphing program used in a fifth-grade class deepen students' understanding of mathematical concepts?

The point is this: expected outcomes of specific projects need to be articulated and assessed. This is not only a more manageable and controlled assessment task than attempts to assess the effects of technology overall but also more likely to be successful.

John Cradler's Classroom Intervention Plan (CIP) provides an interesting model for such efforts (Cradler, 1992). As part of the planning and resource acquisition process, teachers are asked to specify technology projects, including objectives and methods of assessing effectiveness. Teachers are then expected to implement their assessment plans and to report on their results.

Aggregate Findings Across Projects

The methodological problems inherent in evaluating many new technology-using projects underscore the futility of expecting definitive results from any single evaluation. Nonetheless, those concerned with today's schools can build their knowledge base by aggregating data across studies, deriving confidence when results from experimentally fallible studies do converge. Meta-analysts (Glass, 1977; Rosenthal, 1984), of course, have been advocating quantitative synthesis for years, and meta-analyses aggregating findings across a very large number of studies of computer-assisted instruction (CAI) have provided confidence that these programs are effective in improving students' basic skills (Kulik, Kulik, & Bangert-Drowns, 1985; Kulik & Kulik 1991).

Meta-analysts caution that only methodologically strong studies be included in these aggregations. However, even with less-than-ideal methodological studies, agreement strengthens the evidence base. For example, several small studies show that microcomputer-based laboratories (MBLs) enable students to understand scientific concepts more thoroughly (Linn, Layman, & Nachmias, 1987; Wiser, 1986). Similarly, a number of studies (U.S. Congress, Office of Technology Assessment, 1988) have demonstrated the effectiveness of graphing programs and their effects on student understanding, and the effectiveness of simulations. Furthermore, when studies provide good information about the context and process of implementation, aggregate analysis can clarify the conditions essential for success. Thus, for example, looking across a number of technology projects intended to stimulate inquiry (simulations, MBLs, and the like), study after study finds that appropriate instructional support from teachers is lacking. Such findings have strong implications for the design and appropriate use of technology and for the formulation of sound policy about technology in the classroom.

Focused research across laboratory and classroom settings represents another promising avenue for deepening educators' understanding of how and why technology works. Ann Brown's design experiments, for example, systematically move between classroom and laboratory settings (Brown, 1992). Hypotheses developed in one setting are verified in the other, merging concerns for external and internal validity by moving between controlled and real-world settings. Brown's work demonstrates the value of combining qualitative and quantitative methodologies, as well as the insights to be derived from different research environments.

Redefine the Meaning of Data

Technology-using projects intended to stimulate or support school reform require sensitive assessment strategies and expanded evaluation paradigms combining qualitative and quantitative methodologies. Teachers, administrators, and researchers must all look across issues of program implementation, instructional processes, and student outcomes to discover the best ways to use technology to improve the lives and learning of teachers and students. Although much of the data needed will come from formal research and empirical study, educators should not discount the value of the working knowledge of the teachers and administrators who have already been heavily involved in reforming schools and implementing technology or the value of the insights of the qualitative and other researchers who have been involved in studying these projects. If evaluation is to provide data for practical decision making, all concerned with education reform must be attuned to all feasible data sources and to the power of informed insight.

Consider a case that takes a leaf from Delphi methodology in order to suggest how a school might make decisions about equipment allocation. Schools wanting to get involved with technology—say, for example, computers and word processing—are faced with an immediate decision: whether to aggregate most of the equipment to a single technology center or to distribute it to classrooms, a critical decision given current financial constraints. No school or district I know of is willing to put this question to a true empirical test, nor should they. Yet by conducting focus groups with schools that have taken one option or the other, the school or district would find an answer emerging.

For example, for schools in which most teachers are novice users of computers, the technology center approach seems to hold clear advantages. Tech centers provide settings where teachers and students together can comfortably learn to use technology and where a teacher's whole class can be engaged in technology-based instructional activities that are central to the curriculum. In contrast, when technological novices have only a few computers spread throughout their classrooms, they tend to see the computers as supplemental to instruction and as a management strain. Moreover, by providing settings for staff development and for teachers to meet and share ideas, tech centers can act as centers of innovation and sharing, as well as be the physical and intellectual hub of an innovative project.

Redefine Questions of Cost Effectiveness

Finally, it is clear that schools must get a better handle on the teaching effectiveness of technology before they can sensibly respond to questions of its cost effectiveness. Schools need farsighted approaches that consider both the ultimate aims of education and the ways in which current and future technology may influence those ultimate aims (U.S. Congress, Office of Technology Assessment, 1988).

At the most primitive level, questions about cost effectiveness must ask whether particular technological applications accomplish at lower cost the same ends as existing alternatives. Here, for example, military studies comparing the cost effectiveness of computer-assisted instruction with that of traditional training show clear advantages for CAI, on the order of one-third less than the cost of conventional instruction (Fletcher & Orlansky, 1986). School studies also show advantages for CAI compared with traditional instruction on basic skills (Hawley, Fletcher, & Piele, 1986) and cost effectiveness relative to some alternatives but not to others (Levin, 1986).

But learning theorists and futurists tell us that students need more than basic skills: they need sophisticated skills for future success (Benjamin, 1989; Lucas, 1985). To thrive in an information age, they will need to access, organize, and apply knowledge in order to solve problems. Thinking about cost effectiveness only in terms of basic skills attainment is shortsighted. Yet schools currently lack appropriate measures to do otherwise.

Furthermore, schools must be attuned to the new avenues and potentials that technology opens. How should schools consider the cost effectiveness of functions and uses that were impossible in the absence of technology? What is the cost effectiveness of electronic networks that link schools in California with those in Idaho, Japan, and Italy? What is the cost effectiveness of simulations that enable students to experience scientific concepts, or to experiment with lethal chemicals, or to access the latest data from space?

Again, schools have to think in terms of long-range goals and long-range implications. Consider dramatic technological break-throughs from the past and whether they met the test of short-term consequences: Was it cost effective to move from slates and chalk to pencil and paper? Over the life of a student, would the cost of reams of paper and many pencils outweigh that of several slates? Was it cost effective to move to printed books? The printing press changed the nature of society and the nature of access to information, and on a per book basis, costs certainly went down, but did anyone stop to ask whether it was cost effective to put the power of information into the hands of the common public? Regardless of the relative costs, students' preparation for the future requires their acclimation to technology.

And what of students who are at risk? How shall this society judge the cost effectiveness of such affective outcomes as educational efficacy, motivation to attend school, the development of career plans, and the like? These are areas where the use of technology in school reform shows promising effects, yet they are areas traditionally devalued by the policymaking community. Are they trivial? Should they be ignored in cost effectiveness equations? Not if one believes that they ultimately affect students' predisposition to stay in school and succeed.

Conclusion

This chapter has summarized many of the difficulties in measuring the effects of technology in school reform. These recurring evaluation problems also contain the seeds of their potential solutions. Among these solutions are the following:

- A single study cannot provide the answers. Teachers, administrators, researchers, and policymakers must look across studies and across cases to understand the effects of technology in schools.
- Student outcome measures must be carefully crafted to match intended outcomes.
- Evaluation designs must investigate the process as well as the outcomes of technology.
- Evaluation designs must be grounded in theories of action that explain the nature of effective programs and suggest how to replicate them.
- Evaluations should include a variety of qualitative and quantitative indicators of technology's impact, triangulating on changes in instructional processes and student outcomes.
- The key aspects of the operation of specific projects and the

nature of their outcomes must be clearly articulated so they will not be lost in the noise of poorly specified programs and overall school effects.

- Answers to cost-effectiveness questions must consider comprehensively the full range of outcomes that will influence students' and the society's future success.

However, even with more sophisticated assessment and evaluation strategies, the search for effects may still come up short. It is clear that technology in and of itself is not a magic remedy for current failures in educational effectiveness. It is simply a tool. In the hands of good teachers, integrated into a sound instructional program, technology can enhance effectiveness. Studies in which I have participated have revealed many examples of good, reform-minded teachers who seize the power of technology to reinforce their goals (Baker, Gearhart, & Herman, 1991; Gearhart, Herman, Baker, & Whittaker, 1992). In the hands of less competent teachers, however, technology may be just another add-on to (or, worse, a distraction from) other more basic changes that are necessary to improve the teaching and learning process in schools.

Technology cannot effortlessly transform education. Productive reform will require sustained attention to curricular and instructional change and to technology solidly grounded in effective theories of action. Just as technology must be built on significant and meaningful curricula, so efforts to integrate technology into schools must be combined with professional development for teachers in effective curriculum design and instruction. Transforming education will require that reformers get smarter about how best to use technology to support effective instruction as well as about how best to assess that technology. This reform will take time.

References

Baker, E. L. (1989, March). *What's the use? Standardized tests and educational policy*. Paper presented at the annual meeting of the American Educational Research Association, San Francisco.

Baker, E. L., Gearhart, M., & Herman, J. L. (1991). *The Apple Classrooms of Tomorrow: 1990 UCLA evaluation study* (Report to Apple Computer). Los Angeles: University of California, Center for the Study of Evaluation.

Baker, E. L., Herman, J. L., & Gearhart, M. (1989). *The Apple Classrooms of Tomorrow: 1988 UCLA evaluation study* (Report to Apple Computer). Los Angeles: University of California, Center for the Study of Evaluation.

Barron, L. (1989). *Enhancing learning in at-risk students: Applications of video technology* (ERIC Digest). Syracuse, NY: ERIC Clearinghouse on Information Resources. (ERIC Document Reproduction Service No. ED 318 464)

Benjamin, S. (1989). An ideascape for education: What futurists recommend. *Educational Leadership, 7*(1), 8–14.

Berman, P., & McLaughlin, M. W. (1977). *Federal programs supporting educational change. Vol. III: Implementing and sustaining innovations* (R-1589/8-HEW). Santa Monica, CA: Rand Corporation.

Brown, A. (1992). Design experiments: Theoretical and methodological challenges in creating complex interventions in classroom settings. *The Journal of the Learning Sciences, 2*(2), 141–178.

Brown, J. S., Collins, A., & Duguid, P. (1989). Situated cognition and the culture of learning. *Educational Researcher, 18*(1), 32–42.

Burbules, N. C., & Reese, P. (1984, April). *Teaching logic to children: An exploratory study of "Rocky's Boots."* Paper presented at the annual meeting of the American Educational Research Association, New Orleans, LA.

Cognition and Technology Group at Vanderbilt. (1990). Anchored instruction and its relationship to situated cognition. *Educational Researcher, 19*(6), 2–10.

Collins, A. (1991). The role of computer technology in restructuring schools. *Phi Delta Kappan, 73,* 28–33.

Cradler, J. (1992, June). *Classroom intervention plan: Personal communication.* Paper presented at the National Educational Computing Conference, pre-conference symposium, Dallas, TX.

Dwyer, D. C., Ringstaff, C., & Sandholtz, J. (1990, April). *The evaluation of teachers' instructional beliefs and practices in high-access-to-technology classrooms.* Paper presented at the annual meeting of the American Educational Research Association, Boston.

Fletcher, D., & Orlansky, J. (1986, April). *Cost effectiveness of CBI in defense training.* Paper presented at the annual meeting of the American Educational Research Association, San Francisco.

Gearhart, M., Herman, J. L., Baker, E. L., & Novak, J. (1992). *A new mirror for the classroom: A technology-based tool for documenting the impact of technology on instruction* (Tech. Rep. No. 336). Los Angeles: University of California, Center for the Study of Evaluation.

Gearhart, M., Herman, J. L., Baker, E. L., & Whittaker, A. K. (1992). *Writing portfolios at the elementary level: A study of new methods for writing assessment* (Tech. Rep. No. 337). Los Angeles: University of California, Center for the Study of Evaluation.

Glass, G. V. (1977). Integrating findings: The meta-analysis of research. *Review of Research in Education, 5*, 351–379.

Goodlad, J. I. (1984). *A place called school: Prospects for the future.* New York: McGraw-Hill.

Hall, G. E., & Loucks, S. S. (1981). Program definition and adaptation: Implications for inservice. *Journal of Research and Development in Education, 14*(2), 46–58.

Hawley, D., Fletcher, J. D., & Piele, P. K. (1986). *Costs, effects and utility of microcomputer-assisted instruction* (Tech. Rep. No. 1). Eugene: University of Oregon, Center for Advanced Technology in Education.

Herman, J. (1988, April). *The many faces of meaning: Students', teachers', and administrators' views of the effects of computer saturation.* Paper presented at the annual meeting of the International Association for Computing in Education, New Orleans, LA.

Herman, J., Gearhart, M., Baker, E., & Whittaker, A. (1992, April). Portfolios: An approach to the assessment of technology-supported composition. In D. Dwyer (Chair), *Understanding technology impact in schools: New approaches to student assessment.* Symposium conducted at the annual meeting of the American Educational Research Association, San Francisco.

Herman, J., & Golan, S. (1991). *Effects of standardized testing on teachers and learning: Another look* (Tech. Rep. No. 334). Los Angeles: University of California, Center for the Study of Evaluation.

Hord, S. M., Rutherford, W. L., Huling-Austin, L., & Hall G. E. (1987). *Taking charge of change.* Alexandria, VA: Association for Supervision and Curriculum Development.

Kulik, J. (1990, September). *Assessment of computer-based instruction.* Paper presented at the Conference on Technology Assessment: Estimating the Future, University of California, Center for the Study of Evaluation, Los Angeles.

Kulik, C.-L. C., & Kulik, J. (1991). Effectiveness of computer-based instruction: An updated analysis. *Computers in Human Behavior, 7*, 75–94.

Kulik, J., Kulik, C.-L. C., & Bangert-Drowns, R. L. (1985). Effectiveness of computer-based education in elementary schools. *Computers in Human Behavior, 1*, 59–74.

Levin, H. (1986). Costs and cost effectiveness of computer-assisted instruction. In J. A. Culbertson & L. L. Cunningham (Eds.), *Microcomputers and education: Eighty-fifth yearbook of the National Society for the Study of Education, Part I* (pp. 156–174). Chicago: University of Chicago Press/National Society for the Study of Education.

Linn, M. C., Layman, J., & Nachmias, R. (1987). Cognitive consequences of microcomputer-based laboratories: Graphing skills development. *Journal of Contemporary Educational Psychology, 12*(3), 244–253.

Linn, R. L., Baker, E. L., & Dunbar, S. B. (1991). Complex, performance-based assessment: Expectations and validation criteria. *Educational Researcher, 20*(8), 15–21.

Lucas, C. (1985). Out at the edge: Notes on a paradigm shift. *Journal of Counseling and Development, 64,* 165–172.

Pogrow, S. (1990). Learning dramas: An alternative curricular approach to using computers with at-risk students. In C. Warger (Ed.), *Technology in today's schools* (pp. 103–118). Alexandria, VA: Association for Supervision and Curriculum Development.

Resnick, L. B., & Resnick, D. P. (1990). Tests as standards of achievement in schools. In G. R. Anrig (Ed.), *The uses of standardized tests in American education: Proceedings of the 1989 ETS Invitational Conference* (pp. 63–80). Princeton, NJ: Educational Testing Service.

Rosenthal, R. (1984). *Meta-analytic procedures for social research.* Beverly Hills, CA: Sage Publications.

Sacramento City Unified School District. (1990). *Research and evaluation report: Model Technology Schools Project, 1989–90.* Sacramento, CA: Sacramento City Unified School District, Research and Evaluation Office.

Scardamalia, M., & Bereiter, C. (1991). Higher levels of agency for children in knowledge building: A challenge for the design of new knowledge media. *Journal of the Learning Sciences, 1*(1), 37–68.

Scott, T., Cole, M., & Engel, M. (1992). Computers in education: A cultural constructivist perspective. *Review of Research in Education, 18,* 191–251.

Sheingold, K., & Hadley, M. (1990). *Accomplished teachers—integrating computers into classroom practice.* New York: Bank Street College of Education, Center for Technology in Education.

Shepard, L. A., & Cutts-Dougherty, K. (1991, April). *Effects of high-stakes testing on instruction.* Paper presented at the annual meeting of the American Educational Research Association, Chicago.

U.S. Congress, Office of Technology Assessment. (1988). *Power on! New tools for teaching and learning.* Washington, DC: U.S. Government Printing Office.

Van Haneghan, J., and others (1992). The Jasper series: An experiment with new ways to enhance mathematical thinking. In D. Halpern (Ed.), *Enhancing thinking skills in the sciences and mathematics* (pp. 15–38). Hillsdale, NJ: Erlbaum.

Wiser, M. (1986). *The differentiation of heat and temperature: An evaluation of the effect of microcomputer teaching on students' misconceptions* (Tech. Rep. No. 87–5). Cambridge, MA: Harvard University, Educational Technology Center.

Wittrock, M. C. (1986). Students' thought processes. In M. C. Wittrock (Ed.), *The handbook of research on teaching* (3rd ed.) (pp. 297–313). New York: Macmillan.

Chapter Seven

Realizing the Promise of Technology: A Policy Perspective

Jane L. David

Technology holds great potential for revolutionizing education. This claim has been widely heard since microcomputers first appeared well over a decade ago. Since then, technology's rapidly increasing power, portability, and connectivity, and its decreasing costs, have surpassed the wildest dreams of educators in the early 1980s. Yet inside classrooms across the country, there is little evidence that any kind of revolution has occurred, and remarkably little technology is evident.

The Unfulfilled Promise of the 1980s

The primary reason technology has failed to live up to its promise is that it has been viewed as an answer to the wrong question. Decisions about purchases and uses of technology are typically driven by the question of how to improve the effectiveness of what schools are already doing—not how to transform what schools do. Consequently, choices about instructional hardware and software are based on whether the technology is likely to increase standardized test scores. Choices about administrative technology are made to facilitate existing financial and record-keeping systems. Moreover, as has been typical with innovations of the past, scant attention has

Note: I am indebted to the participants in the 1992 Christa McAuliffe Institute Summer Conference, sponsored by the National Foundation for the Improvement of Education, who took time from their busy schedules to answer my questions.

been paid to preparing teachers and administrators to use new technology well and even less to their preferences about hardware and software. Instead, the acquisition of technology has been viewed as an end in itself, and the more "teacher-proof" that technology the better.

Systems designed specifically to increase standardized test scores on basic skills and do record keeping as well have grabbed the largest share of the educational technology market. Schools' and policymakers' focus on raising test scores and a corresponding lack of investment in educating teachers and administrators about technology and about effective ways of learning have made school districts easy targets for hardware and software vendors' marketing claims. Vendors who can demonstrate that their technology is aligned with existing curricula and tests are more likely to make large sales than are those who push technology as a tool to transform teaching and learning. The bewilderment of educators and policymakers in the face of varied claims for technology simply adds to the appeal of individualized, self-paced student learning systems that require little, if any, teacher involvement. Moreover, such systems are typically placed in a computer laboratory with its own teacher or aide, further isolating classroom teachers from the technology.

Imagine how different U.S. schools might look today if the main goal for purchasing and using hardware and software during the 1980s had been to transform teaching and learning instead of to increase the efficiency of current practices. The education reform agenda of the 1990s offers this opportunity for transformation because it is driven by a new conception of what students should know and be able to do, how people learn, and correspondingly, how schools and school systems should be organized.

Why the 1990s Are Different

The systemic reform agenda of the 1990s no longer aims to improve what schools are already doing. National and state policymakers, including governors as well as educational and business leaders, now imagine a restructured educational system that qualitatively increases the performance of *all* students. The language of the reform agenda communicates a very different image of teaching and learning from the traditional image in which teachers "deliver" knowledge and assign seatwork. The new image captures a much more dynamic view of schooling in which teachers guide students through individual and collaborative activities that encourage inquiry and the construction of knowledge. Table 7.1 summarizes some major ways in which educators, students, and communities are being asked to change their beliefs about instruction. Moreover, this new conception of teaching and learning is much more compatible with the early visions of technology's promise than are the traditional views of teaching and learning.

Table 7.1. Shifts in Teacher Beliefs and Practices.

Area	Traditional Beliefs and Practices	→	Constructivist Beliefs and Practices
Classroom activity	Teacher centered Didactic	→	Learner centered Interactive
Teacher role	Fact teller Always expert	→	Collaborator Sometimes learner
Student role	Listener Always listener	→	Collaborator Sometimes expert
Instructional goals	Facts Memorization	→	Relationships Inquiry and invention
Concept of knowledge	Accumulation of facts	→	Transformation of facts
Demonstration of success	Quantity of memorized facts	→	Quality of understanding
Assessment	Norm-referenced Multiple-choice instruments	→	Criterion-referenced Portfolios and performances

Source: Dwyer & Ringstaff (1992).

There has been an equally dramatic and analogous shift in the conception of how organizations change and the appropriate role of policy in that process. Previous waves of reform have amply demonstrated the futility of mandating a challenging curriculum without changing the rest of the system in ways that support teachers. Policies to transform teaching and learning must transform the organization of schools and school systems as well. This new view of parallel organizational and instructional transformation shifts the role of the policymaker, like that of the teacher, from telling others what to do to leading and supporting others to continually learn and improve. Policy changes from a tool for prescribing and controlling behavior to a tool for empowering people and facilitating change with appropriate checks and balances.

The goal of systemic change, of creating an education system in which all students can reach much more challenging performance standards than before, puts the potential of technology in a very different light. For education reformers, the question is no longer how to use technology to do the same thing better. The question now becomes, How can technology be used to change educational practice to reach new goals? How can technology become a catalyst for change; a tool for creating, implementing, managing, and communicating a new conception of teaching and learning; and a system that supports the new conception? In this new system, the old learning goals, as assessed by standardized achievement tests, do not fall by the wayside. In fact there is evidence that basic skills, as defined by these tests, are learned at least as well, if not better, through the more intellectually challenging experiences available to students in the new system (Knapp, Shields, & Turnbull, 1992).

Numerous examples exist, covering a wide variety of students and settings, that show how technology can be used to transform teaching and learning. These examples demonstrate that, under the appropriate conditions, technology can stimulate and facilitate the introduction of project-based activities, student and teacher collaboration, and cross-disciplinary work. The examples also document a range of outcomes far broader than those measured by typical multiple-choice tests (see, for example, Pogrow, 1990;

Stearns, David, Hanson, Ringstaff, & Schneider, 1991; Tierney and others, 1992; Zorfass, Morocco, Tivnan, Persky, & Remz, 1991).

Each of these examples demonstrates that technology can be the vehicle for significantly changing what happens in classrooms and for greatly expanding how and what students learn. For example, Tierney and others (1992) reported that high school students, after four years of exposure to computers as tools for exploration, "became independent and collaborative problem-solvers, communicators, record-keepers, and learners with the computers" (p. 11). Although the interventions cited here differ in technology applications, subject matter, student characteristics, and numerous other features, they also share three significant features. First, they are based on the premise that the development of students' understanding and problem-solving skills requires activities that engage students in constructing knowledge. (This view does not obviate the need for practicing basic skills in a tightly structured environment. In fact, it enhances the learning of such skills by providing a context that gives them meaning.) Second, these interventions incorporate intensive support for teachers' professional development. Third, they involve only a small number of classrooms or schools.

In fact, the success of these intervention projects has had less to do with the technology on which they rely than with the philosophy of learning and conception of professional development that they embody. Project staff provide ongoing assistance, facilitation, and professional development to teachers in support of transforming their practice. These knowledgeable staff are available on site and on line to answer questions, guide, and cajole as well as to offer specific training, development, and support. The support staff are learning alongside teachers what it takes to create inquiry-based learning environments. This is a far cry from the traditional workshop/ training model of professional development in which the instructor is the authority. Instead, it is much closer to the kinds of learning opportunities the project teachers are asked to create for their students.

The very reasons for the success of these small interventions are the reasons they have not been possible on a large scale. First, their goals and assumptions about teaching and learning are at best out of sync and at worst in direct conflict with school, district, and state goals for student learning. Second, they require a huge investment, some of which goes into technology but much of which goes into the people and the time to support major changes in practice.

Creating these kinds of new educational practices is difficult in the best of circumstances. In an inhospitable environment, it is impossible. In the current system, such interventions run counter to a multitude of existing policies and attitudes including the curriculum; what is tested and how; the ways teachers are evaluated; the expectations of students, parents, and administrators; the school calendar and schedule; course requirements; and so on. The system is like an interlocking jigsaw puzzle. Attempts to change the piece in the center—where students and teachers interact—without changing the configuration of all the surrounding pieces is ultimately futile. With tremendous effort, the shape of the central piece can be changed, but over time the pressure from the other pieces of the system will force it back into conformance. Significant changes in teaching and learning thus require significant changes in the entire system.

Creating a New System

The systemic reform agenda of the 1990s takes on all the pieces of the jigsaw puzzle. It aims to change every part of the educational system in order to support the creation of challenging learning environments in all schools. To the extent that systemic reforms make progress in changing the goals, structure, and supports of the system, reformers' efforts to introduce powerful uses of technology will have a much easier time. Systemic reform and innovative uses of technology will be working toward the same goals instead of working at cross-purposes.

Changing the goals, structure, and supports of the education system is a long-term undertaking that requires sustained leadership and patience. It is also requiring a new approach to policymaking.

Policies designed to stimulate systemic reform cannot take the familiar form of a new program, a new set of requirements, or a new set of goals and policies superimposed on the existing system.

Essentially, systemic reform requires turning the education system on its head. Instead of a system in which the top (whether district, state, or federal level) prescribes, regulates, and monitors schools, reformers envision a system in which the top sets goals and provides schools with the flexibility, time, know-how, and assistance to achieve the goals. Schools assume responsibility for reaching the goals and also accept the consequences of failure. In such a system, the same patterns and principles are replicated at each level—classrooms, schools, districts, and state agencies. Each level must balance direction and control from its top with professional autonomy and responsibility at its bottom—a balance totally out of kilter with the present top-down bureaucratic organization of schools, districts, and state education agencies. At each level of the reformed system, people will be asked to take on more authority and responsibility—students for their learning; teachers for their effectiveness and professional growth; administrators for providing the necessary conditions for teachers; and policymakers for providing the direction, standards, and resources to guide and assist administrators, teachers, and students.

Translating these grand ideas into practice requires major changes in roles and responsibilities, changes that for many challenge their beliefs about teaching and learning as well as their beliefs about management. To make these changes, administrators, teachers, and students need on-the-job access to role models and expertise. They need the flexibility to create schedules and learning opportunities based on the particular context of a particular school and the needs of the individuals, teams, and faculties in that school. Class periods less than an hour long, for example, do not provide enough time for either students or teachers to undertake meaningful learning activities.

Learning opportunities for teachers, like those for students, need to be authentic and collaborative tasks like curriculum development, not traditional menu-driven workshops and packaged training programs (Little, 1992). Only under a system with opportunities to learn new ways of leading and teaching, and the flexibility to put them into action, is it possible to imagine the process of school transformation unfolding (Ray, 1992).

In a nutshell, policies to stimulate local educators to transform their schools and thus transform the education system must accomplish the following major tasks:

- Create challenging performance goals for all students through a broad-based participative process that includes educators and local communities.

- Reinforce learning goals with conceptually compatible curriculum guides, performance assessments, materials, and opportunities for educators to participate in the creation of all these tools.

- Empower and enable school faculties to transform their organizations, through decentralized budgets, flexibility, and access to ongoing professional learning opportunities.

- Develop a system of shared responsibility in which each level of the education system is accountable for meeting its goals.

Such massive changes will not happen quickly, and the barriers are formidable. Following decades of start-and-stop reforms, educators—especially teachers—are wary of new reform efforts. Teachers and administrators as well as students and their parents are accustomed to a system packed with demands and signals about what to do, many in conflict with each other. People have developed powerful coping strategies for functioning in this environment. Consequently, systemic reform must send a clear and consistent set of signals over a long time to have any chance of piercing this protective cover.

The vision of technology as a powerful tool for teaching and learning will not be realized under the present organization of schools and traditional instruction practices. The time and adaptability required for provocative exchange among teachers and between teachers and students, coupled with the limited resources available to public education, requires a dramatically different image of schools. This new image would present schools as community centers and as lifelong learning organizations for everyone. If schools are used by the broader community, throughout the day and year, the public might be more willing to pay for public education. Moreover, multiple uses of the facility can increase sources of funding and create cost savings that will make technology affordable. Redefining school and district staff roles and responsibilities, and drawing on the human resources of the local community, will also be essential elements of education reform.

Local Conditions for Effective Technology Use

Once the goals and structure of systemic reform are in place, the vision of technology as a powerful tool for learning and managing can begin to be realized. Inside classrooms, a range of technologies from camcorders to computers can support inquiry-based learning. Video and computer technology can make possible such new forms of assessment as student and teacher portfolios. Telecommunications can support the two-way flow of information necessary for decentralized decision making. Hypermedia, video, and networking technology can guide teachers' professional development as well as open doors to new ideas, practices, and information resources for teachers (see, for example, Ball, Lampert, & Rosenberg, 1991; Newman, 1992.) In fact, technology may be essential for fully realizing the goals of systemic reform by supporting activities that would otherwise be impossible or prohibitively expensive (David, 1991).

However, the policy structure for systemic reform is only the starting place. For technology to be used as a powerful learning tool and as a support for reform, certain local conditions must be in place. Whether it is used for administrative, managerial, or instructional purposes or for personal productivity, the technology must be readily accessible and functionally suited to the task at hand, and the user must have the necessary training, knowledge, and technical support to use the technology appropriately (see Figure 7.1).

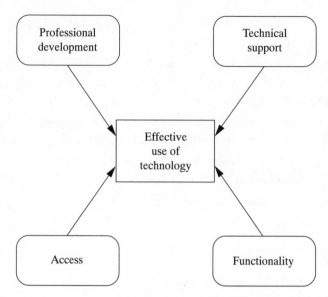

Figure 7.1. Requirements for Effective Use of Technology.

Access to technology requires that it be readily available for use as needed, not simply for uses that can be predicted in advance and squeezed into a fixed time slot. For example, teachers are far more likely to use video for instruction when the choice and timing are under their control. Similarly, teachers and administrators are less likely to use telecommunications networks when they must go to a remote location to do so. Nor can students exploit the full power of word processing if they must wait for their daily or weekly scheduled time in a lab. The technology must be readily accessible for use when it is needed.

The technology must have the *functionality* to support the use for which it is intended. For example, use of graphics requires computers with sufficient memory and speed; use of networks requires a sufficient number of telephone lines. This is a critical issue in the context of the continually expanding capacity of technology and the corresponding additional purposes that technology can serve. Moreover, it is critical that those who make decisions about technology purchases be aware of the functional needs of the tasks for which the technology will be used. No school system can afford to keep up with the latest technology. Therefore, it becomes crucial to match older equipment with tasks for which it is well suited. For example, older computers may be totally inappropriate for algebraic graphing and simulations of scientific phenomena but may be fine for students who are learning keyboarding and composing skills in the early grades.

Computer, telecommunication, and video technologies offer an unlimited range of potential uses. The challenge for teachers is to make appropriate choices of technologies based on goals for student learning (David Dwyer, personal communication, 1992). Open-ended, challenging collaborative projects are appropriate for certain goals, whereas independent seatwork is appropriate for others. Similarly, integrated learning software that structures and sequences learning and tracks individual progress is appropriate for some goals, and whole-class presentations by the teacher are well suited for others.

Judgments about appropriateness require both knowledge about the technology and knowledge about teaching and learning. Therefore, the third prerequisite to effective use of technology is *professional development* that encompasses a range of activities not typically considered professional development. Introductory "how-to" workshops on specific kinds of hardware and software have a place, but the critical development and supports are those available as needed right in the school. They range from opportunities to grow professionally through collaborative work with colleagues (on-site as well as via personal and electronic networks), participation in previewing and selecting hardware and software, and observation of others' use of technology to support teaching and learning.

Teachers as technology users also need *technical support* for operating hardware and software and diagnosing maladies. Like professional support, technical troubleshooting and assistance needs to be readily available. When malfunctions occur in the middle of a lesson, it is not feasible for the teacher to leave the room to telephone someone in another building. However, this problem is likely to diminish over time as more and more students become technically proficient and as teachers become more comfortable turning to students as sources of expertise (Ringstaff, Sandholtz, & Dwyer, 1992).

If access, functionality, technical support, or professional development for the task at hand is missing, the likelihood that the technology will be used effectively is significantly reduced. Moreover, once individuals experience ineffective technology use, they can become frustrated and less willing to change in the future.

Policy Issues and Implications

Creating federal, state, and local policies that embody systemic reform is only the first step. Transforming roles, relationships, and organizations in ways that reflect the new goals and creating the local conditions for technology use pose the real challenges. Imagining how technology could be introduced and used in ways that will support, and be supported by, the goals of systemic reform surfaces all the thorny issues facing systemic reform itself. The rhetoric of decentralizing decision making, for example, masks the complexities of balancing individual preferences with group needs and ensuring that those who make decisions are well informed.

Can policy become a tool to provide the conditions that lead to change inside classrooms, instead of being merely a set of prescriptions and mandates? What follows is a discussion of some of the issues and trade-offs that may be involved in policies for technology acquisition in the context of systemic reform. I discuss these issues under four broad concerns: the shape of technology planning, the locus of decision making, the character of professional development, and the need for equity. At the end of each discussion, I supply some rules of thumb for readers to consider.

Technology Planning

The rapid pace of technological evolution precludes traditional long-range planning. It is difficult to know what technology will be available next year, much less what the options will be five years down the road. Two current trends, however, are likely to continue: what exists now will become less expensive, and new products will be smaller, more powerful, and easier to use. The result will be two pervasive and permanent conditions: technology users will always desire newer equipment, and schools will always be out of date.

Owing to these conditions, strategic planning for technology purchases must be ongoing, and it must focus on the broad goals for the education system, the envisioned role of technology in achieving those goals, and mechanisms for maximizing use of technology and, therefore, cost effectiveness. Rather than specify a series of steps, particular hardware and software, and a schedule, useful plans will describe a set of principles on which purchase decisions must be based. For example, the Kentucky Department of Education's *Master Plan for Education Technology*, published in 1992, is built around a set of design principles called "strategic decisions." These principles express the goals for Kentucky's educational technology system without unduly constraining educators' choices about technologies.

The principles embody the vision of a coordinated statewide system that includes both instructional and administrative uses. The system is intended to be flexible and to expand incrementally by building on distributed networks of small computers. It is designed to have open systems standards that will support a variety of vendor hardware and software. Another principle is that of connectivity. Student and teacher workstations and student and school management systems, as well as district and state administrative systems, are all to be part of a single network. In addition to integrated major applications, the intent is to develop a common user interface throughout the system. Finally, the system is designed to be highly accessible to students, staff, and parents, and highly protected in ways that ensure security without limiting access.

Ideally, decisions about technology should be driven by what will be, not by what is, and by how technology can contribute to the goals of systemic reform. Thus, for example, decisions about networks need to consider the information and communication needs of an education system that is becoming more decentralized. Likewise, decisions about hardware and software should anticipate the expansion of student performance assessments and portfolios and a corresponding reduction in the reliance on standardized test scores.

Decision makers should feel less pressure than they do now to base major technology purchases on a particular technology's track record in raising standardized test scores in the short run and should concentrate instead on the contributions the technology will make to lasting improvement in students' understanding, problem-solving, and thinking strategies. Imagining future instead of present organizational structures also makes possible more cost-effective uses of technology. For example, if four teachers are jointly responsible for 120 students in four rooms, only one room might need to house the technology if that room is readily accessible to all. Without team planning and collaboration, however, such sharing of technology will be cumbersome at best.

It is equally important to make the ongoing planning process both iterative and participatory at each level of the system, so that the process itself becomes a vehicle for continuous communication and education about available technologies and their potential. However, policymakers must also balance breadth of participation in the planning process against the need to make decisions and act on them: the broader the participation, the longer the process takes.

Rules of Thumb for Technology Planning

- Build in flexibility to respond to rapid changes in technology. For example, choose open-ended, multiple-use hardware, not dedicated or restricted-use systems. Stagger purchases and assume a maximum five-year replacement cycle.

- Create an iterative and participative planning mechanism that ties technology acquisition to challenging goals for student learning and organizational change.

Decision Making

The rhetoric of decentralization calls for decisions to be made at appropriate levels of the system rather than primarily at the top. So, for example, decisions about transportation are probably most appropriately made at the district level, whereas decisions about most software purchases belong at the school, team, or individual level. Creating a telecommunications system probably requires decisions at the state level and, perhaps, at the federal level as well.

Decentralizing decisions is no guarantee that decisions will be better, however. A decentralized system presumes that the resources and the know-how rest at the level at which decisions are made. For decentralized decision making to be effective, decision makers must have access to information, and there must be policies in place to facilitate communication throughout the system. Moreover, if technology-related decisions are to be delegated to schools, such decisions must be accompanied by access to new knowledge about teaching and learning, by access to new knowledge about technology, and by sufficient time to test new approaches and observe others, for example. These learning opportunities ensure better decision making.

Whatever the quality of the decisions, when those who must live with the outcome of the choices are also those who make the choices, they will feel more ownership in the choices and the decision-making process. For example, in one district, the curriculum coordinator—an expert in constructivist teaching and learning but a novice in computer technology—mistakenly ordered computers without hard drives, precluding their use by teachers for the very ends he imagined. When state and district personnel make such decisions, they do not directly experience the consequences of poor decision making. When teachers are not part of the decision making, they are less likely to feel responsible for the results and therefore feel free to ignore equipment that does not meet their needs.

Decisions about technology may necessitate a larger cast of characters than is typical for most school purchases. Ultimately, these decisions should be driven by student learning needs, but a knowledge of technology is also needed. As illustrated in the example just described, *both* technical and instructional expertise are important, as is knowledge of product reliability and compatibility with other products. A school may even decide that different decisions about technology are appropriate to different groups. For example, California's Cupertino-Fremont Model Technology Schools Project created two school-based mechanisms for faculties to choose technology tied to goals for student learning (David,

Stearns, Hanson, & Schneider, 1989). First, teachers develop and continually revise Personal Learning Plans that describe their individual goals for learning about technology, including goals for productivity and instructional applications. The plans include flexible time lines and descriptions of how goal attainment will be demonstrated, as well as hardware and software needs. Then, in grade-level teams or departments, groups of teachers jointly create Departmental Technology Plans for technology acquisition based on their individual Personal Learning Plans, team or departmental goals, and the need to share equipment.

Rules of Thumb for Decentralizing Decision Making

- Give schools technology budgets, delegate decisions about hardware and software to schools, and give schools access to information about technology choices.
- Facilitate communication and information sharing up, down, and across the school system and with the community. Create districtwide and statewide networks to give schools and districts immediate access to budget and other data related to staffing and management.
- Encourage school planning that ties technology choices to learner outcomes either directly, through instructional applications, or indirectly, through applications to increase staff productivity, learning, and communication.

Professional Development

Technology provides tools and an impetus for the creation of challenging curricula and instruction. However, teachers need to know how to create these new environments, administrators need to know how to lead and inspire such creative efforts, and both need to be able to employ a range of technologies. Both teachers and administrators thus need a different kind of professional development—one driven by individual and team choices made as needed. Like effective instruction for students, effective professional development provides authentic tasks in collaborative settings and the time to do the tasks well. Hence, designing curricula, creating technology-based projects with a team, and developing assessment tasks are powerful ways for educators to develop their instructional and technological expertise.

Educators face a tension between learning how to use technology before "going public" and learning alongside students. Each individual has a different sensibility, but most educators prefer to master at least the basics of a new technology before beginning to use it in front of others. Consequently, a powerful form of professional development tied to technology is to give teachers computers they can take home. A number of districts now do this in conjunction with introductory training—teachers who attend summer training institutes receive a computer for home and school use. Experience at Apple Classroom of Tomorrow (ACOT) sites, which have had large infusions of technology over the years, suggests that, over time, teachers become more comfortable learning new tools alongside their students (Ringstaff, Sandholtz, & Dwyer, 1992).

Telecommunication systems extend teachers' potential for collegial work beyond the school. In fact, given the isolation of teachers from each other within buildings, creating professional networks can be easier outside a school than inside. However, to benefit from the vast world of information and people just a few keystrokes away, teachers need access to a computer, telephone line, and modem. In organizations that have yet to put telephones on teachers' desks, this is no small requirement. In Texas, where a statewide network (TENET) was introduced last year, 10,000 teachers signed up during the first year, but of those interviewed, many used the network at home but not at school owing to lack of access to telephone lines (Web Associates, 1992).

Rules of Thumb for Professional Development

- Invest at least as much in professional development as in technology. If funds are limited, use what is available for professional development and seek other funding sources, including grants and business partnerships, for acquiring technology.

- Focus on ensuring teachers' access to and comfort with technology for their own uses before expecting teachers to use technology extensively with students.

- Invest in developing school principals as leaders of change, supporters of teacher development, and modelers of technology use.

- Leverage professional development by investing in trainer-of-trainers models, including lead cadres of teachers (one or more from each school) who are supported in their efforts to share expertise with colleagues.

- Give school faculties (as a whole, as teams, and as individuals) the flexibility to select the training and other development opportunities appropriate to their needs and preferences.

Equity

Reforming the education system and realizing the potential of technology is extremely difficult in the best of circumstances. Realizing technology's promise in rural schools and inner-city schools in neighborhoods devastated by poverty greatly intensifies the challenge. The biggest risk the U.S. education system faces is that this promise will be realized only in wealthy communities, greatly increasing the already large and growing gap between rich and poor. The federal government has traditionally played an important role in ensuring educational equity through providing resources and protecting rights, and pressuring states to do the same. To achieve the vision of systemic reform, all levels of the system must strive together to transform the system in ways that will benefit *all* children.

Equity rests first on a fair system of school finance that does not penalize property-poor districts. Equitable access to technology for all students requires not only access to hardware and software but to teachers who use technology effectively. If teachers have no reason to change their practices, computers will be used as workbooks, video technology will be used for presentations, and telecommunications will be used, if at all, to pass along administrative dicta. Consequently, equitable access for all students rests to a significant degree on opportunities for teachers and administrators to learn new practices. Current instructional practice leans more heavily on drill and basic skills for students of poverty than for those of wealth. Uninformed choices about technology and lack of knowledge about principles of learning could maintain that discriminatory distinction.

Ultimately, telecommunication and video technology may be the most cost-effective vehicle for giving teachers, wherever they are, access to best practices. Through downloading curricula, interacting with experts and colleagues on line, and watching (individually or in working groups) master teachers and instructional videos, more teachers may have access to new ideas and collaborative work than would be possible or affordable face-to-face. For students, equitable access to materials, information, and other resources may be more readily achieved through networks than under current distribution systems.

Schools can also work toward equity by using their learning technology to provide education to parents and communities. Such extended education has multiple advantages. It broadens support for new uses of technology with students, maximizes the use of technology and the school facility, and provides needed skills to adults. Instead of restricting use of costly technology to the thirty hours a week when school is in session, schools that employ their technology on evenings and weekends for adult learning can acquire additional sources of revenue for technology purchases.

Rules of Thumb for Equity

- Ensure equity in access to technology and professional development, both across and within schools, through state and federal policies and resources.
- Ensure access to challenging curricula and instruction for children of poverty.
- Provide parents and the community with access and training to use the technology.

Conclusion

The conditions necessary for the long-anticipated technology revolution in education are now close at hand. On the technology side, low-cost, easily portable notebook computers have arrived, as have easy-to-use software programs for manipulating words and data. Multimedia technology and video production equipment, which can readily be shared among many students, are also within reach. On the reform side, there is a growing consensus around the need for more challenging performance-based goals for students and a massive overhaul of the whole system to create learning environments that will allow students to reach those goals. To the extent that efforts are made to reform the system through the creation of performance-based goals and assessment and through corresponding curriculum frameworks and professional preparation and development, the promise of technology tied to those goals can be realized.

However, systemic reform is a major undertaking. Although concerned about the quality of education, our society has not yet faced the need to transform an entrenched public institution. Public support for such a venture is spotty at best. In particular, changing authority relationships in the education system and providing teachers with ongoing access to information, knowledge, and colleagues will not come easily. By itself, technology cannot transform the system, nor can it change public opinion, but it can contribute to educators' overcoming some of these major barriers.

Educators are not likely to take on the reform challenge unless they have internalized a new set of goals requiring such change and have the necessary supports, including the time, access to knowledge, and flexibility, to learn new ways of teaching and of organizing schools. State and local policies cannot force change, but, with sustained leadership, they can set the stage, provide the direction, and offer the supports.

References

Ball, D. L., Lampert, M., & Rosenberg, M. L. (1991). *Using hypermedia to investigate and construct knowledge about mathematics teaching and learning.* Unpublished manuscript. East Lansing: Michigan State University.

Council for Education Technology. (April 1992). *Master plan for education technology.* Kentucky Department of Education.

David, J. L. (1991). Restructuring and technology: Partners in change. *Phi Delta Kappan, 73*(1), 37–81.

David, J. L., Stearns, M. S., Hanson, S., & Schneider, S. (1989). *Implementing the teacher-centered model of technology use: The first 15 months.* Menlo Park, CA: SRI International.

Dwyer, D., & Ringstaff, C. (1992). *ACOT overview.* Cupertino, CA: Apple Computer.

Knapp, M. S., Shields, P. M., & Turnbull, B. J. (1992). *Academic challenge for the children of poverty* (Summary report for the U.S. Department of Education). Menlo Park, CA: SRI International.

Little, J. W. (1992). *Teachers' professional development in a climate of educational reform.* Paper prepared for the Consortium for Policy Research in Education. Berkeley: University of California.

Newman, D. (1992). Technology as support for school structure and school restructuring. *Phi Delta Kappan, 74*(4), 308–315.

Pogrow, S. (1990). Challenging at-risk students: Findings from the HOTS program. *Phi Delta Kappan, 71*(5), 389–397.

Ray, D. (1992). Educational technology leadership for the age of restructuring. *The computing teacher, 19*(6), 9–14.

Ringstaff, C., Sandholtz, J. H., & Dwyer, D. (1992). *Trading places: When teachers utilize student expertise in technology-intensive classrooms* (ACOT Report No. 15). Cupertino, CA: Apple Computer.

Stearns, M. S., David, J. L., Hanson, S. G., Ringstaff, C., & Schneider, S. A. (1991). *Teacher-centered model of technology integration: End of year 3.* Menlo Park, CA: SRI International.

Tierney, R. J., and others (1992). *Computer acquisition: A longitudinal study of the influence of high computer access on students' thinking, learning, and interactions* (ACOT Report No. 16). Cupertino, CA: Apple Computer.

Web Associates. (1992). *TENET: The first year* (Draft report for the Texas Department of Education). Naples, FL: Author.

Zorfass, J., Morocco, C. C., Tivnan, T., Persky, S., & Remz, A. R.(1991). *Evaluation of the integration of technology for instructing handicapped children* (Final report for the U.S. Department of Education). Newton, MA: Education Development Center.

Chapter Eight

Tomorrow's Schools: Technology and Reform in Partnership

Barbara Means and Kerry Olson

The preceding chapters have dealt with aspects of technology and education reform ranging from the potential of multimedia to enhance instruction to the connection between network hardware and software choices and their likely impact on instruction and restructuring to the training of teachers for restructured classrooms, the development of assessment methods, the evaluation of programs, and the kinds of decisions and support needed from policymakers. Having pulled apart the concept of technology-supported education reform in order to consider each of these issues in detail, this chapter now puts the pieces back together, by providing descriptions of particular school programs that illustrate many aspects of using technology in the context of education reform.

The schools we describe here were visited in the spring of 1993, as part of an ongoing SRI International research project funded by the Office of Educational Research and Improvement. By describing these schools, we seek to illustrate, first, the kind of powerful teaching and learning that can go on in classrooms in which the goals of

Note: This chapter is based on research supported by the Office of Educational Research and Improvement of the U.S. Department of Education. The views expressed are those of the authors and do not necessarily reflect Department of Education policy. We wish to thank the staff and students of the schools described in this chapter for allowing us to observe their classrooms at length. We received outstanding support from Jackie Munoz, project coordinator at Frank Paul Elementary School; Robert Blatt, principal of the Open School; and Jane Barton, associate teacher of communications at Saturn School of Tomorrow.

education reform and the use of technology are both brought to bear, and second, the many different ways in which such innovations may come into existence. After considering a range of examples, we draw some inferences about the factors that appear to be important in producing effective technological support for education reform and about some of the barriers and challenges that reform efforts are likely to face.

Classroom Illustrations

We begin by describing two specific activities in particular classrooms, as a way of illustrating how skillful teachers can bring the elements of education reform and the power of technology together to give students meaningful, challenging instruction.

Learning About Local Heroes at Frank Paul Elementary School

Our first illustration is a fifth-grade classroom project conducted in an elementary school in Salinas, an agricultural town in California. The community served by the school is considered one of high risk because of its poverty, crime, drugs, and gangs. The student population is 86 percent Hispanic, 7 percent African American, 4 percent Anglo, and 3 percent Asian American; 33 percent of the students qualify for migrant education; 64 percent are classified as limited English proficient.

Like all classrooms in this school, the one we describe here adheres to the school's goal of producing students who are literate in both English and Spanish. Some students may do their content reading in English while others read comparable materials in Spanish. Other aspects of the school's philosophy that show up in the classroom include the attempt to provide a homey atmosphere, with soft lighting and reading corners where kids can lounge on pillows as they read, an ethic of respect for each individual's contributions, and extensive use of collaborative learning and small-group work.

The teacher, Cliff Gilkey, holds a bilingual credential and has twelve years of teaching experience, including nine at Frank Paul. His prior teaching experience included using computers with primary school students, and he welcomed the opportunity to have four computers in his class of thirty-one at this school. Sharing the school's emphasis on thematic instruction and collaborative learning, Gilkey did not find it difficult to manage the introduction of these few computers (too few for the whole class to use at once). Some of the initial uses he found included word processing and telecommunication with distant classrooms through the National Geographic Kids Network. In the rest of this example, we describe a project in which Gilkey's class used technology to develop curriculum materials on local minority leaders. The project illustrates the approaches to learning that make up the conceptual model for student learning and school reform presented in Chapter One.

Authentic, Challenging Tasks. The classroom's project grew out of two very real needs. In the past, students at this school had participated in a week-long science camp during their sixth-grade year. Funding cuts had meant suspension of this activity in the 1992–93 school year, and the fifth-graders did not expect to have this activity funded for them in their sixth-grade year either. However, the trip was important to them, so they began to think about raising the money themselves.

The second need was for appropriate curriculum material featuring contemporary Hispanic leaders. Materials available in textbooks and libraries were very limited. Gilkey reported that the role models that available materials provided for the Hispanic community tended to be either outdated from the students' point of view or primarily representative of success in the entertainment world. When appropriate material was located, the reading level was too high for his students who were just transitioning to English reading. The class members not only wanted to find appropriate materials for their own use but also became convinced that there was a real need for this kind of material in other schools serving similar student populations. They conceived the idea of a multimedia project on people they called local heroes. The project involved identifying local Hispanic, African-American, and Vietnamese leaders including politicians, businesspeople, researchers, and educators; conducting and videotaping interviews; and composing written highlights from the interviews. Technology made it possible for students to aspire to producing materials of a quality that would tempt others to purchase copies of them.

Advanced Skills Practice. The multicultural heroes project involved students in a range of tasks that required higher-level thinking skills. In preparation for conducting the interviews, the students first conducted a library search of interviews with famous people, and they analyzed these interviews to develop a set of questions that would fit their purpose and be likely to generate interesting responses (for example, questions about discrimination the heroes faced while growing up and how they overcame barriers). Through this process, the students learned concepts (such as the difference between open- and closed-ended questions) and techniques (for example, the importance of maintaining eye contact during an interview). Thus, the project provided a meaningful context for learning and practicing complex skills in a variety of cognitive, social, and technical domains as students planned and organized their activities, engaged in video recording and editing, and identified and solicited appropriate local leaders for participation.

Heterogeneous, Collaborative Work Groups. Students went out to interview their subjects in teams of three. One student served as the interviewer, a second acted as cameraperson, and a third served as recorder (initial practice convinced the students that it is hard to conduct a good interview and take notes at the same time). After the fieldwork was conducted, each student team reviewed and critiqued its own videotaped interviews. Within their groups, students engaged in discussions about additional questions that should have been asked and ways to improve their technique. They also worked on a written document, transcribing and summarizing key points from the videotape and the recorder's notes. While entering text into the computer for later editing and formatting, individual students on the team focused on different aspects of the task (for example, typing, spelling, and remembering and repeating what was said on the videotape).

Teachers Who Are Facilitators and Coaches. As we observed the classroom, Gilkey moved from group to group, checking on progress, monitoring students' practice, and giving groups questions to explore. Working with a group at the video monitor, Gilkey helped the students look for ways to improve their interviewing technique, asking them for example, "What could you have asked when she mentioned that she had dropped out of school? What will the listener want to know?" Moving on to another group, Gilkey sat on the floor as group members practiced opening an interview, using an imaginary microphone and camera. Simply introducing themselves and asking their initial questions was something that brought on waves of self-consciousness in these fifth-graders. Gilkey had them work on eye contact and discuss the reasons why an interviewer should ask the initial questions without looking down at the prompt sheet. Coaching, as practiced by Gilkey, does not mean fading into the background. He provides the structure that challenges his students, and he actively supports their performances and reflections.

Extended Blocks of Time. The project began in January 1993 and was expected to continue through the rest of the school year. In fact, Gilkey talked about seeking outside funding to help support the project and also to test the water in terms of schools' and libraries' interests in purchasing the materials. At the time of our visit, he was contemplating extending the project into the next year by teaching a mixed fifth-grade/sixth-grade class so that he could continue to work with a core of students from the first year of the project.

Building a City of the Future at the Open School

Our second example comes from a California elementary school with a very different history of school reform and technology implementation. The Open School, part of the Los Angeles Unified School District, was established in 1977 by a group of parents and teachers who wanted an alternative to the highly structured back-to-basics approach that dominated public education at that time. Their desire to establish a school based on the principles of Jerome Bruner and the British infant schools coincided with the decision of the Los Angeles Unified School District to set up a series of magnet schools to comply with court-ordered desegregation guidelines. The school's 385 students are drawn from across the entire Los Angeles area, selected at random within a set of geographic and ethnic strata to obtain a student population that is 39 percent Anglo, 21 percent African American, 20 percent Hispanic, 18 percent Asian American, and 3 percent from other ethnic backgrounds.

The city-building learning activity at the Open School illustrates both the kind of instruction that the school was designed to foster and the school's perspective on the use of technology. The activity is conducted in a classroom of 64 children, eight to ten years in age. The curriculum combines elements usually taught in the third and fourth grades, with an emphasis on the fourth-grade material. One of the classroom's two teachers, Dolores Patton, has more than twenty years of teaching experience. The other team member, Denise Cole, was in her first year as a certified teacher at the time of our observations. She had been a student teacher in the classroom the previous year and was selected as the replacement when Patton's teaching partner retired.

Authentic, Challenging Tasks. Each year, many of the students' activities in this cluster are centered around planning a City of the Future for the land site surrounding the school (a section of central Los Angeles). The city-planning task is a complex one. Students are asked to make projections about the size and composition of the Los Angeles population of the future, to think about all the needs that must be served, and to draw inferences from current trends about the types of problems that will be critical and the technologies and resources that will be available. Their planning task is difficult in part because they are required to house 1,500 people on the piece of land designated for their city.

Although they are familiar with *SimCity*, the popular software program that has students build a city, Patton and Cole do not use this software in their class. Their city-building project is a much more integral part of their curriculum than a prepackaged program could ever be; the technology they use encompasses the same software tools that adults might use to design or run a city or any other organization.

Multidisciplinary Curricula. The city-planning project, based on a curriculum developed by Doreen Nelson (described at length in Nelson, 1984), combines elements of social studies, language arts, science, and mathematics. Social studies topics include the structure and functions of city government, which students learn by taking on specific roles (for example, mayor or head of the Public Works Commission) and acting in those capacities for the classroom. Science topics are incorporated as students consider the natural disasters (notably earthquakes) that might threaten their city and seek to design in safeguards (for example, buildings with flexible bases). Opportunities for using mathematics are abundant. For example, a student who proposes a certain structure for a piece of land places an appropriately scaled color-coded piece of paper on the site (different colors represent different uses, such as residential or commercial). The student has to measure the piece of paper, compute the size of structure that the paper represents (one-half inch equals six feet), and then judge whether that size would be appropriate for the proposed building.

Heterogeneous, Collaborative Work Groups. Students are divided into neighborhood groups charged with planning for different portions of the land site. In composing these neighborhood planning groups, the teachers take care to get a mix of ages, genders, ethnicities, and ability levels.

Advanced Skills Practice. Within the neighborhood group, each student has his or her own parcel of land. Each student then builds a HyperCard stack that includes a representation of the parcel plot, as well as city, state, country, and world maps, and representations of the buildings he or she designs for the parcel. Students also produce plans for the structures to be built on their parcels of land, using the computer for scale drawings and text *if they wish.* Computers are viewed as available tools in this classroom, just as they would be in the home or office, rather than as a special privilege or reward for completing an assignment early. Each student presents his or her plans to the other members of the neighborhood for discussion and critique.

In addition to the neighborhoods, the classroom is broken into eight commissions, representing such city functions as Parks and Recreation and Environmental Quality Control. The commissions issue regulations in their own domain. For example, the Building and Safety Commission issues regulations on the height of buildings. As in the real city, neighborhood groups and bureaucratic commissions can interact. In the preceding year, the classroom Building and Safety Commission's height restrictions made it impossible for the neighborhoods to accommodate their quota of housing and still have room for other necessary services such as hospitals and commercial establishments. Several of the neighborhoods petitioned the commission and got the regulations changed.

Additional Authentic Tasks. The commissions also perform logically related functions within the classroom. For example, the Historical Commission is responsible for collecting documents representing the activities of the class and displaying them on the History Wall, as well as within a HyperCard stack. When we came to the class, a member of that commission was assigned to act as our informant regarding the history of the project. During the same week, the Education Commission represented the class in communicating with other schools on the Apple Global Education network.

The city-building curriculum existed before the introduction of technology at the Open School, but the addition of technology augments the project's authenticity. As the teachers and students in this cluster became comfortable with technology tools, it was natural for them to think about applying those tools to their most important project. The professional appearance of the parcel plots they can produce on computers adds to the students' sense that they are working on something important. In addition to the sense of confidence students gain from being able to produce products that many of their parents could not duplicate, the teachers believe that the use of computers to manipulate scale and other features of objects helps students acquire skills that are among the learning objectives for this unit—for example, thinking in terms of operations that can be performed on different content and in terms of mappings between objects before and after application of some operation such as magnification or mirror-image reversal.

Student Exploration. The teachers' strategy is to create a structure within which students discover concepts and apply new skills rather than to tell students how tasks should be done. One of the teachers' practices is to have the students begin the project by quickly building an "instant city" that represents their ideal for the future. Each student works separately on creating the layout for his or her individual parcel of land. The students then come together as a group, the parcels are connected, and the teachers lead the students in a discussion to analyze and critique the results of their uncoordinated efforts. Students note such inevitable problems as the fact that none of the roads are connected and that some services are overrepresented (twelve hospitals within a two-mile radius, for example) while others are missing altogether (no McDonald's!). The teachers note that the extra time it takes to "do" rather than to "tell" is worth it; students leave this activity ready and motivated to work together because they have discovered for themselves the importance of collaboration.

Interactive Instruction from Teachers Who Are Facilitators and Coaches. Students decide what they would like to put on their individual parcels of land and prepare a plan showing the layout, size, and functions of the buildings they propose. They are required to design something that reflects the needs and capabilities of the future rather than simply replicating something that exists today. Although students are extremely active in generating ideas and reasoning about them, the teachers are pivotal in planning and orchestrating the learning activities. As students share their initial plans within their neighborhood groups, the teachers guide the discussions, keeping the students on track and drawing them into the process of making inferences about future conditions and the relationships among elements in the city environment. One extended neighborhood planning meeting we observed covered topics ranging from school security to transportation to making inferences about the likely size and needs of the elderly population and discussing the issue of the right to die. This kind of interactive instruction calls on the teacher to respond flexibly to the innumerable topics and logical problems that student explorations unearth.

Use Extended Blocks of Time. The city-building project takes over six months to complete. Over their winter break, students do such preliminary work as taking note of the existing buildings on their land parcel and counting traffic. Then, when they return to school, they spend some four months building the city. After it is built, they enact life in the twenty-first century in their city and then use that experience to make final revisions. In the spring of 1993, the class was planning to use QuickTime (a software program that incorporates digitized video images along with text and graphics) to produce a record of their city-building experiences.

Reflections on the Contributions of Technology to Teaching and Learning

In the two projects we have described, it is clear that technology per se is not the driving force behind either curriculum planning or skillful instruction. The teachers' selection of challenging projects and their skills in orchestrating students' work with or without technology appear to be much more important than the availability of hardware or software. Nevertheless, our observations also suggest that the introduction of technology in these two classrooms has had a number of positive effects, amplifying what the teachers can do. Some of our tentative propositions about these contributions (which will be tested further as we complete case studies for our project) are discussed here.

Technology implementation often stimulates teachers to present more complex tasks and material. Technology appears to stretch teachers' expectations concerning what their students might be able to accomplish. The functionality of the technology suggests complex tasks, and teachers see these tasks as feasible given technological supports. At both the Frank Paul Elementary School and the Open School, some of the activities students performed appeared to be inspired by the availability of technology. Cliff Gilkey's project for producing curriculum materials is a good illustration. Other examples, drawn from our observations of additional classrooms at the Open School, include an activity in which students designed creatures for a two-dimensional "planiverse" and reasoned about how those creatures could function (for example, how would the creatures move and how would it be possible for two of them to pass each other in two dimensions), and a project in which students used desktop publishing skills to produce a calendar featuring an environmental fact for each day of the year. In some cases, such as the planiverse activity, technology appears to provide an advanced entry point, allowing students to engage in content areas and inquiries that might otherwise be inaccessible to them until a much later point in their academic careers. In more traditional activities, such as writing a research report or creating a calendar, technology can extend and enhance what students are able to produce. In addition, technology appears to stimulate problem-solving and thinking skills as students engage in the process of selecting appropriate tools and manipulating those tools to achieve their ends.

Technology tends to support teachers in becoming coaches rather than dispensers of knowledge. In classrooms where students spend large blocks of time using technology to design, compose, or solve complex problems, lecturing by the teacher is minimized. Both Frank

Paul and the Open School feature student-centered classrooms in which students spent most of their time working independently or in small groups while the teacher provided structure and support. In neither school, however, did we get the impression that the introduction of technology was the vital force in creating this classroom structure. Rather, it seemed to us that the teachers came to technology with these teaching approaches already well in hand. Because they were able to use these strategies, they could easily incorporate meaningful student projects supported by technology.

Use of technology increases teachers' sense of professionalism and achievement. Interviews with teachers in both schools confirmed findings of earlier studies that teachers' growing mastery of technology and its incorporation into instructional activities gives teachers a sense of achievement (Sheingold & Hadley, 1990). In both schools, opportunities were provided for teachers to hone their teaching and technology skills and to discuss their innovations in settings or contexts that reflected a respect for their accomplishments. For example, Frank Paul teachers went on corporate-style retreats, and Open School staff held Apple consultantships (these consultantships are discussed in more detail later).

Technology can motivate students to attempt harder tasks and to take more care in crafting their work. One of the major factors that motivates teachers to use technology is their observation of its effect on their students. At these schools, as at those studied by others, students become engrossed in their technology-supported tasks (Collins, 1990; Sheingold & Hadley, 1990). They stay inside during recess to continue their work; they delight in showing parents or visitors their products. The teachers we observed reported particularly marked effects on student writing, including students' having a greater interest in writing, writing longer text, doing more revision, taking more care in correcting mechanical problems, and, at Frank Paul, exhibiting an increased willingness to write in English.

Using the technological tools of the professional community adds significance and cultural value to school tasks. A strong impression left on us by both of the classrooms described here is that students see value in their technology-supported work. Creating parcel plots with a reasonable resemblance to those found in city records and creating official-looking building certificates makes the city-building task not just more realistic but more important in students' eyes. Students are not only learning to use the real technological tools of the workplace, they are coming to envision themselves as participating in significant work roles. Such experiences may be particularly important for students from economically disadvantaged backgrounds, who are likely to have little access to a variety of professional role models outside the school.

Implementation Issues: Alternative Pathways to Combining Use of Technology and Education Reform

Having provided several illustrations of the kinds of learning activities that are possible in classrooms that have embraced both the student learning goals of education reform and the use of technology, we turn to a consideration of the broader educational system within which such innovations take place. By examining the implementation histories of schools that have attempted to use technology as part of their education reform efforts, we seek to identify lessons learned that will be helpful to other schools, districts, and states as they embark on technological innovations.

Technology's Role in Restructuring a Traditional School

In thinking about the local heroes project that Cliff Gilkey conducted in his fifth-grade class, we asked ourselves, What made it possible for Gilkey to attempt a project of this kind? Among the more obvious features, we found the following:

- The teacher felt free to innovate and to try a high-risk/high payoff activity.
- Students were accustomed to working in cooperative groups: norms for turn taking, offering constructive comments, and being courteous were well developed; the teacher was accustomed to operating as a roving coach.

- Technology was available to the classroom: students could use four permanent computers, a mobile bank of eight Macintoshes, a multimedia center, a telephone, and video equipment.

Although the qualities that Gilkey brings to his class as a teacher and a role model for his students are critical, what we particularly want to discuss here are the ways in which the other layers of the education system—the school, the district, the state, federal programs, and the community—have made it possible for this kind of technology-supported innovation to occur. The Frank Paul Elementary School was established as a traditional, graded elementary school, and for many years the main feature that set it apart from other traditionally organized elementary schools was the demographics of its student body and its concentration of bilingual teachers. Over the last five years, however, the school has been consciously engaged in school reform and restructuring.

The initial impetus for reform came from work with a private foundation. In 1988, the school was one of the initial grantees in the Mid-California Science Improvement Program (MCSIP), funded by the Packard Foundation. The goals of this project were highly consonant with the education reform agenda: the project sought to stimulate integrated thematic instruction in science through multidisciplinary projects built around scientific themes (such as the study of whales) and lasting for extended periods of time. Teachers were encouraged to move away from standard textbooks and to develop their own materials. To achieve its aims, the project made extensive investments in teachers' professional development. Participating teachers received two weeks of summer training plus additional release time to develop curriculum materials. The project also funded a teaching coach to come to the school twice a month during the project's first four years. After five years, nineteen of Frank Paul's twenty-four teachers had gone through the MCSIP training. In addition, a number of the school's teachers had been trained as MCSIP coaches and were acting in that role for other schools.

In 1990, the school responded to another outside stimulus for school restructuring. The school district's superintendent had developed a contact with the president of Pacific Telesis at a Business Roundtable meeting and found that Pacific Telesis was preparing to provide selected schools with grants to experiment with site-based management to become the School of the Future. The superintendent encouraged Frank Paul to apply for a grant, and the application was successful. This project had a clear education reform focus: Pacific Telesis provided training and resources for participating schools to try site-based management and to experiment with new ways to teach and run a school. Part of this process was to develop a vision or plan that described where the staff wanted the school to be in eight years and to maintain a school portfolio. Another part of the process involved developing a site-based council and giving teachers many of the decision-making powers formerly held by the principal. The Pacific Telesis grant was not primarily about technology, but the Curriculum Action Team of teachers and aides set up as a result of the project made technology a priority. Although the project's original emphasis was on development of student literacy skills, the team grasped the idea that technology provided tools that could be applied in any curriculum area.

The funding and impetus for innovation that Frank Paul received from outside sources was complemented by resources from the district, state, and federal education systems. When the State of California held a grant competition for school restructuring, Frank Paul won a planning grant for the 1991–92 school year and an implementation grant that started in 1992–93. Preparation of the plan and the implementation proposal provided a focus for the staff's continuing dialogue about their goals and how they could improve. Funds from the grant supported hiring a coach who came twice a month to help teachers improve their thematic instruction skills. In 1993–94, the school initiated a Head Start program and other family services on campus. Current plans also include placing a set of computers in the library and making them available for evening use by parents, very few of whom have computers in the home.

The district assisted the school's reform efforts in tangible ways, such as a $50,000 Chapter 1 technology grant for the purchase of additional computer equipment and the provision of training in hardware and software use from the district technology coordinator. Although described by some Frank Paul staff as sometimes reluctant to allow Frank Paul to be different from other schools in the district, the district has in many ways given the school permission to change. For example, Frank Paul has been allowed to trade its vice principal position for part-time project coordinator and parent liaison positions. The district has also been cooperative in accepting the school's assertion that scores on standardized tests do not provide good measures of what the program is trying to do or of the real achievement of its students, most of whom are limited in English proficiency.

Integrating Technology into an Alternative School

The Open School was started with many of the features that reformers are now trying to bring to more traditional schools. The purpose of this alternative school was to encourage students to learn through exploration and to work in teams of varying size and composition. Students were organized into multi-age clusters, each taught by a team of two teachers. Each cluster's curriculum was organized around multidisciplinary thematic units, and each cluster had a "grand theme" which fit into the school's overall curriculum theme. (At the time of our visit, the overall theme was entitled "Survival: Man's Interaction with the Environment.") The school day was designed to be very flexible, with a rough division into four large blocks of time. Within this structure, teachers planned projects that would last over a period of days, weeks, or months.

Although there was limited use of computers in some classrooms from the school's beginning, the serious introduction of technology began in 1986, after Alan Kay, an innovator in human-computer interface design and an Apple Computer research fellow, selected the school as the site for a research project he named "The Vivarium." Kay wanted to use the school as a testbed for new ways to interact with intelligent software. His notion was that if you design something powerful yet simple enough for kids, it will be good for adults as well. For a school to be an appropriate testbed, it had to have enough technology around so that access was not an issue.

Kay originally proposed to use one or two classrooms for his research. The Open School's principal, however, objected to this plan, despite the offer of a classroom full of computers. It was her conviction that any introduction of technology had to be done on a whole-school basis so that it would unite the school rather than fragment it. Therefore, Kay and the school agreed that technology would be introduced into all of the clusters in such a way that it would be easily accessible as a tool but neither the focus of instruction nor an intrusive part of the classroom environment (Kay, 1991). Over time, Apple Computer placed approximately thirty computers into each of six cluster classrooms of sixty-four students each. Most of the computers are recessed into specially designed tables that can be used for other kinds of student work when the computer is not needed. Technology integration is now at a mature stage in this school. Students use technology in every classroom and have become so accustomed to it that there is no novelty value.

Apple provided the school with an extraordinary measure of support. In addition to the computers, CD-ROM and laserdisc players, networking and other technology, the corporation supported a full-time technical support person and a portion of the time of several other staff members who provided assistance with technological activities through the end of the 1992–93 school year. During this six-year period from 1986 on, Apple also paid the school's teachers as consultants over the summer and winter breaks. Thus, during these periods, the teachers were able to spend time receiving coaching on technology use and developing materials for their classrooms.

Building a New Technology-Supported Break-the-Mold School

At both the Open School and Frank Paul Elementary, the introduction of technology took place gradually, within the context of previously established instructional environments. Within these contexts, technology was adopted selectively to support and facilitate ongoing educational goals and practices within classrooms. At the same time, technology expanded and transformed various aspects of the schools' goals and practices.

In contrast to Frank Paul and the Open School, the Saturn School of Tomorrow, a magnet middle school in St. Paul, Minnesota, illustrates the history of a school founded to embody both the implementation of technology and educational restructuring. Built from the ground up as a "fundamental redesign of the way we deliver educational services" (Preskill, 1990, p. 4), Saturn was established by the St. Paul School District as a model for the coupling of technology use and education reform. Planners described the Saturn concept as a "high tech, high teach, high touch" program in which students would engage in a combination of computer-supported, teacher-led, and collaborative project-based learning activities.

The impetus for the creation of Saturn came from a keynote address given by Al Shanker, President of the American Federation of Teachers, to St. Paul teachers and district administrators in 1986. During what one teacher later described as "a terrific and disturbing" speech, Shanker noted the failure of traditional education to prepare students for life in the twenty-first century. He called for the retooling of the public school system, citing General Motors' Saturn plant as an example within industry of the kind of innovative approach needed within education. Shanker's message struck a resonant chord with the school superintendent and other members of the St. Paul educational community, and within months a planning committee to explore the creation of a Saturn School was formed.

Tom King, the leader for the collaborative effort to establish the Saturn School of Tomorrow and a member of the St. Paul school district administration, devoted much of his time during the ensuing three-year planning period to soliciting and orchestrating the needed resources, funds, and equipment. The Minnesota Federation of Teachers, the College of St. Thomas (located in St. Paul,

Minnesota), and the Minnesota Educational Computing Corporation (MECC) were the initial and primary partners. The Minnesota
Federation of Teachers was actively involved in the planning
process and supported the contract revisions that were necessary to
implement Saturn's concept of leadership by master teachers holding year-round teaching positions. The College of St. Thomas sponsored an internship program at Saturn and was awarded a three-year
grant by the Bush Foundation to conduct the formative evaluation
of the Saturn implementation. MECC provided software and technical support and was responsible for an evaluation of the technology component of the program during Saturn's second year of
operation. A wide range of corporate sponsors that included Apple
Computer, IBM, Tandy, Control Data, Pioneer, Cray, Jostens, Computer Curriculum Corporation (CCC), Sunburst, and Optical Data
provided hardware and software donations or discounts.

Saturn opened in temporary quarters in the fall of 1989 with
grades four through six (grades seven and eight were added in 1990
and 1991, respectively). The school moved to its permanent location in a renovated downtown YWCA building in January 1991.
The Saturn building itself is nontraditional in its layout, having
been designed especially to fit Saturn's instructional program by an
architect who worked closely with the lead teaching staff. The
building features a variety of spaces designed specifically for technology-supported learning—for example, cooperative learning
areas, computer labs, and a video production studio. Every classroom is equipped with a telephone and a teaching station that
includes a Macintosh system (linked to a school network) and a
video monitor to display in-school broadcasts and VCR or videodisc
presentations.

Although the magnet school enrollment process succeeded in
establishing one of the most ethnically diverse student populations
within the district (60 percent Anglo, 40 percent minority groups),
there has been a disproportionately high number of male students
(65 percent) since the school's inception. Saturn staff attribute this
gender imbalance to Saturn's reputation within the community as a
technology-oriented school as well as to the possibility that Saturn

may be viewed as an alternative to traditional programs, in which a greater number of male than female students are having difficulties.

Project leader Tom King articulated three guiding principles in the original proposal for the school:

Instructional content should be oriented around the needs of individual students. One corollary to this principle is the planning team's conviction that students learn best when working with content that is really interesting to them; hence, needed skills were to be embedded in content of individual students' own choosing. A second corollary is that learning plans must be individualized and that instruction should be organized around these individual plans.

Teachers should be highly professional leaders. The original Saturn plan called for no school principal. Instead, the school's leadership was to be invested in a lead teacher, a concept similar to the British notion of a headmaster. The school's core teaching staff of four (the lead teacher and three associates) were to take responsibility for program design and curriculum development in addition to their teaching duties. They were to be compensated for this work with a year-round salary.

State-of-the-art technology should be used to "ensure individual student mastery and agreed-upon achievement levels" (St. Paul Public Schools, 1987). The Saturn planners sought to harness the power of technology to make Saturn a "school of tomorrow." The intended role of technology in the Saturn program was broad and wide ranging. Recognizing the increased level of risk involved in giving students so much leeway to follow their own interests, the school founders envisioned technology as an "insurance policy" that would see that all students attained appropriate levels of basic skills. In addition to individualizing tutorial instruction, technology was to support a range of activities including exploratory learning (using, for example, *Lego LOGO*), general applications such as word processing, and instructional management systems.

Although it has taken longer than originally planned, the individualization of instruction is the area in which Saturn's implementation is probably closest to the original concept. Students are surveyed each term concerning the courses they would like to take.

Individual responses are compiled and discussed in staff meetings, with teaching staff volunteering to teach new courses requested by students (for example, marine biology). Thus, course offerings range broadly and change constantly, reflecting student demand. Most courses are open to all grade levels (four through eight). Mentorships, independent studies, and off-site learning opportunities (at the Science Museum and the Minnesota Museum of Art, for example) are central to the program. The course of study for each student is worked out in a process called Personal Growth Planning (PGP). Using a computer-based management system, students define their academic and personal goals and enter them into the system, which then searches key words to identify relevant courses, resources, and mentorships. The system includes electronic mail and reporting (hard-copy) functions that facilitate communication between teachers, students, and parents. The system can also help the teacher create a syllabus, and it can monitor, evaluate, and report on the progress of individual students. Development of the PGP has been a major project and is still in progress.

The second principle, the professionalization of teachers, did not play out exactly as the planners expected. The year-round positions for four lead and associate teachers provided critical time for planning and reflection. However, the resulting differential staff structure, which upgraded the jobs of "lead" and "associate" teachers but left "generalist" teachers and "education assistants" working on nine-month contracts and excluded from many program decisions, produced fragmentation within the program and resentment inside and outside the school on the part of regular teachers. Although the plan to proceed with no principal was modified to incorporate a half-time principal, some observers believe that the school has suffered from the lack of a strong principal who could build political support for a radically innovative school throughout the district. (Preskill, 1990, 1991, 1993, provides extensive discussion of these staffing issues in the school's formative evaluation reports.) The St. Paul school district discontinued the lead and associate teaching positions at the end of the 1992–93 school year, bringing Saturn staffing into closer alignment with that of the rest of the district.

Finally, although the overall goal to use state-of-the-art technology remained intact, the way in which this third founding principle was realized evolved over time. The school's founders put a great deal of effort into obtaining an integrated learning system (ILS) laboratory, with more than fifty stations featuring both CCC and Jostens basic skills curricula. A second major component of the technology plan was two Discourse systems and specially designed classrooms for their use. These classrooms resemble corporate training rooms with tiered rows of seats and writing areas. In front of each student is a keyboard that can be used to respond to teacher questions. So, for example, a teacher can pose a math problem, have each student respond individually through the system, and then see immediately how many students reached the correct answer and what incorrect answers were most common.

Teachers were not on board when decisions regarding specific hardware and software choices were made. In the words of one teacher, "this forced [the teaching staff] to have, use, and struggle with a technology that they might not have selected." Many of the teachers working at Saturn came to the school initially with little or no technological experience. Hired only six weeks before the opening of the school, the lead teaching staff was faced with a long list of priorities, such as developing the curriculum, organizing the schedule, and designing new approaches to monitoring and evaluating student progress. These critical issues, coupled with the daily responsibilities associated with teaching once the school was in session, took precedence over learning to use and integrate a variety of unfamiliar technologies.

In some cases, teachers reshaped the technology to fit their approach. For example, one Saturn teacher received vendor and district support in making modifications to the Discourse system that would allow her to use it as a tool for collaborative activities such as group brainstorming. In other cases, Saturn teachers have found that they have needed to rethink their approaches to a particular technology. Initially, the ILS lab functioned almost completely independently as the primary vehicle for the delivery of instruction in math and reading. Teachers, for the most part, took little interest in the

ILS program, and some felt that it did not fit well with the school's overall philosophy, that is, students' learning skills within the context of personally meaningful tasks. ILS was never intended to operate as a stand-alone system, however, and ultimately it failed to carry the weight of the basic skills curriculum that was placed on it. (In 1990–91, student performance on standardized tests of reading and mathematics declined from fall to spring.) The ILS lab continues to be used at Saturn, but it is now used more selectively with particular students, and efforts are under way to integrate ILS activities with other aspects of the curriculum. For example, lessons are being programmed to coincide with math course activities.

Although the technologies that received the most emphasis in the original planning have been downplayed, other technology uses are well entrenched within Saturn's instructional program. Students are encouraged to use technology to prepare and to present their projects and final products in the context of courses and self-directed learning activities. In the process of preparing a research project, for example, a student might photocopy written material to highlight for later reference, gather information from a CD-ROM, conduct a telephone interview with an informant, prepare written text on the computer, and use the scanner, the interactive videodisc, or HyperCard to incorporate graphics, sound, or animation. At Saturn, students are given a great deal of flexibility in determining how they will go about their project work and which tools they will use in the process. This high level of self-selected access to such a wide array of equipment has resulted in what one Saturn teacher has described as "technology-hungry students" who are skilled and comfortable in their use of technology and who find ways to incorporate it into their work as a matter of course.

Reflections on Implementation Issues

After considering the three implementation histories described here, we have drawn the following inferences concerning barriers to and facilitators of technological innovations within the context of school reform.

Authentic, challenging tasks are best supported with flexible technology applications rather than canned instructional programs. As described in Chapter One, educational uses of technologies comprise not only tutoring and exploration but also use as tools and for communication. Ironically, although the first two categories of technology applications are those designed specifically for instructional purposes, our observations support the view that the latter two categories are more conducive to the kinds of instructional activities called for by education reformers. Educational software designed outside the classroom nearly always has limitations in terms of its match to the teacher's curriculum and the endurance of its appeal to students (after a student has solved the problem several times, it is no longer motivating). However, general purpose tools such as word processing, communication, data base, and spreadsheet applications can be integrated into an infinite variety of long-term curriculum projects, as illustrated by the local heroes and city-building projects we have described. The evolution of technology use at Saturn is consistent with this view that some technologies have a more enduring utility than others.

Schools should have project-based, cooperative teaching and learning skills in place. The kind of technology-supported, complex, collaborative projects we have described require multiple skills on the part of both students and teachers. Because the subject matter is open ended, it is challenging and can never be totally mastered. At the same time, both the teaching and the learning roles pose challenges. The teacher must be able to launch and orchestrate multiple groups of students, intervening at critical points to keep each group on track, diagnose individual learning problems, and provide feedback. The students must learn to regulate their own learning and to work in a group, coping with such issues as turn taking, accommodating diverse points of view, and allocating work fairly across group members who differ in levels of skill and motivation. Moreover, at least initially, the technology itself poses challenges as students and teachers learn to set up equipment, remember software commands, and troubleshoot system problems. Observations in another school studied by SRI suggest that it is too much to ask students and teachers to learn all of this at the same time. For example, when a teacher decided to experiment with cooperative research projects that would use books on laser disk and a CD-ROM encyclopedia, she found that the activity broke down because of students' lack of skill in working together (Ringstaff, Stearns, Hanson, & Schneider, 1993, Case Study 2). Classrooms in which teachers and students are already accustomed to collaborative learning and a project-based curriculum are much easier proving grounds for the introduction of general applications and communication technology.

Technology implementation can be a safe context that allows teachers to become learners again and share ideas about curriculum and method. Smith and O'Day (1990) have noted that one reason real education reform is so problematic is that teachers perform their functions in isolation. No matter what the urging of academic researchers or state education departments, teachers' overwhelming tendency is to "close their classroom doors and teach as they were taught" (p. 238). Through time-honored tradition, teachers are the rulers of the classroom, deprived, for the most part, of the opportunity to collaborate with adult colleagues on the central issues of teaching method and content and often anxious about submitting their practices to outside scrutiny. One of the most striking things about several of the schools we visited, and the Open School in particular, was the coherence of the instructional program and the way teachers talked to each other about what they are teaching and how. We argued earlier that new technology can be a catalyst to stimulate teachers to think about new projects and curriculum possibilities. At the same time, teachers learning about technologies face inevitable trials and tribulations. Both experiences can stimulate discussions among teachers going through this process of learning and experimentation together. As Roberta Blatt, the principal at the Open School, expressed it, "If we've gotten nothing else out of this [implementing the technology], it [has given] the teachers an invitation to share their ideas about instruction. Technology is something they were not expected to know already. It is not competitive."

Teachers need time to develop their own technological skills. Although the introduction of technology offers teachers an opportunity to examine and modify their practices, serious changes in practice do not happen overnight. Studies of technology implementations suggest that these projects generally require three to five years for a significant proportion of the teachers involved to become sufficiently comfortable with the technology to incorporate it skillfully into their teaching. Our observations certainly did not contradict this conclusion. Technology was well integrated into all the classrooms at the Open School, but the teachers had over six years of extensive access to equipment and an unusually high level of technical support. Moreover, even in this school, some tools, such as CD-ROM, that had been available for several years did not receive significant use in a number of classrooms. The technology implementation at Frank Paul Elementary School is at a younger stage: although some teachers have thoroughly assimilated technology into their classroom activities, others still treat computers as isolated objects pulled out occasionally for enrichment activities or student practice with keyboarding skills. Similarly, at Saturn, despite its origins as a technology-oriented school, some of the more recent teachers were unfamiliar with technology when hired and have not had time to explore the school's technology and the ways they might incorporate available applications and tools into their teaching.

Easy access to technical assistance is critical, especially in the early years. None of the schools we observed had selected teaching staff on the basis of computer skills. An important aspect of technology implementation, then, is providing resources for teachers to learn computer basics, obtain computers for their own use, and receive technical support while trying new applications (see, also, Chapter Seven). Teachers at the Open School were particularly enthusiastic about the support they had received from the on-site technology coordinator paid by Apple Computer. The key to the effectiveness of this support appeared to be the school's having a sympathetic, technically knowledgeable person available to teachers as they explored and experimented with new ways to integrate and use technology within their practice.

Technological innovations are more effective when teachers feel ownership. There will always be tension between those who propose top-down initiatives for change versus those who want to work from the bottom up. In Chapter Seven, Jane David notes that when individuals outside the school decide what technology to purchase, teachers feel little or no obligation to make use of that technology. The implementation histories reviewed here, particularly Saturn's experience with the ILS lab and the Discourse system, corroborate her assertion. At the same time, because many teachers lack familiarity with many technologies and, therefore, may have difficulty envisioning uses for the technologies, there is a role for outside input when technology is introduced into a school. We have argued elsewhere (Means and others, 1992) for "mixed initiatives" in which higher levels of the education system provide a structure for reform by setting a reform agenda and offering funding, technical assistance, and waivers from regulations while leaving the details of individual reforms to the local levels (p. 125). We believe that schools need to reinvent themselves and that teachers need to assimilate technology into their curriculum and instructional strategies in much the same way as students are expected to construct new knowledge.

Schools need permission and support for innovation from the district, state, and federal levels of the education system. We have come to appreciate the ways in which education occurs within a complex system of mutually reinforcing pieces such as curriculum guidelines, assessment systems, and funding policies (Smith & O'Day, 1990). Chapter Seven highlights the difficulty of changing one piece of the education system without also changing the other parts that have shaped it and, notably, the futility of trying to change the curriculum if high-stakes student testing reflects a different set of priorities.

Our case studies support this proposition to varying degrees. Both the district and the state provided significant encouragement and financial support for the reform activities at Frank Paul. The activities of the Open School received no significant financial support from either of these sources, but the school was given *permission* to be different by both the district and the state. (After years of receiving numerous waivers of regulations every year, the school became one of California's first charter schools in March 1993.) The

Saturn School would not have been founded without the impetus and financial support of the St. Paul school district. However, despite its origins as a district initiative, the school had difficulty in maintaining district support in the years following its opening as test scores declined (as discussed later), observers criticized the differential staffing model, and other schools within the district began to challenge the perceived concentration of resources on Saturn.

Innovative programs need to build a constituency of supporters and should not expect to show dramatic effects on standardized test scores in the short term. In Chapter Six, Joan Herman discussed the mismatch between the basic skills measured in most mandated standardized testing programs and the instructional goals of many projects that link use of technology and education reform. Given this mismatch, plus the years it takes for teachers to become comfortable, effective users of technology for instructional purposes, innovators should be wary of letting their supporters on the school board, in the district office, in the corporate community, and among students' parents get the impression that innovation will result in improved standardized test scores. The three schools described in this chapter had very different experiences with regard to this issue, but all their experiences point to reformers' need to build a constituency that will support the innovation on other grounds.

At Frank Paul Elementary School, where the largely limited-English-proficient students generally score poorly on standardized tests, the district accepts the school's arguments that these scores are not good indices of educational effectiveness. The students' parents, who hold great respect for the educational establishment, have not focused on scores. At the Open School, test scores are high, but there has been no effort to attribute those high scores to the use of technology. When district personnel are asked why they support the school, they cite the high satisfaction of the students' parents rather than test scores. The parents, who are a vital part of the school's decision making and functioning, seem to share the staff's emphasis on other indicators of educational value. Both the principal and the parents are skilled at taking their story to the school board and district offices in order to maintain support for the school.

Despite favorable attention to the school in the national press, Saturn's relations with the administrators and community within its own district have been more troubled, and standardized test scores have been a major factor in the controversy. The concentrated infusion of technology and the school's investment in educational reform had set the stage for high expectations. At the end of the 1990–91 school year, just one week after President Bush paid a high-profile visit to Saturn in honor of its break-the-mold efforts, falling standardized test scores were reported to the press. At the national level, Secretary of Education Lamar Alexander came to the school's defense, stating that "whenever people experiment, there will be failure. . . . One of the problems with American education is everybody thinks everything has to be one hundred percent from the start" (Weisman, 1991). Locally, the news of falling test scores and the ensuing negative press took a debilitating toll on Saturn: community support declined and pressure from the district to treat the test scores as a bottom-line measure of the success of the program mounted. The perception within the community that Saturn had received more than its share of limited district resources during a period of severe budget cutbacks only intensified the issue (many were unaware of the level of external support given to Saturn).

In retrospect, the teachers at Saturn felt that they could have taken a number of steps that would have alleviated some of the difficulties they encountered. While teachers were exploring and experimenting with alternative methods of assessment, they neglected to keep the district informed of their important work in this area. They did not perceive, and therefore did not address, the value placed on standardized testing at the district level. In their concentrated effort to get the program up and running, they also failed to perceive the importance of communicating their progress to the rest of the community. Saturn teachers have recently sought to be more proactive in sharing their program with the school board, with other schools, and with the local community. Presentations to the school board on Saturn teachers' use of portfolios to document student progress, for example, have been well received and have stimulated discussion regarding the role of standardized testing.

Outside funding and support may be required to provide teachers with the level of technical assistance and professional development they need to implement technology-supported education reform. The cases we have described here testify that school reform and appropriate uses of technology to support student learning can be productive partners within public schools, including schools that serve high proportions of children from economically disadvantaged homes and from a diversity of cultural and linguistic backgrounds. At the same time, we have been struck by the importance of support from sources outside the education system. Foundation and business support was critical not only in putting the Frank Paul Elementary School on the path of school reform but also in providing the school staff with opportunities that shaped their thinking about and increased their skills in thematic instruction, site-based management, and the use of technology. Apple Computer played an essential role in stimulating and supporting the technology implementation within the Open School's program. The Saturn School benefitted from numerous corporate donations of technology. These schools and their districts had leaders who were able to identify outside funding resources, secure funds, and make the funded activities work for each school's particular setting and goals. These leadership skills may become increasingly important in an era of inadequate school budgets.

Technology and Reform as Partners

The complexity of the school experiences described here precludes such simple prescriptions as "computers improve learning" or "give technology to teachers first." There is no one right answer, either in terms of specific technologies or uses of technology or in terms of how to introduce technology into a school. Rather than provide specific prescriptions, this volume has attempted to clarify the issues of technology in relation to reform in ways that will help future innovators avoid some pitfalls of the past.

However, one thing is clear. Technology by itself is not the answer to this nation's educational problems. We believe that the power of technology will come from its combination with serious education reform. Schools must first rethink their missions and structure, starting with the needs of students and a set of instructional principles, before they can understand the ways in which technology can help them. When technology is integrated into a broad effort for school reform, and is considered not as the instigator of reform or a cure-all but as a set of tools to support specific kinds of instruction and intellectual inquiry, then educators, students, parents, and communities have a powerful combination that may, indeed, bring necessary, positive change to this nation's schools.

References

Collins, A. (1990). The role of computer technology in restructuring schools. In K. Sheingold & M. S. Tucker (Eds.), *Restructuring for learning with technology.* New York: Center for Technology in Education, Bank Street College of Education; and Rochester, N.Y.: National Center on Education and the Economy.

Kay, A. C. (1991). Computers, networks, and education. *Scientific American, 265*(3), 138–148.

Means, B., and others (1992). *Using technology to support education reform* (Report prepared for the U.S. Department of Education, Office of Educational Research and Improvement). Menlo Park, CA: SRI International.

Nelson, D. (1984). *Transformations: Process and theory.* Santa Monica, CA: Center for City Building Education.

Preskill, H. (1990). *Saturn School of Tomorrow: Formative evaluation report, year 1 (1989–90).* St. Paul, MN: College of St. Thomas.

Preskill, H. (1991). *Saturn School of Tomorrow: Formative evaluation report, year 2 (1990–91).* St. Paul, MN: University of St. Thomas.

Preskill, H. (1993). *Saturn School of Tomorrow: Formative evaluation report, year 3 (1991–92).* St. Paul, MN: University of St. Thomas.

Ringstaff, C., Stearns, M. S., Hanson, S. G., & Schneider, S. (1993). *The Cupertino-Fremont Model Technology Schools Project: Years 4 and 5.* Menlo Park, CA: SRI International.

Sheingold, K., & Hadley, M. (1990). *Accomplished teachers: Integrating computers into classroom practice.* New York: Bank Street College of Education, Center for Technology in Education.

St. Paul Public Schools. (1987, June). *The Saturn School of Tomorrow: A proposal to the Bush Foundation.* St. Paul, MN: Author.

Smith, M. S., & O'Day, J. (1990). Systemic school reform. In S. H. Fuhrman & B. Malen (Eds.) *The politics of curriculum and testing* (pp. 233–267). London: Falmer Press.

Weisman, J. (1991, July). Amid publicity over declining scores, acclaimed Saturn School faces review. *Education Week, 10*(40), p. 12.

Name Index

Subject Index

A

Alternative assessment. *See*
    Performance-based assessment
American Association for the
    Advancement of Science, 83, 88,
    115, 130
American Association of Colleges for
    Teacher Education, 101, 105
American Educational Research
    Association, 101, 105
Anchors, videodisc-based, 83–84
Apple Classroom of Tomorrow (ACOT),
    185
Apple Computers, 198, 206–207, 216,
    220
Apprenticeships, cognitive, 28–30
Assessment: as agent of change, 111;
    traditional, 112. *See also*
    Performance-based assessment
At-risk students, 23–24, 163, 192–195;
    authentic tasks for, 8–9; cognitive
    apprenticeships for, 28; and higher-
    order learning development, 45;
    intrinsically motivating activities for,
    43–45; and literacy problem, 24–27;
    and technology-based learning
    scaffolds, 46–47; vocational versus
    remedial schooling for, 27–28
Authentic tasks, 193–194, 196–198,
    201, 214; and classroom
    management, 99–100; for
    disadvantaged students, 8–9;
    performance-based assessment of,
    112, 121; as reform instruction, 5–7,
    83; tools for, 13–14

B

Bank Street College of Education,
    10–12
Bulletin board systems, 76
Business Roundtable, 2, 205

C

CAI programs. *See* Computer-assisted
    instruction programs
California Learning Assessment System,
    112–113, 116
California Technology Project (CTP), 60
California's Cupertino-Fremont Model
    Technology Schools Project,
    183–184
CBAM. *See* Concerns Based Adoption
    Model
Charlotte Middle School, Rochester,
    New York, 14–15
City-building learning activity, 196–200,
    203
Classroom, student-centered. *See*
    Constructivist learning approach
Cleveland State University, teacher
    education program, 96
Cognition and Technology Group at
    Vanderbilt, 3, 28, 46, 50, 52, 53, 83,
    84, 87, 100, 106, 133, 136–137
Cognitive apprenticeships, 28–30
Cognitive skills, development
    technology in, 47–48
Collaborative projects. *See* Project-based
    curriculum
Complex tasks, 6–7. *See also* Authentic
    tasks